FLAUBERT

"La race des gladiateurs n'est pas morte, tout artiste en est un. Il amuse le public avec ses agonies."

Letter to Feydeau, October 1859

Flaubert about 1870

FLAUBERT

A Biography

by

PHILIP SPENCER
Fellow of Clare College, Cambridge.

★

THE GROVE PRESS
NEW YORK CITY

First published in mcmliii
by The Grove Press
59 West Ninth Street
New York, 11
Printed in Great Britain by
Western Printing Services Limited, Bristol

To

E. E. S.

and

W. H. S.

Author's Note

I am heavily indebted to the previous biographers of Flaubert,
in particular to MM. René Dumesnil, René Descharmes,
Edouard Maynial, and Gérard-Gailly. I should also like
to thank Les Amis de Flaubert, especially the Secretary, M.
René Martin, for their help; M. Edmond Ledoux for information unobtainable elsewhere; Lt.-Col. Ivan Latil for facts
about Emile Judée; Mrs. Coombe Tennant for reminiscences
of Gertrude Collier; Dr. M. G. P. Stoker for medical data;
Dr. D. Russell-Davis for generous advice on psychopath-
ology; Mr. Alexander Allan for shrewd criticism; Mr. E. M.
Forster for permission to quote from his biography of Goldsworthy Lowes Dickinson; and my wife for considerable
patience.

July 1951   P.H.S.

Contents

The frontispiece shows Flaubert in 1870. Flaubert was very hostile to the camera, and only two photographs of him are believed to be extant, of which this is perhaps the more characteristic.

Chapter One

ROUEN

'Nous portons en nous notre passé; pendant toute notre vie nous nous sentons de la nourrice.' Letter to Mme Flaubert, 14th November 1850.

F laubert's life is the history of a predicament: his predicament first as a man and then as an artist. Exactly why it began or persisted we cannot tell: strong forces were working on him from his childhood, and while their trends are apparent, their nature is hidden. But at least it is clear that by character and temperament he connived at their operation and put himself in their power, at first unconsciously, but later with his eyes open.

Flaubert belongs to Rouen as Joyce belongs to Dublin, and in Rouen the pattern of his servitude was sketched out. It is a city of contrasts: essentially drab in spite of its cradle of woodland scenery, and emphatically contemporary in spite of its medieval past. The ancient Cathedral is counterbalanced by the docks, the picturesque rue de la Grosse-Horloge by the industrial suburb of Saint-Sever. The visitor today can still form a picture of the city as it was at the beginning of the nineteenth century if he thinks away some of the outer boulevards and imagines narrow streets and precarious houses in the bare space around the Cathedral. Then, as now, Rouen was synonymous with commerce and commerce at its most uninviting: a greyness of spirit seemed to droop over the river and seep into the hearts of the inhabitants. Practical wisdom triumphed in an embodiment of anti-Romanticism.

Flaubert's father, Dr. Flaubert, was a notable of the place. Since 1818 he had been head of the Hôtel-Dieu, and he was universally respected in the locality and beyond. But local fame did not satisfy

him; he had been sent to Rouen from Paris by Dupuytren, whose
solicitude about his health was probably reinforced by a desire to
be rid of an able and ambitious junior. As a result, Dr. Flaubert,
who considered himself the equal of any Parisian doctor, exercised
a caustic wit on the leaders of his profession. What status he
achieved he owed to himself, and he was scornful and no doubt
envious of those who rose by birth or money. He was a Cham-
pagnois, and his family, which included farriers and veterinary sur-
geons as well as, more recently, a doctor, had been gaining in
credit generation by generation. By upbringing, therefore, he was
not inclined to pay undue respect to the powers of the land, and
his sceptical, rebellious attitude was confirmed by his medical
training. He had been a colleague and friend of Magendie's,
belonging to the group who reacted against Broussais's biological
theories and revived the tradition of Cabanis and Bichat. From
Cabanis, in particular, he took over a belief in physiological deter-
minism and this, coupled with his natural self-confidence, brought
him to the orthodox position of men with his social and intellectual background: a dogmatic anticlericalism.

He was the first doctor of his district, honoured and esteemed;
but the memory of his personality is drowned in the chorus of
approval and it is hard for us to distinguish the man behind the
screen of his conventional virtues. Even when his son describes
him as Larivière in *Madame Bovary*, the portrait does not go far beyond his external characteristics: 'his long woollen *douillette* and
broad black coat, whose loose facings half-covered his hands—
fine hands, always ungloved, as though to probe more swiftly into
distress. Scornful of honours, decorations, and Academies, hospi-
table, generous, paternal to his needy patients, practising a virtue
in which he did not believe, he would almost have passed for a
saint had not the sharpness of his mind made him feared like a
demon. His glance, keener than his own scalpels, cut straight to
your heart and laid bare every lie concealed beneath assertion and
half-statement.' There are, however, significant hints of emotional
instability: he did not spare his colleagues and he tyrannized over
his pupils; on both he exercised a fiery temper.

His son Gustave was born in the annexe of the Hôtel-Dieu on

12th December 1821, the fourth of six children, of whom three survived.

Of his temperamental similarity to his father Gustave only became aware as he grew older. 'I am', he once told a correspondent, 'the son of an extremely humane man, sensitive in the good meaning of the word. The sight of a dog in pain brought tears to his eyes. Yet he performed his surgical operations with undiminished competence—and some of them were terrible.' To a child, however, Dr. Flaubert must have been a grim figure, almost a god; and Gustave's awed respect surely persists even in the portrait of Larivière, as though the omniscient gaze before which no deceit was possible and the impeccable life that admitted of no criticism were articles in the forgotten theology of childhood.

Mme Flaubert, on the other hand, supplied a supporting strain of continuous, unfluctuating affection; but when we examine her features at this distance of time, they are, like her husband's, blurred. She came of solid middle-class stock.[1] Her mother died in giving her birth and she lost her father, a doctor, when she was nine. At thirteen she came to live in the Hôtel-Dieu with the family of the *chirurgien en chef* and five years later, in 1812, she and Dr. Flaubert were married. Misfortune had brought her to early maturity and she made a self-effacing wife, quiet and well bred, excellently suited to the social and administrative duties of her position. She seems to have glided through life almost imperceptibly, absorbed in husband and children, exerting an influence that was tacit but unescapable. But behind her demure manner one has glimpses of an uneasy personality, haunted by fear, distrusting life, frightened that the pattern of bereavement might recur; a small dark woman, for whom grief had been so bitter that she was suspicious of present peace of mind and peered into the future with a secret, unremitting anxiety. If she baffles us a century later, she already baffled her children. 'There is in her whole being', Flaubert wrote, 'an imperturbable quality, naïve yet chilling, which confounds you.'

Her eldest son Achille, Gustave's senior by eight years, was overshadowed by the figure of his father. He made up his mind that he too would be a doctor and concentrated on the task. A dry

personality, sincere, hard-working, and conventional, he was undoubtedly able, but lacked the faculty of being liked. Even his
father nurtured a secret animosity towards him, and when Achille
received his degree, Gustave saw Dr. Flaubert brandishing a fist
behind his back and muttering, 'If I had been in *his* place, at *his*
age, with the money *he* has, what a man I should have been!' Because of the gap between their ages Achille and Gustave were
hardly children together. By the time Gustave was out of his
swaddling clothes Achille was at school, and when Gustave
went to school Achille was reading medicine in Paris.

Caroline, however, the youngest of the family, possessed the
sensitivity Achille lacked. She was a delicate, imaginative child
who responded easily to any stimulus, and although she was three
years his junior, Gustave made her his confidante, involving her in
his enthusiasms, using her as a sounding-board for his emotions.

A challenge was thus implicit in the circumstances of Flaubert's
childhood. With a dominating father whose authority was unques-
tioned and an elder brother who had no difficulty in finding and
pursuing his vocation, he was pushed back on his mother and
sister: but for his vitality he would have been cast in the social and
intellectual mould of his family.

This mould would have bruised and distorted his personality
had he submitted to it, for the Flaubert household was obstinately
provincial. Disappointed as he was at his limited fame, rawly conscious of the greater success of inferior men, Dr. Flaubert mocked
at everything that came from Paris and ridiculed metropolitan
manners, morals, and ideas. Aesthetically he was a Philistine, regarding literature and art with good-natured disapproval as non-
pathological manifestations of nervous instability. With all his
merits and foibles he was essentially bourgeois; and like many
other members of his class, which had suffered severely from
twenty years of virtually uninterrupted war, he was profiting by
the return of more settled conditions to build up a fortune. He saw
to it that his family was never short of money. His wife had brought
him a respectable dowry, consisting mainly of land, and he added
to it year by year so that in 1875 his property at Deauville alone
fetched 200,000 francs.[2]

To Mme Flaubert, who was even more conventionally bourgeois than her husband, position and respectability were the cardinal virtues, and in bringing up her children she was primarily
concerned to inculcate in them her own social tact. Caroline
received a superficial grounding in religion, largely for form's
sake, but Mme Flaubert was herself a deist and had neither the
wish nor the power to combat the crude materialism Gustave im-
bibed from his father. Provided her children spoke well and behaved properly she was satisfied.

But although she guided those vital early years, one is left to
guess at the relations between herself and Gustave. The bond
between them was close, but not abnormally so, and her affection
for him did not involve any coldness towards the other children.
Perhaps he caught from her the habit of anxiety and dimly learnt
the first lesson of hypochondria. There are, too, indications of an
Oedipus complex in his ambivalent attitude to his father and in his
hostility to his brother, onto whom some of the resentment may
have been transferred. But these are conjectures, and even if correct, they do not much advance our knowledge of Flaubert's
youth. Indeed what information there is comes from two sources:
the reminiscences of Flaubert's maturity, in which he looked back
on his childhood with wistful longing and spread over it a veneer
of literary idealization, and the stories related by his admirers,
especially his niece, who knew him as a writer of some stature and
told pleasant but unreliable anecdotes about his burgeoning talent.

Flaubert's recollections are naturally important—important because he remembered these events so long, ascribing to them an
influence they can hardly have possessed. He liked to describe how,
when Dr. Flaubert had driven off on his rounds, Caroline and he
would explore the hospital, scampering along the grey corridors,
hovering round the wards, peering into the court. In summer they
could see a few patients strolling along the paths or sitting on the
stone benches while occasional attendants and sisters of mercy
hurried past; in winter there was only the glimpse of a brown coat
or a bandaged head at one of the windows. Periodically a covered
stretcher was carried across the court to the dissecting-room and
by climbing up the vine in the garden Gustave and Caroline could

gaze through the window at the bodies stretched out on slabs in a haze of flies, till Dr. Flaubert noticed them and waved them away with his scalpel. When he was about six Gustave caught sight of a group of mad women, naked to the waist, tearing at their faces with their nails.

No doubt the grim, familiar scenes of a hospital are not the most suitable background for a growing child, but there is no reason why they should become a decisive influence on his mind. Flaubert, however, regarded environment rather as Taine regarded it—a force operating on man in spite of himself—and when he recalled his youth he always spoke of the Hôtel-Dieu as one of the factors conditioning his later outlook. Not that he admitted a mechanical connexion between fact and opinion, for that would rob opinion of its objective validity. Rather, he considered the environmental influences of his youth as pointers to an ultimate disenchantment; but simply by maintaining that point of view and declaring disenchantment to be the only sensible conclusion, he implied that the influences were not haphazard. Even to perceive in a hospital the frequency of death and the permanence of suffering argues a certain maturity and, in a child, a peculiar cast of mind. But already as a child and perhaps especially then, Flaubert selected the influences that coloured his development. As he rejected the bourgeois Philistinism of his home and neighbours and rebelled against his father's exclusive concern with medicine, he did what was entirely natural to him. There was nothing in his physical environment he did not share with his brother and sister and if the Hôtel-Dieu was significant its significance lay in the echo it called forth in his personality. It influenced him because he was willing to be influenced, because his mind was already turned unconsciously to an awareness of the cruelty latent in life. 'It is strange', he wrote to a friend in 1846, 'how I was born with little faith in happiness. When I was very young I had a complete presentiment of life. It was like a nauseous smell of cooking escaping from a vent. You don't need to eat it to know that it will make you sick.'

The other pictures of Gustave are less characteristic. He was highly strung, easily aroused. Even more than most children he was immersed in his imagination. If he could only persuade the maid Julie to tell him folk-tales about the witches and magicians in her native valley of the Andelle or to recall some of the fiction she had read, he listened contentedly for hours at a time; and when he had grown out of that, he used to run across the rue de Lecat to old M. Mignot, a friend of the family, eat his wife's sweetmeats and ask to hear fantastic stories. The best had to be told over and over again and thanks to M. Mignot's good taste Gustave soon knew a great deal of *Don Quixote* by heart. On the other hand he was not at all interested in learning the alphabet and made much slower progress than Caroline. When Mme Flaubert reproved him he asked 'Why bother, since Papa Mignot can read?'

In 1821 Dr. Flaubert had bought a country-house at Yonville,[3] just where a lane struck off the Déville road for the Bois-l'Archevêque; he added two wings, set a bust of Hippocrates in the middle of the façade, and transported his family there whenever he needed a change from the prosaic drabness of the Hôtel-Dieu. Sometimes too Mme Flaubert took the children to Pont-l'Evêque,[4] where she possessed a farm, and about every two years they all piled into a post-chaise and rumbled off to Nogent, on a visit to the Champagne branch of the family. Here Gustave found another welcome companion in his uncle, the goldsmith François Parain, who contrived to be on excellent terms with Dr. Flaubert and yet entirely different from him. He had a keen and subtle mind with a pleasant turn for wit, and his wide reading and the gusto with which he took his pleasures were more to Gustave's taste than the depressing purposefulness of Rouen.

In Rouen, however, a malicious irony made him attractive to people he disliked. He was plump and rosy and caught the eye of any motherly woman; once, when the Duchess of Berry was visiting the city, she saw him held up in his father's arms and stopped her carriage to give him a kiss. Yet although he was spoilt and humoured by both his parents he was in some ways inferior. Achille, by contrast, was a model son, working diligently and already showing signs of becoming his father's successor. As for Caroline, she was quick and receptive, a docile pupil and lively companion. But Gustave, who felt that he was different, had neither his brother's application nor his sister's vivacity. In himself he was sure that he was the equal of both, but it had yet to be proved; and the need for self-justification, which amounted to a desire to demonstrate his superiority, led him to discover his talents at a remarkably early age and to exaggerate and exploit qualities not shared by the rest of the family. He had a resilient, self-assertive originality; but if he could not establish it, he was in danger of being crushed. He knew already how good he was at telling stories; when he returned from M. Mignot he would repeat to Caroline what he had heard and watch her face for expressions of pleasure, excitement or fear. And now, unconsciously obeying the imperative of his nature, he rationalized his independence and proved to himself that the humdrum people around him were not so infallible as they seemed, that they sometimes behaved foolishly and talked nonsense, and that if he wanted to feel superior to them he could easily find reasons. So the first of his letters that has been kept, written on 31st December 1830 when he was just nine, starts abruptly 'You are right in saying that New Year's Day is silly', and goes on 'As there is a lady who comes to see Daddy and always tells us a lot of rot I'll write it down'.

This letter was addressed to Ernest Chevalier, Gustave's best friend. He was a year older, a bad correspondent but a cheerful companion. Twice a week he came to the Hôtel-Dieu, and though without Gustave's ferocious powers of criticism he was better qualified for orthodox success: he had a quick wit and a long memory, together with an interest in everything that was modern, and the desire to please. He fell in readily with Gustave's idea of writing plays.

Perhaps the idea originated with Parain or Mignot; perhaps Gustave hit on it himself. Certainly Dr. Flaubert's practice kept him far too busy to attend the theatre unless he were on a trip to Paris, and Mme Flaubert was the last woman to encourage literary ambitions in her son. At any rate Gustave asked Ernest to collaborate in a series of comedies. The reply was some time in coming and he followed his letter with another modifying the proposal. 'I told you I was going to write plays, but no, I'll write some novels that I've got in my head about the fair lady of Andalusia, the masked ball, Cardenio, Dorothea, the Moor, the nosy-parker, and the cautious husband.' The novels, however, were no sooner mentioned than forgotten, whereas the plays became an institution.

Next to the lounge, on the first floor of their house, the Flauberts had a little-used billiard-room and Gustave persuaded his mother to let him use it as a theatre. When a performance was imminent, posters were pinned up, invitations sent out, and chairs arranged in rows. The billiard-table, pushed up to the window, served as a stage, onto which the actors climbed over an old garden seat. Caroline was wardrobe-mistress, constructing togas from Mme Flaubert's discarded shawls. Chevalier, who never wrote plays and had 'dreams' instead of ideas, took leading parts and shifted the scenery. As for Gustave, he was actor, producer, and author rolled into one, commissioning plays, allotting roles, drilling the cast and even arranging for an usher to be at the door. As impresario he promised his friends a spirited performance of some trifle by Scribe, Carmontelle or Berquin, and they might even be treated to *L'Amant avare* or *Poursognac* (*sic*)—by Gustave Flaubert.

There were other games as well, for a hospital as important as the Hôtel-Dieu had considerable possibilities. Gustave and his friends abstracted a few skeletons, dressed them up, leaving the skull uncovered, and placed them in prominent positions; or lurked in the corridors at night, waiting for some unsuspecting passer-by, and then, slipping a lamp inside a skeleton, cast sudden shadows on the wall.

But although there was always in him something of the histrion and something of the ghoul, his essential nature was not expressed in his social activities. He was most himself when alone; in fact he cultivated solitude and the grey mood of reverie, finding more pleasure in his day-dreams than in his companions. He possessed an extraordinary and seductive capacity for visualization. According to his mother he used to sit for hours at a time with his finger in his mouth like a simpleton; if he was reading he became so absorbed that he sometimes overbalanced on to the floor. Once he cut his nose falling against the glass front of a bookcase.

But the imagination that delighted in Mignot's tales and the adventure stories of childhood was already oddly flavoured, spiced with precocious dissatisfaction. 'I came into the world bored', said Flaubert; 'it is the disease that eats me up.' Day-dreams held out a more satisfactory world than the one in which he was living; but for a long time he believed that Rouen was not typical and that far-away towns and people existed as he would have them be. Up to Rouen the Seine is tidal and along the quays ships of all sizes, rigs, and nations used to moor, while in the dark streets that contained the lodging-houses he could meet sailors from all over the world. He never threatened to run away to sea, but at least he sent his imagination on long voyages to the East; later he would follow and savour the real delight instead of the substitute.

In February 1832, however, his independence was curtailed and he was sent as a boarder to the *collège* of Rouen, now the Lycée Corneille. He detested it. The class-rooms were cold, high and uncomfortable, and most of the form had to sit on oak benches that dated back to the Jesuits, and, with an inkhorn in one hand and a quill in the other, write by balancing a notebook on their knees. The military discipline, as elsewhere, was emphasized by the beating of a drum at the end of each period, and on Thursdays the whole school marched out for a walk. As for the teaching, it was almost entirely of one kind: the days passed in a long series of Latin proses, Latin translations, Latin stories, and Latin essays, with occasional exercises in the writing of Latin verse. French grammar entered the curriculum as a baffling mass of rules which had to be learnt by heart but were never put into practice; and in the higher classes some time was devoted to history, literature, and nature-study. The staff consisted mainly of diehards, though leavened by one or two men with new ideas. There was Pelletier, cool, bespectacled, and correct, who taught a clear and orderly French; Giffard, who wore a Newgate frill to prevent a stiff neck and could not turn his head fast enough to keep order; Gerbal, sharp and observant, who confiscated some of Flaubert's books; Chéruel, at the outset of a distinguished career as an academic historian; Magnier, whose class-room reverberated with his denunciations of the Romantics; and Pouchet, the learned and original naturalist, whose form, when he drew animals on the board, broke into appropriate cries till the course became intolerable and had to be suspended.

The pupils themselves had two main interests: politics and literature; and ceaseless wars raged between rival factions. The overthrow of the Bourbons and the enthronement of Louis Philippe in July 1830 was considered a mere sop to the bourgeois and did not satisfy a clique of Robespierrites, who demanded a genuine revolution with guillotine and victims. The year before Flaubert entered the school there had been a revolt among the boarders, and on speech-day the prize-winners had publicly renounced their prizes so that the money could be sent to help the Polish insurrection. Meanwhile, although the battle of Romanticism had been fought and won in Paris, mopping-up operations continued in the provinces. The adherents of classicism were shocked by the flamboyant way in which the new literature invaded contemporary manners. Like Dumas's Antony, the *collégiens* of Rouen carried daggers in their pockets. A friend of Flaubert's swore he would turn Mohammedan and go off to Algeria to fight for Abd El Kader; a certain Barbelet blew out his brains for love; another, disgusted with life, was found hanging by his tie.

All this was immensely to Flaubert's taste. He hated being incorporated in the mass and treated like everyone else; he despised most of the staff and resented working for them; and so he rallied to the standard of revolt. Already in 1830 he had been composing radical speeches about the constitution; now he became one of the most ruthless enemies of the *classiques*, declaimed Hugo, praised Byron, and slept with a dagger under his pillow. But although he made a number of friends his only real intimate was Ernest Chevalier. Superficially he was less lonely at school than he had been in the Hôtel-Dieu; but in fact he wished he could escape from the company that was imposed on him. The indiscriminate society of school forced into consciousness his feeling of separateness and moral isolation; he could no longer ignore the abnormal sensitivity with which he was endowed. Once, as he was going home for the week-end, he passed a recently used guillotine; a man was undoing the basket and there was blood on the paving-stones. The scene recurred with terrifying vividness all night.

23

But he knew that the quickness and depth of his response meant not only acuter anxiety but keener pleasure.

Every year, from the third week in October to the beginning of November, the Foire Saint-Romain was held in Rouen; booths and stalls sprang up all over the boulevard north of the school, stretching from the Place Beauvoisine to the Boulingrin. The *collégiens* always asked for a half-holiday to go to the fair and never obtained it. So at four o'clock, when a drum-roll announced the end of the last period, the whole school poured out of the gates, overran a near-by cake-stall, and swept northwards. It was hard to choose the greatest attraction. Bells were clanging and barrel-organs grinding; jugglers juggled and clowns clowned; hoarse voices implored spectators to try their luck and acrobats leapt about in improbable positions. But one of the favourite shows was a puppet-theatre run by a perennial impresario, the Père Legrain, and called *La Tentation de saint Antoine*. The saint's temptation comprised the whole repertoire; its characters were the hermit, his pig, Satan, and God the Father, with a supporting cast of angels and devils; and by bellowing out the traditional lines, spicing them with his own pleasantries and calling on the audience for the chorus, Legrain showed how Saint Anthony was tempted by the Devil, but resisted his wiles and was ultimately justified.

Flaubert was a devotee of the puppet-show. As actor and author he delighted in the tale and its manner of telling, and every year he was to be found on the benches, joining fervently in the saint's appeal.

> *Messieurs les démons,*
> *Laissez-moi donc!*
> *Messieurs les démons,*
> *Laissez-moi donc!*

Notes to Chapter One

1. Flaubert liked to claim originality for three of his ancestors: they were supposed to be a *chouan*, a pirate and an Iroquois squaw.

But the first died in 1785, seven years before the *chouans* began to operate and was merely the namesake of a famous warrior; the second was the grandfather of Flaubert's great-great-aunt by marriage and a harmless man anyway; and the third was purely conjectural.

2. According to Moreau de Jonnès, a contemporary statistician, in 1856 the average yearly earnings of a family of four were 1,232 francs in the towns and 562 francs in the country. Average industrial wages were from two to three francs a day. Somewhat later Zola told Cézanne that if he wanted to come to Paris he would need 1,500 francs a year. A member of the middle class could live quietly on 3,000 francs and a comfortable income would be about 10,000.

3. The 'Yonville' of *Madame Bovary* is not this Yonville but Ry, about a dozen miles from Rouen.

4. Pont-l'Evêque is largely the scene of *Un Cœur simple*.

Chapter Two

TROUVILLE

*'Les plus grands événements de ma vie ont été quelques pensées,
des lectures, certains couchers de soleil à Trouville au bord de la
mer, et des causeries de cinq ou six heures consécutives avec un
ami qui est maintenant marié et perdu pour moi.'* Letter to
Louise Colet, 18th September 1846.

Flaubert's precocity was emotional: judged by academic standards he was neither clever nor a dunce. But he discovered
abnormally early the solitariness of human destiny, at least in
so far as he was involved in it, and he rendered the feeling articulate and vocal. Beginning as a consciousness that his personality
was valid in its own right, the feeling was complicated and intensified by the problems of adolescence, which took a form almost
incapable of solution.

Every summer the Flauberts went to Trouville on the Channel
coast, where they possessed a good deal of land. In the eighteen-
thirties it was almost unknown to holiday-makers; the elder
Dumas, who made frequent trips to the locality, had not yet popu-
larized it and apart from a few painters who stayed in the village
and a handful of writers like Sainte-Beuve and Alfred de Musset
who put up at Ulrich Guttinguer's house farther along the coast,
there were no tourists. Deauville, on the other bank of the
Touques, consisted merely of a farm, one or two cottages and a
chapel almost lost in the dunes, and Trouville was just a fishing-
village. There was only one inn, L'Agneau d'Or, on the corner
of the quay and the rue du Commerce, and the Flauberts always
stayed there, attracted as much by its position as by the Mère
David's excellent cuisine.

At Trouville you had to amuse yourself. The Flauberts usually bathed in the morning or, if the tide was out, collected shells and sea-urchins on the foreshore; in the afternoon, unless the sun was scorching, they went for walks, perhaps as far as Hennequeville; otherwise they rested in their shuttered rooms till the heat had abated. Gustave liked to stroll along the pebbled road through the village; in the doorways fishermen in red and blue were often hanging up their water-worn nets, brushing away the half-naked children who played outside. As he grew older, he got to know the personalities of the place and cultivated them with fascinated curiosity. He called on M. Couyère, who was to become mayor in 1837, sampled the rum he always offered visitors and attended, on his invitation, some of those copious Norman feasts that lasted for six or seven hours. He argued with the Abbé Bourgeois, the local priest, who had little education, much industry, and an enormous appetite. He begged stories from the retired sea-captain Barbey and listened to the morose imprecations of his hunchback daughter La Barbette. And he gossiped with the Davids about the guests at their inn.

Among these guests there was, in 1835, Henry Collier, the British Naval Attaché, who had come on holiday with his wife, son and two daughters.[1] Henrietta, the younger girl, became great friends with Caroline, and Gustave naturally took an interest in Gertrude, who was his own age. She was small, podgy and cheerful, just the right companion for a few weeks by the sea; and when Gustave discovered that she liked reading, he pressed on her all the novels and plays he had brought with him and engaged her in long discussions on literary subjects. As Herbert, her younger brother, could safely be left with Henrietta and Caroline, Gertrude and Gustave were free to go on long walks together; and they developed a mutual sympathy that was too exciting for mere friendship ·but not self-conscious enough for love. The word 'love' was never mentioned: they chattered and played like children and wrote verse together. If Gustave kissed her Gertrude burst into tears.

Parting caused them no great distress, and when Gustave was back at school in the autumn he soon had other matters to think of. He had now reached the fourth form, having started in the eighth, and was maturing fast. It was only two years since he had been to the theatre in Paris and told Ernest: 'Seven people die. It's a lovely play.' But from his reading he had borrowed a richer and more pretentious vocabulary and a more adult set of ideas. When he wrote to Ernest ennui was a word that sprang readily to his pen: the ennui of being alone, deprived of his friends' company, with only the tiresome platitudes of the bourgeois to listen to. But although he attributed his ennui to the stupidity of his fellow-citizens, its cause lay in himself and the attitude he had already adopted. As a mature artist he declared that he was not interested in facts but in their interrelations, and even as a boy he was only concerned with things in so far as they aroused his emotions and gave each other significance. By his exclusive emphasis on intent living he abjured minor pleasures, and imprisoned as he was in his own solitude, he perceived only the differences between himself and the mass of Rouennais. Like Baudelaire he felt 'l'horreur de la vie et l'extase de la vie'; but though his horror was for the real life of every day his ecstasy lay in the illusory life of fantasy. So he spoke glibly of 'that foolish joke we call life' and sought consolation in Art; 'greater than peoples, crowns and kings, Art is eternally present, sustained by enthusiasm, decked with a godlike diadem'.

Art and school were not, however, easily compatible. The previous year he had begun a journal with himself as editor and sole contributor, but it was discouraged, and now he turned his attention to history. Largely because Napoleon's distrust of anything approaching independent thought had been inherited by succeeding dynasties, history was not a subject often taught in schools; but the *collège* of Rouen had been fortunate in adding a former pupil, Chéruel, to the staff and in his lessons he conveyed some of the warmth and colour he had caught in Paris from his master and friend, Michelet. Tall, brisk, and self-assured, he spoke clearly and without notes. In the fourth form he dealt with Roman history, relying on Michelet's recently published book and recommending it to his pupils; in the third he passed to the Middle Ages, on which he could claim to be a specialist. Flaubert, who shared to the full the contemporary admiration for Michelet's prose, enjoyed Chéruel's lessons and found in history, even at the cost of being unhistorical, a life and glow that Rouen signally lacked. He worked with a will, producing plans, sketches, and essays, some of which are still extant, and as a result he won a first prize for history in 1837 and 1838, and a second in 1839.[2]

There were of course other influences that were salutary, though unwelcome: influences that were imposed. Giffard, the master of the third form, who taught literature, had an especial fondness for the balanced and subtle prose of La Bruyère; Pelletier, who took the second, boldly encouraged his pupils to choose for discussion their own passages from the classics, welcomed imaginative work and insisted on a clear and easy French. In later years it was Pelletier's teaching that the *collégiens* remembered with most gratitude and Flaubert cannot have remained indifferent to methods so strikingly opposed to current pedagogy.

If, however, he had known of Flaubert's favourite authors Pelletier would have pulled a wry face. A schoolmaster who loved to quote Rivarol—'Ce qui n'est pas clair n'est pas français'—must have felt some misgivings when a pupil steeped himself in Byron, Hugo, Lamartine, Rousseau, Rabelais, and Montaigne and derived an almost perverse enjoyment from Scott and Shakespeare. For Flaubert was aggressively Romantic in his tastes; he was young enough to inherit the Romantic triumphs without having to fight for them, and he varied his literature with vehement politics. 'I see with indignation', he says in a letter of 1835, when he is still not fourteen, 'that censorship of plays is to be reintroduced and the liberty of the press abolished! Yes, this law will go through, for the representatives of the people are nothing but a crowd of venal rascals.'

Somewhere about this time he got hold of Goethe's *Faust*, which had been translated in 1828 by Gérard de Nerval. Leaving school on Easter Eve, he did not go straight home, but, according to his niece, wandered across the river to the Cours la Reine, sat down on the bank, and as the bells rang out from the city opposite, turned over the pages of the book. Even if the setting is fictitious the essential fact is true. Goethe's poetry overcame him

29

like wine; his head swam and his eyes blurred; as he staggered home Rouen was less real to him than the cell of the despairing philosopher.[3]

His other discoveries were less dramatic but equally personal: they were the means of knowing himself. He smuggled candles into the school dormitory and devoured forbidden literature late at night, quenching the flame and shamming sleep when he heard the night-watchman approaching on his rounds. Possibly it was during this period that he read Chateaubriand; at any rate one of his friends declares that a few years later he knew *René* by heart.[4]

Secretly he had no doubt about the real bent of his personality, the natural direction of his life. Literature claimed him wholly and his response to it was such that his instinctive demand was for beauty. How to achieve beauty on his own account was a question he hardly dared set himself; but besides his work for Chéruel he turned out a mass of short stories, trying his hand at phrases, experimenting with contrasts, dabbling in colours, and expressing half-unconsciously the sanguinary imagination of the little boy who had dreamed nightmares at the sight of a guillotine.

Meanwhile his sister Caroline was developing a frail and exquisite beauty, and when she and Gustave were out together passers-by turned to watch them. Gustave himself, with his smooth complexion, high forehead, and round sea-green eyes, arrested the attention: a little strange, perhaps, with his gusts of laughter and extravagant gestures, but unusually handsome as he swaggered by with a sailorlike roll of his shoulders.

So he was, when he returned with his family to Trouville in 1836; but what tender memories he preserved of Gertrude were soon overwhelmed in a new and devastating experience.

As yet Trouville possessed no bathing-machines: people either undressed on the shore or came straight from their rooms, wearing coats. One day, as Flaubert was walking along the beach at a spot much frequented by bathers, he noticed that the incoming tide was licking the edge of a red cloak lying on the sand. He picked it up, saw that it belonged to a woman, and carried it out of the reach of the waves. At lunch he was thanked, and he was never to forget the person who thanked him.

She was tall and well-built, with long tresses of black hair, a straight nose, and dark, smouldering eyes; he noticed a slight down on her upper lip and a tracery of blue veins across her neck; when she spoke, it was with a soft, rich-toned voice. She had a certain carelessness of manner which was displeasing to other women; but it contained a promise of passion.

He soon found out that she was called Mme Schlésinger and was on holiday with her husband. As for M. Schlésinger everyone knew him: his life was one continuous self-advertisement and he struck Gustave as a cross between an artist and a commercial traveller. Born in Berlin of a Jewish family in 1797, he had wandered about Europe in various capacities, now fighting as a Hussar, now meddling in Republican intrigues, till he had arrived in Paris and set up as a music-publisher in the rue Richelieu. The business prospered, and though most of his associates, whether artists, composers or customers, were sure that for the greater part of the time they were being outrageously tricked, Schlésinger contrived to make even the justest claims against him seem faintly unreasonable. His tortuous business methods baffled even Wagner, who complained bitterly that Meyerbeer left him 'at the mercy of this monstrous personage'; and before many years Schlésinger was an indispensable contact for any aspiring musician who came to Paris. But he owed his success as much to his virtues as to his vices; for though he could behave like a Shylock, he was at other times extravagantly generous and no one reproached him if he subsequently turned his generosity to good account. By nature he was contradictory and unstable: in later years when his wife had no stockings to wear, he lavished money on a fur-coat she did not need; and despite his proud and continuous affection for her, he spent his life pursuing other women.

Drawn to Trouville by his friend Alexandre Dumas, Schlésinger had arrived in a coach with his wife, child, and dog, and twenty-five bottles of Rhenish wine; and he divided his time equally between them. Flaubert, however, had fewer distractions; realizing that acquaintance with the wife could only be bought by friendship with the husband, he cultivated Schlésinger—emphasized the amusement and hid the irritation caused him by this flamboyant and expansive personality. Gustave was not yet fifteen: his ideas had largely been derived at second-hand from literature. Swept without warning by an infinite tenderness utterly different from his jolly companionship of a year before with Gertrude Collier, he innocently sought out the woman whose presence could shed upon him some of her own sweetness; he lurked by the shore to watch her bathe and almost choked with delight as she walked past him with drops of water pattering off her body. On one occasion he nearly broke his neck catching her dog and kissing it where she had kissed it.

Schlésinger liked and encouraged him; indeed he virtually adopted Flaubert for the duration of the holiday, consenting to be known as 'la mère Maurice'. So there were ample opportunities to talk to Mme Schlésinger—'Elisa' as her husband called her. Though not unconventional enough to smoke, she offered Flaubert cigarettes, treated him as a friend, and unaffectedly gave the breast to her baby girl in his presence. One afternoon when it was too hot to go out, they all stayed at the inn, sipping grog and talking about art with some painters. Flaubert was delighted to find that she shared his point of view. At Maurice Schlésinger's suggestion, he went boating with her one fine evening in the bay; after taking her home, he remained on the shore till the light in her room had gone out. She must be alseep. But as he gazed fondly at her window, the picture of her coarse and jovial husband rose suddenly in his mind and obscene and intolerable ideas assaulted his imagination. He felt miserable and alone.

This was the dominant emotional experience of his life. He gave his heart to Elisa, a woman he could only desire and not possess; and the pattern of his psychology acquired a fresh clarity and rigour. Unconsciously he chose a feminine ideal so remote that there would be no dishonour in failing to achieve it; falling in love with a married woman eleven years older than himself protected him from the rivalry of his contemporaries, helped to justify his theoretical addiction to pleasures forbidden by society and fostered his dreams of adultery. Above all, it expressed his vaulting desire: he pursued the unattainable, knowing it was beyond his reach.

But at first Elisa was only a sweet memory. There was always the loyal Ernest Chevalier in whom to confide, but Flaubert shrank from imparting so intimate an experience. With Ernest he liked to talk of more ordinary things: they would lie flat on the grass either at Déville or Les Andelys, where Ernest's family had a house, and smoke pipes and discuss the *collège*; or Ernest came up to Gustave's room in the Hôtel-Dieu and, brandishing a pair of tongs, disfigured the fireplace while he enlarged on his plans for the future. But if Flaubert were to open his heart it must be to someone older of whose emotional maturity he could be reasonably sure; and he found the man in Alfred Le Poittevin.

M. Le Poittevin, Alfred's father, was Gustave's godfather and Dr. Flaubert stood in the same relation to Alfred himself. Laure, the sister, who was almost exactly the same age as Gustave, used to come to the plays performed in the billiard-room, and sometimes she brought Alfred. But although he took a polite interest in the proceedings and even composed a few short pieces, he did not become friendly with Gustave till about 1837. By this time he was twenty. He had left school the same year that Gustave began it, but, because of his delicate health, remained in Rouen with no particular occupation, dallying with literature, philosophy, and art, and finding that time lay heavy on his hands. The discovery that Gustave had largely the same interests, and no doubt the welcome respect paid to his opinions, led him to visit the Hôtel-Dieu with Chevalier on Thursdays and Sundays; it was an opportunity for expansion and emotional release.

Alfred Le Poittevin was a victim of his epoch. Timid, proud, and sensitive, he had devoured Romantic literature and thus intensified the dislike he already felt for life; what began as an instinctive reluctance to participate in the struggle for existence was enhanced and extended till it became an overwhelming lassitude and disgust. He recoiled, brooded, and reviled. But his pessimism sharpened his curiosity and he probed the depths of his own nature, experimenting with bizarre and morbid sensations, deriving a painful pleasure from an examination of his defects. 'I am', he told a friend, 'a Greek of the Lower Empire.' The collapse of his aspirations had been too sudden for him to accept it and recover; behind his disillusion and cynicism he remained secretly and unconsciously Romantic, full of resentment at a world which failed to accord with his idea of it. His manner was bitter and incisive; because his own effort had failed, he delighted in exposing the futility of all other effort; convention he regarded as mere hypocrisy and, dismissing personal responsibility, he blamed his own unhappiness on fate, his parents, and friends. The period was one when despair was fashionable and was taken to signify a noble and interesting nature rather than a maladjusted personality; unhappy though he was, Alfred Le Poittevin merely followed the mode.

He was, however, original in his metaphysical approach. The Romantic movement had been accompanied by a resurgence of occultism, a renewed concern with mystics like Boehme and Swedenborg and a revolt against the dry rationalism of much eighteenth-century thought. Without wallowing in the crude sentimentality that often did duty for religion, Le Poittevin had read widely in occult literature; his cast of mind being particularly suited to metaphysics, he had also acquired some familarity with Descartes, Malebranche, Kant, Hegel, and, above all, Spinoza; and he was beginning to work out a philosophic system of his own. In some ways very similar to Balzac's hero Louis Lambert, perhaps distinguishing with difficulty between what was real and what was imagined, he was a convinced spiritualist with a strong belief in reincarnation. When he talked, he liked most of all to indulge in metaphysical speculation, seeking universal laws in the flux of life and discussing the mysterious transition from matter to idea.

The impact of his personality was decisive for Flaubert, who had never before heard abstractions dealt with so clearly and critically; indeed when he was an ageing man and had met all the famous thinkers of his time, he still maintained that none of them handled philosophic notions with the ease and mastery of Le Poittevin. Clouded with affection though this judgement may be, it is significant: Flaubert stood in urgent need of an intellectual basis for his ideas, and this Le Poittevin afforded, leading him into a bewildering world of strange symbols and tremendous concepts.

Their characters, however, were radically different. Whereas Le

Poittevin burned with an intellectual ardour, Flaubert strove for a harmony in his jarring emotions; and so their mutual influence, in the exact sense, was small. It was rather that each fortified the other's desire for self-realization. Thus although Le Poittevin introduced Flaubert to Spinoza, Flaubert only retained the ideas congenial to his temperament—Spinoza's doctrine of pantheism and his forthright rejection of any anthropocentric view of the universe; and he was more stirred by the revelation of Creuzer, whose *Religions de l'antiquité* (1825-41), still in process of publication, unveiled not only a startling beauty but a deep significance in the myths of antiquity. As for Le Poittevin's own theory of reincarnation, it left him indifferent. Both of them, however, fell victims to ennui and self-disgust; both of them detested the bourgeois and railed in unison; and both had ambitions to write.

Le Poittevin's family owned a house at Fécamp to which Flaubert paid occasional visits, and it left him some of his happiest memories. Apart from the arguments, practical jokes and ambitious schemes hatched during long evenings by the fireside, he recalled a little room on the second floor where he first read Hugo's *Feuilles d'automne* with Alfred's sister. In Rouen, too, literature often occupied them, and Le Poittevin himself published verse in *Le Colibri*, a small but eclectic paper which tilted quixotically at authority in all its disguises. In one of his poems he prescribed a cure for boredom:

> *Alors je redemande à l'Orient magique*
> *Des âges primitifs le souvenir antique,*
> *Par fum qu'on ne respire plus.*

They were lines that would appeal to Flaubert: indeed *Le Colibri*'s flavour of sincere but outmoded Romanticism accorded well with his own taste, and it may have been through Le Poittevin that he obtained an introduction to the editor. The result was the publication of *Bibliomanie* in February 1837—a hair-raising tale about a Barcelona bookseller who commits arson and murder because of his passion for rare editions. It was followed next month by *Une Leçon d'histoire naturelle. Genre commis*, in which the appearance, habits, distribution, and peculiarities of the genus office-clerk are described in scientific detail; the natural historian responsible is indicated by a modest F at the end of the article.

Whenever Flaubert described his youth, a veil of melancholy slipped over his eyes; he interpreted it with a mature awareness of its implicit conflicts and disappointments; he remembered his misery and isolation, the grim background of the Hôtel-Dieu and the stupid bourgeois of Rouen, and his recollection of happy moments with Le Poittevin and Caroline was clouded with the threat of later bereavement. At the time, however, he was boisterous and energetic; a learned friend of the family who disapproved of his work and opinions remarked that despite his sincerity and imagination he lacked judgement: 'He only ever had one idea in his silly head—to be a buffoon.' And the spirit of buffoonery came out nowhere more clearly than in the creation of *Le Garçon*.

Le Garçon had entered the world as a satirical portrait of the bourgeois—a fantastic creature who, in the billiard-room of the Hôtel-Dieu, defended the more flagrant crimes against society in the name of order and morality. He thundered and besought and platitudinized. But from these humble beginnings he expanded and dilated, transcending and overwhelming his original conception till he attained an almost legendary importance and became the supreme embodiment of everything that was foolish and humdrum and conventional. When Flaubert and his friends went about Rouen, they took it in turns to personate *Le Garçon*. Passing in front of the Cathedral, one of them would say 'That Gothic architecture is grand, it inspires you', and *Le Garçon* would bellow 'Yes, it's grand, and so were the Massacre of Saint Bartholomew and the dragonnades and Revocation of the Edict of Nantes—they were grand too!' He acquired a characteristic laugh, high and piercing, and set, mechanical gestures; his ideas represented the quintessence of every current folly, from the cautious pomposity of the conservative to the inept enthusiasm of the Romantic; sometimes he even parodied the cherished notions of Flaubert and his circle. Around him there grew up a rich mythology. He possessed a house to which were consigned all the most odious characters of Rouen; and he kept a hotel, 'L'Hôtel des Farces', which was run in contravention of every established custom. As each guest walked in, he was welcomed by six masked men who beat him black and blue; the central heating only worked in summer, and in winter visitors froze to death. Flaubert howled with uncontrollable mirth when, on one of his journeys years later, he discovered that the proprietor of the hotel he was staying at was a certain M. La Garçon (*sic*).

From his correspondence, however, it is not hard to see that despite his parade of scepticism and worldly knowledge he remained at heart simple and easily moved; he denounced hypocrisy and cant because they really shocked him; indeed they were to shock him till the day of his death. But partly to protect himself, partly to disguise the delicacy of his feelings, and partly to overcome his subservience to what he regarded as a bourgeois morality, he assumed a mask: he pretended to be indifferent, even hostile, to his environment. It was a Romantic pose and in some ways it worked. It capitalized his loneliness and enabled him to mock and criticize without being involved in the foolishness around him; just as he had, at the age of nine, rejected the festivities of New Year's Day precisely because they represented the society in which Achille and Caroline were at home and he was a stranger, so now he learned to take a malicious pleasure in the moral foibles of those who appeared to be his superiors. When the vice-principal of the *collège* was discovered in a local brothel and hauled before the governing body, Gustave chortled with glee; by standing aloof from this society he could laugh at it with impunity. *Le Garçon* was an exaggerated symbol of his scorn.

But the pose which he adopted to deceive others also deceived himself: by wearing a mask he modified his own features. At an age when most boys are still innocent of any systematic guile, Gustave had learnt to simulate a Romantic personality, a personality partly true and partly false. What had begun as a kind of bitter joke was soon to be taken in deadly earnest. Ceasing to be a mere source of amusement, the bourgeoisie became excruciatingly funny when absurd and appallingly sinister when in action; it absorbed the complex of violent emotions that had racked Flaubert in his earliest years; he saw it as a force implacably opposed not only to his conception of life but to his mere existence and in his less reasoned moments he concentrated on any member of the class all the disgust, all the fear and hatred that the hunted animal must feel for its pursuer.

Meanwhile he tried to relate his acute sense of beauty to the ugly everyday world; and, encouraged perhaps by Le Poittevin's disillusion, he concluded that no connexion existed between the two. In the preface of *Cromwell* Victor Hugo had proclaimed the grotesque as an essential of Romantic art. But for Flaubert it was something more: the eternal contrast between beauty and ugliness, existing independently and side by side, was a fundamental secret of life. In June 1837, for instance, he wrote to Ernest Chevalier: 'The loveliest of women is not very lovely on a dissecting-table, with her intestines on her nose, one leg skinned and half a burnt-out cigar lying on her foot.' This sense of the grotesque coloured and characterized his whole vision.

But he escaped from ugliness by dreaming his way into the East and into the past; like Le Poittevin in his poem, he found in the imagination a cure for ennui; his desires far outbalanced his needs and such were the delights of those unsubstantial journeys into remote climates and epochs that he poisoned himself with ennui in order to savour to the full the antidote. On this practice he became increasingly dependent. A ship or two tied up in the port of Rouen, a page of Hugo or Gautier—and he had left the grey skies of Normandy and was off to lands of dazzling sun and glittering colour. Like his own hero: 'I saw the East and its vast deserts, its palaces trodden by camels with brass bells; I saw mares bounding towards the sun-flushed horizon; I saw blue waves, clear sky and silvery sand; I breathed the smell of the warm oceans of the South; and then, near me, in a tent shaded by a broad-leaved aloe, some brown-skinned woman with burning eyes would fold me in her arms and whisper the language of the houris.'[5] He fettered himself to his own mechanism of escape.

In 1837,[6] as usual, the Flauberts spent their summer holiday at Trouville and Gustave experienced a painful surprise. Not only was Mme Schlésinger not there, but her husband had left two days before—with another woman. The disappointment drove Gustave back on his memories; wandering along the shore or lying in the

grass, he lived over again the days he had spent with her and conjured up her figure beside him. It was a poor substitute; and
though he had been happy in her company, he realized that now,
when she was no longer present, he truly loved and desired her.
He began to perceive the situation into which he had stumbled;
there was no way out. For a fortnight of high wind and rough
weather he recalled their conversations in the inn, trips on the
river, and walks by the shore; and by constant repetition he
deepened and clarified the traces of that experience. When he returned to Rouen in the autumn, he was no longer sweetly and
hazily affectionate, but wounded and aroused.

It was now, if not earlier, that he confided in Le Poittevin, and
the advice he received did not solve his problem. For Le Poittevin
love had turned sour and he wrote to Gustave: 'I don't know what
you will think of a plan I am carrying out as soon as possible. I
shall go and spend three days at Le Havre or Honfleur with a
whore I'll choose for the purpose; I'll feed her and show her
round and we'll sleep together. It will be a great pleasure to take
her to that part of the country where I was once young and credulous. On our return I'll pay her off.' With such a counsellor it is
small wonder that Flaubert sought in the arms of one of his
mother's maids what he could not find at Trouville. But peace of
mind was not to be purchased so cheaply; the result was to fill him
with self-disgust and remorse as though he had profaned something sacred.

His daily life was smooth and uneventful. As soon as school was
over he joined Le Poittevin in his home in the Grand' Rue or they
strolled down to the quay and chatted to a café proprietor who
put down rum faster than most people would care to drink water.
But apart from his friendships he remained indifferent to the city
and the school and spent most of his spare time writing. Emotionally he had grown up all at once; severe as it was the shock would
not occur a second time, and when he revisited Trouville in 1838,
he merely rehearsed his former feelings and confirmed his reaction.
On his return, striving somehow to shake off the intolerable burden of his longing, he began *Les Mémoires d'un fou* and after a
hesitant and declamatory introduction set down the story of his

encounter with Elisa Schlésinger. It is an uneven book in which lengthy passages of second-hand emotion smother descriptions of more intimate experience; but it enabled him to numb, at least for a while, the pain of separation.

In the autumn he ceased to be a boarder at the *collège* and became a day-boy. It was a step nearer freedom, for he could puff his pipe in the morning, smoke his cigar in the evening, and linger at the Café National waiting for school to begin. But he was on his own; for both Ernest and Alfred had left for Paris to read law and, deprived of their company, he was more than ever thrust back on himself. Whereas Alfred had excited him with dizzy speculations, Ernest, a coarser and more robust nature, had kept him cheerful and reasonably contented. But now, if he was not working for Chéruel, learning English to read Shakespeare, or concocting obscene stories about priests to tease a new arrival from a Catholic school, he tended to brood: wild desires obsessed him; spurring on his imagination, he indulged in huge orgies and tasted exquisite pleasures; with the whole world, past and present, at his disposal, he squeezed against his palate the quintessence of delight, persecuting with Nero, feasting with Heliogabalus, warring with Alexander, being loved by Helen and Cleopatra. It was a wholehearted self-abandonment to *delectatio morosa*, and it bore fruit in *Smarh*, a turbid phantasmagoria supposedly based on a mystery-play.

But despite his moods of ennui and lassitude, Gustave was never too tired to slate the bourgeois, and the aversion he already felt for his brother was enhanced by the news that, now his doctoral thesis had been approved, Achille was going to marry and settle in Rouen. That his fiancée had all the right ideas was enough to repel Gustave, and after Achille had left the Hôtel-Dieu in June, the relations between the two brothers were never cordial and seldom more than polite. For Achille, Gustave's manner of life was unhealthy and indolent: for Gustave, Achille's existence represented a polypoid adherence to convention.

By reading Rabelais and Montaigne Flaubert had strengthened his scepticism. 'Que sçais-je?' contained all the law and the prophets, and he was annoyed to learn that Ernest had attained a belief in a creative force. But he was not saved the embarrassment of being commended at school for his 'disposition for moral ideas'. In December 1839, however, he had his revenge, for he left suddenly under mysterious circumstances. He had to prepare at home for his *bachot* and despite the petulant incomprehension with which he regarded much of the syllabus and his eagerness to throw down the set books and pick up the Marquis de Sade, he passed the examination in August.

Probably Dr. Flaubert was surprised, but he was certainly pleased, and almost immediately afterwards he allowed Gustave to set out on a trip to Corsica with Dr. Jules Cloquet. Cloquet was Dr. Flaubert's best friend, a Parisian who had written a standard work on anatomy; in 1835 he had taken Achille with him on a tour of Scotland, and though Gustave had at first some doubts about his suitability as a travelling companion, they were soon disposed of; for Cloquet turned out to be genial and even-tempered and thoroughly deserved his reputation for caustic wit.

It was the first time Flaubert had gone south, even in France, and the people and scenery struck him as new and strange. At Bordeaux, scorning the pagan Cathedral, he fingered with veneration the pages of Montaigne's manuscripts; at Biarritz he nearly lost his life trying to save a man from drowning; at Irun he had one tantalizing glimpse of Spain; at Saint-Sernin there was a delightful irruption of the grotesque when the priest, exhibiting his treasures and relics, mentioned that vellum from the missals had gone to make cartridges; and then one morning beyond Nîmes, coming over the crest of a hill, he saw the imperturbable Mediterranean, covered with a slight haze, lapping the grey rocks of Marseilles bay.

Looking for somewhere to stay in Marseilles, they found the Hôtel Richelieu in the rue de la Darse, and from it they made excursions to the port, buying sandals and Turkish pipes. As Gustave was returning one day from a bathe, he noticed a young woman sitting in the hotel court. He saluted her, she smiled invitingly, and there was a sudden upsurge of passion. For Eulalie Foucaud de Lenglade, who was shortly leaving to join her husband in French Guiana, it was a delectable experience unlike anything she had known before; for Gustave it was an explosion of physical desire, agreeable but unimportant, in which he gave more pleasure than he received. He could not break out of the situation in which he was imprisoned by Elisa's memory. Ultimately he was his own victim and chose his own punishment. Because the ideal was beyond his grasp, the sexual relations he had with any woman so cheapened her that he was unable to participate emotionally: he was excited but unmoved. When he wrote to Eulalie he simulated what he did not feel; six years later, turning over the letters she had sent him, he was moved by their warmth and sincerity and put on the outside of the folder: 'Poor woman! Can she really have loved me?'

The sea-crossing to Corsica was rough and Gustave, who was sick, was galled at the sight of four passengers dining with complete unconcern—Cloquet and three priests. When, however, he landed, he fell in love with the country at once. An island where banditry was a title to respect and half the population seemed to be fleeing from justice, was almost too good to be true: he admired the vigorous traditions of the people, their hospitality and pride and their habit of travelling armed; and if the social structure was fiercely primitive, it preserved the tang of a far-off ancient world about which he dreamed. As he rode through the tangled maquis, plucking the myrtle-flowers and the red arbutus berries, his thoughts turned more and more to the East; he longed to be outside Europe; at any rate he must see Greece and Rome; and one evening, as he and Cloquet emerged from the forest of Marmano on to the lofty plateau of El Prato, they looked across the Tyrrhenian Sea and descried a faint white line on the rim of the horizon. It was Italy.

Notes to Chapter Two

1. He is always referred to in books about Flaubert as Sir Henry Collier, but in fact he was not knighted. He was the son of Sir

George Collier, Vice-Admiral of the Blue, and he entered the Navy in 1800, when he was nine. He became a captain on half-pay on 26th December 1822, and his promotion was uninterrupted till 1863, when he retired with the rank of admiral. He married in 1816, and had six children—three sons and three daughters. The sons were George, Clarence (b. 29th July 1830), and Herbert (b. 19th July 1833). The third daughter, Clementine, was the youngest of the family. It is curious and faintly mysterious that Flaubert refers only to Gertrude, Henrietta, and Herbert.

In 1847 Gertrude married Charles Tennant, an economist. She subsequently published *France on the Eve of the Great Revolution*, the journal that her grandfather, Sir George Collier, had kept when he visited Paris and Brussels in the summer of 1773. Her daughter Dorothy became the wife of H. M. Stanley, the explorer.

Henrietta (her names are also given as Harriette Augusta Royer) married Sir Alexander Campbell, Bart., of Barcaldine.

2. He also won a second prize for composition in 1833 and a first prize for natural history in 1837.

3. If this account seems exaggerated, it may be as well to quote a letter of G. Lowes Dickinson, written under similar circumstances: 'Oh Grant, I've begun Faust, of which indeed I will not speak, for is it not as yet unspeakable? Such a rush of music and passion and thought as I have not known for long takes me out of this miserable self into heaven.' E. M. Forster, *Goldsworthy Lowes Dickinson* (1934), p. 46.

4. Chateaubriand's imprint on *Les Mémoires d'un fou* of 1838 is heavy.

5. *Les Mémoires d'un fou*, ch. iii.

6. The year that used to be given for the first meeting with Elisa Schlésinger was 1837, but in 1914 Coleman (*Flaubert's literary Development*, pp. 1-3), collating all the references, suggested that 1836 was more likely. In 1932 Gérard-Gailly (*L'unique passion de Flaubert*, p. 29) showed that the date of birth of Mme Schlésinger's daughter had been falsified and that in fact the child (Marie) was born on 4th April 1836, and not in January. In this discovery he had been anticipated by Coleman, but Coleman did not press home his conclusions. If Flaubert saw the child fed at the breast, it was

probably in 1836, especially as he speaks of it as three or four months old; but as many mothers continued to suckle their children for an unnecessarily long time in the mistaken belief that they would thereby avoid further pregnancies, and as Mme Schlésinger had good reasons for not wishing to increase her family (see Chapter III), 1837 cannot be ruled out. 1836, however, accords better with Flaubert's remark to Edmond de Goncourt that he was 'en quatrième' (*Journal*, v, 99); for he entered the third form, which is senior to the fourth, in the autumn of 1836.

The meeting with the Colliers is thus pushed back to 1835 or even earlier. This is confirmed by Flaubert's remark 'la plus âgée avait quinze ans': Gertrude was born in 1819. The only objection is the following passage from *Les Mémoires d'un fou* (ch. xv: 'Plusieurs temps se passèrent donc de la sorte. Au mois de mai, la mère de ces jeunes filles vint en France conduire leur frère. C'était un charmant garçon, blond comme elles et pétillant de gaminerie et d'orgueil britannique.' In 1835 Herbert was only two. There are two possibilities: either the brother referred to is Clarence or even George, or else there were several encounters with the Colliers and in 1837 or 1838, perhaps in May, Flaubert met Herbert. But neither alternative is quite satisfactory: although he met the Colliers periodically as a student, Flaubert never once refers to the existence of George or Clarence; on the other hand, in 1838, which is the latest date possible for the appearance of the 'charmant garçon', Herbert was only five.

As for Flaubert's return to Trouville in Mme Schlésinger's absence, the year usually given is 1838 and the reason seems to lie in this passage from *Les Mémoires d'un fou* (ch. xxi): 'J'y revins deux ans plus tard; vous pensez où . . .; elle n'y était pas.' It is certainly true that he visited Trouville in 1838; but unless the letter of 22nd September 1837 (Conard edition, i, 28) is wrongly dated—always a possibility—he also went there in 1837; and from Demorest's minute and painstaking analysis (*L'Expression figurée*, pp. 125-7) it is clear that after the summer of 1837 his metaphors immediately became more frequent and vivid. Some intense experience is indicated. The most likely chronology therefore appears to be:

1836. Flaubert meets the Schlésingers at Trouville.

1837. He just misses Maurice Schlésinger and fully realizes his love for Elisa.

1838. He spends his holidays there as usual.

In that case, the 'deux ans' of the *Mémories d'un fou* are not to be taken literally.

Chapter Three

PARIS

'J'ai au fond de l'âme le brouillard du Nord que j'ai respiré à ma naissance.' Letter to Louise Colet, 6th August 1846.

Rouen, on his return, seemed scarcely habitable. Now that he had bathed in the gulf of Valinco and slept beneath the Corsican pines, he chafed at every day of inaction spent in France. 'I was born', he told Chevalier in November, 'to be Emperor of Cochin China, with my fifty-yard pipes, my six thousand wives, . . . Numidian mares and marble fountains; but vast desires I can never satisfy, a frightful ennui and yawns without end comprise my whole kingdom.' Though he knew the futility of his girdings against the city and its inhabitants and poked a kind of insincere fun at his own dissatisfaction, the prospect of staying in Rouen for long depressed him beyond measure. More out of indifference than obedience he had acquiesced in his father's wish for him to go to Paris in the autumn of 1841 to read law: the four years of drudgery would at least bring a change. In the meantime he vegetated.

Compared with Achille, he was an unsatisfactory son, with no particular bent and no marked ability; but Dr. Flaubert did not press for a decision about his career and allowed him to spend 1841 idly at home. The reason lay in his health. At first sight he was alarmingly strong, with broad shoulders, black eyebrows, and a golden beard—handsome enough to earn a round of applause at Rouen playhouse when he went to see *Ruy Blas* and to wring from Cloquet the startled comment: 'He must be Apollo.' But his prolonged and apparently motiveless moods of depression were disquieting symptoms, and when he returned from what should have been an enlivening trip to Corsica and slipped at once into his

46

habitual lassitude, there was cause for anxiety; especially as he now assumed an elephantine girth and puffed and sweated at the slightest exertion.

In summer 1841 he went as usual to Trouville, which was growing popular and had acquired bathing-machines; but he was bored and even looked forward to returning to Rouen: there he could at least get up at four to read Homer. As for his future profession, he neglected it entirely, and although in October he enrolled in the Law Faculty at Paris, his departure from home was further postponed.

Flaubert was fond of his family. Little as he had found in common with Achille, he admitted a reluctant regard for him as a brother, and for Caroline he had a much warmer affection. But the intimacy which had bound them together as children and forbidden the harbouring of secrets was gradually dissolving as they grew older, and while Gustave was able to develop largely in accordance with his own nature, Caroline was being moulded for her future as a wife and mother. In spite of her chilly manner she was exquisite both in looks and character; but Gustave felt a diffidence before her, as though by harmonizing so easily with society she had incurred a particle of his unwilling hostility. It is unlikely that she ever had an inkling of his infatuation with Elisa Schlésinger. Moreover their companionship was impeded by her delicate health; for she had suffered from a long illness—probably tuberculosis—and the purpose of the trip to Trouville in 1841 was to distract and relieve the gloom into which she had settled.

His father seemed remote in interests and temperament, and though there is an evident link between Dr. Flaubert's fits of anger and Gustave's moods of depression, it probably never occured to the son that his own troubles were paralleled in the life of so formidable and distinguished a man as the head of the Hôtel-Dieu. Proximity and admiration blinded him; he conceived of his own uneasy longings and painful desires as intensely personal, experienced only by a few kindred souls like Le Poittevin. If he wanted sympathy, he looked rather to his mother, but he was far too proud and shy to take her into his confidence. Ultimately, in spite of the serene family atmosphere, he was alone; his sensitivity divided him from the rest, and by imagining the gulf to be greater than it was and brooding on it, he did in fact deepen his solitude. But his solitude was entirely a matter of aesthetic values and perceptiveness; in other things he adopted the point of view of his family. Flaubert, the great hater and vilifier of the bourgeois, was himself bourgeois; comfort, stability, wealth—all the advantages of the class were his, and he accepted them without question, rejecting only the vices of self-satisfaction, vulgarity, and insensitiveness which seemed almost always to accompany the virtues. He took over unhesitatingly the Romantic meaning of 'bourgeois' as 'implacably opposed to art', for art had simply no place in his own bourgeois background; and although his ideas, as they developed, led him to a qualified anarchism, his condemnation of the bourgeois was moral and never truly political. His period was one in which the middle classes had obtained power; in industry, politics, finance, and society they were supreme; and what Flaubert stigmatized as bourgeois was essentially power itself, the pompous folly of authority, the complacent dogmatism of a ruling class. In another age he would have denounced the aristocracy or the proletariat.

Most of the year 1842 he spent in Rouen, though he made occasional trips to Paris. In March, during one of these periods of absence, the Mayor of Rouen drew lots on his behalf and Flaubert was given a number that exempted him from military service. But his main worry was not conscription, which could always be avoided, but the future. Although he was willing to go to Paris and read law, he could never see himself at the bar; such a life might suit Chevalier and even Le Poittevin, but for him it would be a capitulation. If, however, he rejected law, what possible profession could he choose? Dared he embrace literature? He jealously hid his writing from his family, and when he mentioned it to his friends, he always declared that his work would not be published. Since the appearance of his two pieces in *Le Colibri* his standards had risen till he felt not only superior in taste and discernment to the reading public but reluctant to expose to their bovine and unsympathetic gaze what was after all the tenderest and most secret part of himself. When he wrote it was for his own pleasure

—to express his deepest feelings in an acceptable form—and a work like *Les Mémoires d'un fou* was never intended for the profane reader.

In his perplexity he sent a letter to Gourgaud-Dugazon, formerly a master at the *collège*, asking for advice. His main interest, he said, was still literature, and the more poetry he knew, the more he discovered in it; but though he felt that the critical moment was upon him, he hesitated to make up his mind. 'Once I have reached a decision, nothing will stop me, even if everyone jeers and scoffs.' He could not, however, be sure of his ability; there was always the horrible possibility that he was deceiving himself, that his delight was not matched by any talent. Three years before he had told Ernest: 'If ever I take an active part in the world, it will be as a thinker and demoralizer'; but now he was more certain that his bent led him to imaginative prose, and he offered to show Gourgaud the work he was engaged on. 'Perhaps it's very beautiful, but I'm afraid it may be thoroughly false, pretentious and stilted.'

What Gourgaud replied is not recorded: probably he took refuge in the usual alternation of warning and encouragement. At all events Flaubert carried on as before, and in the autumn he finished *Novembre*. It is the first of his juvenilia for which he retained any affection later in his life and within its limitations it has remarkable power. Though replete with Romantic phrases, moods, and lamentations and certainly not the masterpiece some have claimed it to be, it is a first-class document by which to judge his state of mind from 1840 to 1842; for, under the guise of a prostitute called Marie, he introduces Eulalie Foucaud de Lenglade, describing in a cascade of metaphors the throbbing desire he had felt for her; he speaks too of his earlier dreams, blighted and desecrated by physical love, and recounts the intense conviction of union with Nature he once experienced while walking by the sea— a transposition onto the emotional plane of the Spinozan love of God. But in spite of the main theme, which is Marie, *Novembre*, like *Les Mémoires d'un fou*, is haunted by the memory of Mme Schlésinger: she was identified with Flaubert's picture of womanhood and could not be displaced by an impermanent rival.

His reluctance to practise law derived partly from his feeling for the grotesque; the spectacle of one man judging another, pretending to be superior in order to condemn, struck him as both comic and pitiful; and though he tried to understand the text-books, he put them down with relief and now and then, as he watched the setting sun, imagined that he had reached Arles for the second time and that his journey would carry him far beyond. On 30th June, however, he arrived in Paris to immerse himself temporarily in the legalistic style of the two great pundits, MM. Oudot and Ducoudray; but though, like a two-headed monster, they even invaded his dreams, he did not satisfy his examiners in August. Cheerfully indifferent, he took refuge in Ronsard, Rabelais, and Homer.

It was decided that in November he must leave Rouen and spend the academic year in Paris; and he was the less sorry to go because the change would bring him in close contact again with Ernest Chevalier. He had also built up an attractive picture of student life: he saw himself surrounded by actresses, leading a flamboyantly bohemian existence, flouting the conventions, shocking the bourgeois, luxuriating in love and art and philosophy— rather in accordance with the ideas he later attributed to Homais. From this picture it was a sad decline to reality. He had obtained rooms in what is now the rue Denfert-Rochereau, not far from the Gardens of the Luxembourg, and furnished them with three chairs and a divan. The cost of living was far higher than at Rouen and when he had paid for his meals and his lodgings there was not much left over. He got up at eight and went to bed at midnight, attending dull lectures and reading tedious books; unlike Stendhal he detested the prose of the *Code civil* and longed for some resonant and colourful French. He had no company and no outings; when he could stand his boredom no longer he tidied the boots in his cupboard and put a brighter polish on them. As for actresses, he soon found out that a poor student could not compete with his opulent rivals of the right bank and that the Latin Quarter only offered pallid shop-girls with chilblains on their fingers and probably other more serious disadvantages.

Chevalier, too, had been ill and made only spasmodic appear-

ances, and, rather in spite of himself, Flaubert was so lonely that
he worked hard. The result was to get him through his examinations in December; but before this he had been toying with the
idea of marriage as an escape from solitude and a means of
acquiring wealth. The episode, referred to in a letter from Le
Poittevin, is a mysterious one; it came to nothing and is never
mentioned again.

In Paris he was very much of a provincial, clumsy and ill at
ease, walking out at eight in the morning dressed in black like a
best man, with a white tie and white gloves. But gradually he
settled down, and by 1843 he had been incorporated in the
student community. Incorporated, that is, as far as his temperament would allow; for he was still aloof, proud, and shy, reluctant
to commit himself or to encroach on the personality of others.
The idea of taking a mistress, of being involved in someone else's
life, was abhorrent to him, the more so as student convention
expected it; he was a seducer in theory, not in practice; but the
mere fact of prostitution titillated him strangely, as though it
afforded a delicate revenge on all the philanthropists in the world,
and he liked to wander along the boulevards at eight in the evening
and watch the girls in their low-necked dresses lingering by the
gas-lamps, seeking custom. The last night of the old year he always
spent in a brothel as a gesture of cynicism, but he derived no
pleasure from it; he picked out the ugliest girl and made love to
her with a cigar still in his mouth, just to show his friends how
little he cared. In fact it showed how much, in other circumstances,
he might have cared. He felt as though there were another personality inside him who observed his acts and emotions with sardonic
interest and mockingly checked any tendency to self-abandonment. His real orgies were not of the senses but of the imagination
and he spent his concupiscence on phantoms far more satisfying
than the conventional *grisette*.

Shortly after his arrival in Paris he had called on the Colliers,
who were delighted to see him. Herbert flung his arms round his
neck, Gertrude was charming, and Henrietta smiled from her sick-
bed. Periodically he visited them at their house near the Rond-
Point of the Champs-Elysées; but in August 1843 they moved to

Chaillot, near the Bois de Boulogne, and Flaubert had neither the leisure nor the means to meet them often. He also renewed his friendship with Cloquet, whose hospitality was unfailing, and recalled with him the more ludicrous episodes of their trip to Corsica.

But his important encounter was with Maxime Du Camp. Flaubert met him in the rooms of a former schoolfellow, and from the first moment each sensed an affinity in the other. Both had welcomed the exciting revelations of Romantic literature and been infected with its concomitant melancholy; both felt a revulsion from their epoch and nation; and when, on a sudden impulse, Flaubert invited Du Camp to his rooms and, emboldened by his own temerity, unlocked a casket and read him *Novembre* from beginning to end, the seal was set on their friendship. Henceforward they were inseparable and hid nothing from each other.

Friendship can be almost as blind as love, and though both men had much to offer, there was an essential divergence in their characters. From one point of view Du Camp was more fortunate: left an orphan at an early age and endowed with considerable wealth, he had persuaded his tutor to let him become an author, and though he was reading law in Paris, he could plan his future with the knowledge that his plans would not be opposed. He was lithe and slim, with sharp features and a biting wit. Intellectually he was quicker and more malleable than Flaubert, absorbing and echoing congenial ideas and turning them into epigrams. But while impressions were easily printed on his mind, they were as easily effaced, and he wore convictions as he did his clothes, discarding them when they were no longer fashionable. With Du Camp as listener, Flaubert felt he had met a spiritual twin, so swiftly and exactly were his own ideas returned; and in Flaubert Du Camp discovered a companion who took literature with a proper degree of seriousness and had already attained a remarkable power of self-expression. It did not occur to Flaubert that Du Camp might not share his unimpeachable integrity in all matters of art, just as it did not occur to Du Camp that Flaubert might not share his own preference for fame as against achievement. For the time being they derived an unalloyed delight in each other's company, and while Du Camp had before him the constant example of a delicate and subtly vibrating sensibility, Flaubert rejoiced in a friend whose avowed ambition was to write and whose conversation was one scintillating shower of wit and paradox. Du Camp represented what he yearned to become, and afforded him an opportunity and excuse to be himself. The real stimulus lay in the other man's situation and interests, and even if Du Camp had been a nonentity, Flaubert would have taken long to notice it.

They organized dinner-parties at a restaurant in the rue de l'Ancienne-Comédie—Flaubert thundering out his admiration for Hugo, Du Camp twitting him on his temporary addiction to Ponsard, Louis de Cormenin juggling with words, and Alfred Le Poittevin, when he was in Paris, murmuring sinuous turpitudes. There was scarcely any subject the conversation left unmolested, from the farces at the little theatres and latest literary scandal to the nature of the self and the personality of God. Only politics were taboo. What was said was always superficial and sometimes unintelligent, but it escaped criticism because it was exciting. On other evenings Flaubert entertained in his rooms; through a fog of tobacco smoke a row of highly polished boots reflected the uneven light of a dozen candles, while you could also distinguish a vermeil cider cup and the inevitable Romantic *memento mori*, a skull.

Despite the surge of boredom and disgust that he always felt when attending lectures, Flaubert still turned up dutifully in the hope that some of what he heard would stick in his mind; and at night, in his rooms, he made exhaustive notes from legal textbooks, often copying mechanically with his mind on other things. He had not the faintest interest in the subject and not the slightest respect for those who had mastered it; the law seemed to him not merely an ass but the devil as well. Out of deference to his family he continued his studies, but with reluctance; every time he returned to Paris from Rouen he felt homesick and missed his sister's company; and when he learnt in 1843 that he had been ploughed, he was not at all surprised; his only regret was that the labours of reading and note-taking, intrinsically worthless, had failed to justify themselves.

Art supplied his only true satisfaction, and in addition to the
dilettanti of the Latin Quarter he had now met some real practi-
tioners, for he had visited the studio of the sculptor Pradier. He
may have received an introduction to Mme Pradier, who was the
sister of one of his school-friends; at any rate he soon felt at home
in the free-and-easy atmosphere of the Abbatiale. Pradier was just
reaching the peak of his fame and his studio was like a public
meeting-house; he looked like Poussin and dressed for the part,
with a black velvet jacket, streams of golden hair escaping from a
broad Tyrolean hat, and a cloak lined with blue silk slung jauntily
over his shoulder. He worked in an uproar; and while roughers-out
hewed at marble, models quarrelled, and visitors gossiped, he persevered with his chipping or strode about telling ribald stories and
winking ostentatiously. In many ways he seemed a charlatan and
Flaubert, dazzled though he was, regretted the essential banality of
his character; but he possessed an undoubted talent, an infectious
gaiety, and a genuine love of the antique, and no one who knew
him well could remain unimpressed by his tireless emphasis on
beauty of line and form.

In Mme Pradier's salon Flaubert met Gertrude Collier together
with more distinguished visitors. In January 1843 he was introduced to Victor Hugo—'the man more than any other that has
thrilled my heart'. Hugo turned out to be human, unpreposses-
sing and rather ugly, and as he talked to Flaubert, they both gazed
self-consciously at the right hand that had written so many famous
lines.

But when Flaubert went to Paris, the person he most hoped to
see was Mme Schlésinger, who was living with her husband in the
rue de Gramont, only a few yards from the music-shop. He may
have met her in 1840, when he was returning from Corsica, but if
so, it was for an hour or two, just sufficient to revive their acquain-
tanceship and remind her of their holiday together. Although
Schlésinger had bought some property at Trouville and probably
came in contact with the Flauberts during his trips to the coast,
Gustave can have felt no certainty of being welcome in Paris or
even of being recognized. How relations were renewed is
obscure,[1] but in March 1843 he mentions to Caroline that he has

been invited to 'a big annual dinner with my friend Maurice. It will calm my nerves.'

In a short time he was an intimate of the household, dining every Wednesday and acquiring a detailed knowledge of Schlésinger's intrigues; and what compunction he may originally have felt about deceiving him must have vanished when he realized the extent of his extramarital attachments. With Mme Schlésinger, however, he was timid. Seven years earlier she had embodied for him everything that was pure and desirable in womanhood, and she was coming to stand as a symbol of his own youth and longings; but she preserved all her charm and beauty, and even if Flaubert's first intention in again seeking her company was curiosity, a wish to appraise his adolescent ideal and see how it had borne the passage of time, his interest was swiftly enhanced till he sought to become her lover. Undoubtedly he declared himself; and it seems from *L'Education sentimentale* of 1869, in which he portrayed Mme Schlésinger as Mme Arnoux, that she hinted at some reciprocal feeling. But in spite of his attractions, of which he was thoroughly aware, and in spite of Schlésinger's habitual and notorious infidelity, there was no question of her giving way. Once or twice his arguments may have seemed more persuasive and she listened with less than her usual reluctance; but each time he encountered an eventual refusal, as though there were some hidden barrier she could not cross. It was the more puzzling because she was evidently fond of him, and yet did nothing to retain his love. In Mme Arnoux, as in Mme Schlésinger, there is this core of mystery, and none of the ordinary explanations—affection for her children, loyalty to her husband, religious scruples, respect for convention—is quite adequate; the reader of *L'Education sentimentale* feels what Flaubert himself felt, that deep in this woman's nature there was some particular impediment that absolutely forbade her to yield to her emotions.

Flaubert himself never knew what this impediment was, and but for the acute and patient researches of M. Gérard-Gailly it is improbable that Elisa Schlésinger's secret would ever have been revealed. Even today the precise details are unknown.

She was the daughter of a retired infantry captain named Foucault and was born at Vernon in 1810. After a simple education in which music played a large part, she chose from among her suitors Emile Judée, who was a second-lieutenant in the baggage-train and had been garrisoned at Vernon; and in November 1829, when she had not long left the convent, they were married. It appears to have been a love-match on both sides. There was some difficulty in making up Elisa's dowry to the figure required by the Ministry of War, for her father had never been wealthy and after his retirement had been forced to augment his pension by working first in the *mairie* and then as a *commissaire de police*; but Judée was accommodating, and for the purposes of officialdom the necessary sum was procured, at least on paper. He and Elisa were to live at Vernon and they seemed to enjoy every prospect of a happy marriage: mutual affection, a settled position, and an assured income—they possessed all the simple prerequisites, and if there was a slight disparity of age—the bridegroom was thirty-three—it was not unusual and certainly gave no cause for anxiety.

No news of them comes till the following year. Then, abruptly, without stating any reason, Judée asks for a transfer to Algeria and obtains it at once. Fighting against the Mohammedans was at its fiercest: with desert convoys daily attacked and ambushed, the death-roll was high and in going to Africa Judée was courting death. Meanwhile his wife, who hitherto had never left Vernon, appears in Paris as Mme Schlésinger.

If Elisa's character were uncertain, the sudden and overwhelming change in her fortunes might be explained by a caprice of passion, an infatuation with the dashing and plausible Schlésinger; but everything we know about her contradicts this suggestion. She was always regarded as a woman of outstanding virtue, steady in her affections, unwavering in her religion, yet devoid of bigotry. Of her friends who were familiar with her secret, not one seems to have felt anything but pity for her in her position. Moreover she was undoubtedly in love with Judée.

Hypotheses could be multiplied. Gérard-Gailly supposes, for example, that Judée committed some crime casting dishonour on his wife and her family. But there is no trace of crime in his record. At all events Judée left the country, and Elisa, with the full knowledge of her parents, began an entirely new life in Paris. As Schlésinger, who was a keen hunter, used to stay with the banker Schickler at a *château* close to Vernon, it is suggested that he learnt a crisis had occurred and proposed a bargain : if Judée would disappear once and for all, he would look after Elisa. It was just the situation that would appeal to him, combining chivalry with business: on the one hand, he saved a beautiful woman in trouble; on the other, he acquired an admirable wife whose own equivocal position would prevent her from pestering him unduly about his other attachments.

Judée, however, survived the war, but caught dysentery and in 1835 returned to France for hospital treatment. His health deteriorated fast and he was given indefinite leave. In 1838, after taking the waters at Barèges and Bagnères, he returned to Vernon, and as Elisa came there regularly to see her parents, it is possible that husband and wife met again. By this time he was only the wreck of a man and the next year, having tried unsuccessfully to kill himself, he died.

When, therefore, Flaubert first met Elisa at Trouville, she was not Schlésinger's lawful wife and her daughter was illegitimate. If her name had appeared as mother on the birth-certificate, Judée would, in law, have been the father, and to overcome the difficulty the child was officially registered as 'Marie-Adèle-Julie-Monina Schlésinger, daughter of Maurice-Adolphe Schlésinger, and of a mother unknown'. Indeed the whole fabric of Elisa's life, outwardly so conventional and secure, was compounded of falsehood, and the poor woman must have had a bewildered sense of her precarious standing in the world, as though any moment might bring exposure and denunciation. The news, however, of Judée's death improved her position, for Schlésinger kept his word and in September 1840, as soon as the period of ten months prescribed by law had gone by, he and Elisa were married in great secret. Schlésinger, in fact, was as good a husband as anyone could expect from such a man, and though Elisa reproached him for his fickleness, he was always extremely fond of her and in deference to her wishes abandoned the Jewish religion and was baptized as a Christian. In return she gave him not love but gratitude; and having no conception of the reasons for this gratitude and its depth, Flaubert was baffled by her loyalty. Why she should support and defend a husband who, in addition to his other shortcomings, gossiped about her physical charms to his friends, was an extraordinary problem which he was forced to abandon unsolved; but since it formed part of the human pattern of frustration, misunderstanding, and futility, he incorporated it in *L'Education sentimentale*. His own role was that of Frédéric.

'She immediately broached the eternal subject of recrimination: Arnoux. It was not his misconduct that shocked her. But she seemed to suffer in her pride, and disclosed her repugnance for this man without delicacy, dignity and honour.

" 'Or rather, he's mad,' " she said.

'Frédéric artfully encouraged her confidences. Soon he knew the whole of her life.'[2]

For once, master of irony though he was, Flaubert fell victim to an irony more cruel than his own: he knew only a fragment of her life.

Notes to Chapter Three

1. A good deal can be inferred from *L'Education sentimentale* of 1869, which is largely autobiographical; but as Flaubert adapts and edits his experience to fit it into the mould of the novel, it is almost impossible to tell where fact ends and fiction begins. Thus in reality he had met Mme Schlésinger by saving her cloak from the incoming tide; in the novel Frédéric Moreau stops Mme Arnoux's shawl from falling over the side of a river-steamer.

2. *L'Education sentimentale*, Part II, ch. iii.

Chapter Four

CROISSET

'*On ne pardonne pas assez à mes nerfs. Cela m'a ravagé la sensibilité pour le reste de mes jours.*' Letter to Louise Colet, 25th October 1853.

Flaubert's father did not allow him to return to the University for the new academic year. In December he visited Paris in an attempt to retrieve his failure in the August examinations, but he might as well have stayed at home. He was paying for his earlier indiscretions: overfeeding which alternated with inadequate snacks, overwork which extended into the small hours and was aggravated by large quantities of black coffee, oversmoking which sometimes amounted to thirty pipes a day, and an overindulgence in reverie caused by his dissatisfaction with reality and making it consequently harder for him to reach a *modus vivendi*—all these habits impaired a constitution that had never been so strong as it seemed and was now frayed with worry and discontent.

In January 1844 he was returning from Trouville to Rouen. He had witnessed some distressing scenes at the house of an acquaintance and the emotional disturbance precipitated a crisis. His brother Achille picked him up at Pont-l'Evêque in a gig and Gustave took over the reins himself. It was a pitch-black night; even the horse was scarcely visible. As they were coming into the village of Bourg-Achard with a distant glow on the right to mark the inn, a carrier's cart loomed out of the darkness, and just when it drew level, with bells jingling and wheels clattering, Gustave slumped to the ground—'as though swept away', he says, 'in a torrent of flame'. Achille carried him to the nearest house and bled him on the spot, fearing indeed that he was dead; but at the third bleeding Gustave came round and Achille hurried him back to the gig and on to the Hôtel-Dieu.

There he passed into the hands of Dr. Flaubert, who declared that he suffered from an excess of vigour, sent him to bed, put a seton round his neck to draw off blood, and subjected him to a rigorous diet. He was forbidden wine, tobacco, juicy meats—in fact all the things he loved—and was frequently bled. For some days his life hung in the balance, threatened as much by his doctors as by his illness; he had four more attacks in a fortnight; once, having just bled him, Dr. Flaubert was so alarmed at not seeing the blood return when he withdrew the lancet that he poured almost boiling water onto Gustave's arm and burnt it badly. The treatment was unpleasant: apart from valerian, indigo, and castor, the seton was maintained and dripped continually down his neck; when he was thirsty he was only allowed an infusion of orange-flowers, and he had to resign himself to the application of leeches. He was in a highly nervous state: at the lightest touch or least excitement his whole body quivered and the swift tension of his muscles was painfully apparent under the skin; scarcely a day went by without his seeing odd shapes drifting by like bundles of hair or Bengal lights.

As for the actual attacks, they have been described by Du Camp, who hastened to Rouen as soon as he heard of his friend's illness. Du Camp is not a reliable witness and there is no means of checking his account. He says that Flaubert first had a feeling of unease and then a flame appeared in his right eye; at this stage he could still run to his bed and lie on it, but afterwards he was helpless. 'I hold the reins', he cried, 'here is the carter, I hear the bells. Ah! I see the lantern of the inn.' Then came a sharp cry and convulsion, followed by deep sleep and an exhaustion lasting several days.

These details are neither confirmed nor denied by the rare accounts Flaubert gave of his malady. He felt taut and over-strained as though his sensibility was screwed up to an abnormal pitch; through closed doors he could sometimes hear the softest whisper. Then, when an attack ensued, a million ideas and images exploded in his mind in the space of a second, like a vast firework display, with a rending pain as if body and soul were being torn apart. Several times he thought he was dead; but although he could not speak, he was convinced that throughout the attack he never lost consciousness. His soul, he said, was turned inwards on itself, like a hedgehog tortured with its own prickles.

The diagnosis of Flaubert's disease has caused much controversy. During his lifetime it was believed by his friends that he was epileptic and after his death Du Camp did not scruple to make the allegation publicly and to deduce from it certain characteristics of Flaubert's art and personality. Epilepsy was then considered a shameful secret, to be hushed up at all costs, and it is at least possible that Dr. Flaubert considered his son to be a victim of *grand mal*. The pathology of the nervous diseases, however, was at an elementary stage, and even if epilepsy was diagnosed it by no means follows that the diagnosis was correct. Taking and examining the evidence afresh, it seems far more probable that Flaubert suffered from some form of grande hysteria.[1] But whatever his illness, it affords no clue to his life and work.

The immediate effect was to end his attempts to acquire a competent knowledge of law; it was clear that for a long time he would be unable to lead a normal life and in April he gave up his rooms in Paris. Fortunately, however, he was not condemned to perpetual seclusion in Rouen; for in 1844 Dr. Flaubert sold his property at Yonville because the attached farm was going to be cut in two by the new railway line, and bought a house at Croisset, a few miles downstream from Rouen, on the right bank of the Seine. It had originally belonged to the Benedictines of Saint-Ouen and a tenacious but unsubstantiated local legend maintained that Prévost had there written *Manon Lescaut*. It was a low white house standing some way back from the river, and an avenue of lindens led across the garden to the wooded hill of Canteleu behind. Hard on the towpath there was an eighteenth-century *pavillon* which still survives.

In June the whole family moved to Croisset from the Hôtel-Dieu and the new atmosphere offered a welcome sense of calm. But although he went boating with Achille and spent much time in the open air, Gustave could not find calm within himself. Periodically he suffered an attack and after being once taken ill in the fields and lying helpless for hours, he resolved never again to go walking alone. The company at Croisset, however, virtually restricted as it was to his family, gave him little pleasure or stimulation. Le Poittevin was in Paris with Chevalier, who was completing a doctoral thesis; and when in May Du Camp left for a year's trip to the Near East, Flaubert's envy was sharpened by the consummation of his solitude.

At the supreme crisis of his life, therefore, he was morally unsupported, his daily companions being an affectionate but ailing sister and a mother who wore herself out with anxiety. He had to struggle against the monsters of his imagination and banish them without the encouragement of his friends or the assistance a psychiatrist might nowadays have afforded; and the battle, ironically enough, was with his own creatures whom he had conjured up to distract his leisure. The figures of his early stories—the despairing suicide of *La dernière heure*, the cruel alchemist of *Le Rêve d'enfer*, the murderous ape-man of *Quidquid volueris*—most certainly returned to torment him, and the hours of fantasy he had spent with the great criminals of history were relived in an atmosphere of nightmarish oppression. His own unhappy recollections —the guillotine with the pool of blood, the mad women tearing at their faces, the corpses in the Hôtel-Dieu—must have been interwoven with macabre scenes from Gautier, Hugo, Hoffmann, and the Marquis de Sade, till in the whirl of ideas and impressions he felt, as he said, that his own personality was foundering like a ship in a tempest. Hallucinations beset him; he was like Saint Anthony plagued by his demons; in his darker moments he feared that his mind might crack and he would go mad. But he clung to his reason and conquered the disorders of his imagination by studying them deliberately and scientifically; sometimes, indeed, he induced states akin to his nervous attacks and endured their pain in order to examine them and satisfy his pride. For pride sustained him more than any other emotion; and thanks to his pride he displayed and developed those two qualities of courage and self-analysis which were for him the only means of escaping from the terrors of a distempered mind.

Once the first few months were over and the disease had somewhat abated, he was slow to make progress; he spent the summer months almost entirely at Croisset, bathing and boating, writing and reading, and he had ample time to take stock of his position. Hitherto he had been able to postpone a decision, but now it was thrust upon him. Whether he wished it or not, the kind of life he had led in Paris would not be possible for years; perhaps it would never be possible again. At Croisset, which was to be his home, there was no Law School—and no Elisa Schlésinger. It is as though circumstances conspired with his temperament to eliminate any approximation to the normal pattern of existence. How acutely he felt the change is not apparent from his letters; but he once told the Goncourts that he would rather serve seven years in the army than have any kind of infirmity. Remote as the pleasures he longed for had always been, they now vanished altogether.

Since February 1843 he had been working on a novel, *L'Education sentimentale*, entirely different from the book he subsequently published under the same title; and as he continued writing, the outlines of a more satisfying and personal credo than he had yet attained sketched themselves in his mind and were transferred to the text.[2] The plot was based on the contrast between two friends, Jules and Henry. Whereas Jules remains in the provinces and loses his heart to an actress who takes no interest in him, Henry goes to Paris as a student, makes love to Emilie Renaud, the wife of the man in whose *pension* he is living, and persuades her to elope with him. Up to this point Flaubert's main interest lies in the keen and ambitious Henry, and the surrender of Emilie, who is suspiciously like Elisa Schlésinger, probably gives even more pleasure to the author than to Henry himself. As soon, however, as the couple become lovers, the writing falters, for it treats a subject outside Flaubert's range of experience; and then, with the twentieth chapter, the emphasis shifts entirely. Jules, who has hitherto appeared as a rather mediocre provincial, without personal charm, practical ability or prospects, steps into the limelight, displacing Henry, who, after some months in America, tires of his mistress, brings her back to France, and plunges into a life of superficial brilliance and essential futility. It is clear that between the writing of the nineteenth and twentieth chapters the author's conception of the book has changed and that social success has ceased to attract him. Here, in fact, is the incidence of Flaubert's nervous disease.

Jules is superior by being an artist; and his art is pre-eminently that of drama, to which Flaubert had always been drawn. The theatre, whether represented by the puppet-show of the Père Legrain, the billiard-room of the Hôtel-Dieu, *Ruy Blas* or *Antony*, still had a lure for him and he thought of himself as a poet—a poet who somehow never wrote verse. But he now sifted the ideas about literature he had accepted uncritically from his contemporaries, rejected some, developed others and tried to link them together. At his best he was never a systematic thinker either by natural ability or by inclination; seeking not to dogmatize about aesthetics but to integrate his personality through art, he expounded his new theories in the second part of *L'Education sentimentale*.

Jules, who in this section of the book is entirely Flaubert's mouthpiece, surveys the feelings and ideas that are habitual to him and discovers that many of them derive from past experiences which he has outgrown. Where his opinions are false, they are incomplete, and they are incomplete because his experience of life is too narrow and superficial. To know the truth is in itself impossible—Flaubert had learnt that from Spinoza—but there is always a further stage of knowledge which can be reached, and for Jules the means of attaining it is art. The study of human nature, however, which belongs to the domain of art, is not only a matter of observation and intelligence; it demands a hardening of oneself —a hardening that Flaubert practised in the analysis of his own malady; and Jules realizes that he can no longer dismiss part of his experience as ugly, but that he must seek in it the beauty and harmony which it certainly possesses. Criticism, therefore, whether of nature or of art, becomes more objective: it is not enough to record one's personal reaction to a poem or a landscape. And creative writing becomes objective at the same time, spurning lyrical effusions and striving for a style that is increasingly subtle and strong and for a vision of the world that is sufficiently true. Indeed, Jules is so convinced of the parallel development of vision and style that he rejects the heretical distinction between form and content, maintaining that once an idea has been adequately conceived, the right expression is thereby found.

Although it is possible to trace in the so-called *école pittoresque* of the Romantics a doctrine of objectivity and although Flaubert was certainly familiar with some of these ideas, the artistic credo which he put into the mouth of Jules was not merely another poetic: indeed Jules 'conceived an absolute scorn for all the poetics that ever existed'. By formulating his own attitude, Flaubert was affirming his own discovery of beauty in nature and art; he denounced Romantic subjectivism because it was so grossly, so blasphemously blind to the beauty of the world and attributed to a personal response what in fact transcended and almost annihilated the individual. No one more than he was aware of the fickleness and unreliability of the human mind; his own faculties often seemed on the verge of dissolution; but that same mind, however feeble, was the vessel of a beauty he was still only beginning to perceive; and his theory of art triumphantly declared the intensity, the 'otherness' of that experience, and afforded him a kind of religion in which the existence of an absolute beauty displaced the existence of God.

Henceforward Jules discards much of Romanticism and its clichés; he comes almost to hate scenes by moonlight, ruins, Venice, the innocent maiden, and the benevolent patriarch; but he concentrates on the grotesque element in society, noting with delight the remark of a well-known Catholic novelist: 'I pay prostitutes with the money earned by my platonic lovers.' Flaubert, similarly, had not abjured the grotesque, but modified his conception of it; while of no intrinsic value as he had thought, the abnormal and exceptional illuminate and clarify the normal and commonplace, establishing a broad context in which the antithesis between the two transcends paradox and conveys a truer notion of the scope of reality. Thus by contrasting beauty and ugliness, art, in Jules's words, achieves a beauty 'greater than beauty itself', for it reaches nearer to the source of infinite intelligence. There are indeed two beauties: the first being limited to the accepted pleasurable response, and the second so great that it enfolds all the manifestations of existence.

Through his philosophy of art, Flaubert became more reconciled to life: whatever pain and unhappiness he might undergo
were fragments of knowledge which amplified and deepened the
vision of the world he had so far held. That human life was of more
importance in the scheme of the universe than animal life, he
doubted; at any rate, no one could tell; but human life was the
only subject of which he could know anything, and from now on
his duty lay in observing and recording the activities of men, not
presuming to comment, but endeavouring to render a picture,
which, by its clarity and depth, would achieve a further stage in
the perception of truth and beauty, ultimately indivisible. And so
he leaves Jules at the end of *L'Education sentimentale* content to
write for his own pleasure, careless of success, conscious only of a
duty to express his thought to the best of his ability.

That *L'Education sentimentale* itself falls far short of Flaubert's
goal is not surprising, for the book was nearly finished before he
realized his purpose; but thanks to his illness, his solitude and
unhappiness, he had at last answered the question he put almost
three years before to Gourgaud-Dugazon, and decided what his
future should be. How far the attack of January 1844 coloured his
ideas it is impossible to say; in any case he would have reached
similar conclusions, though they might not have been so clear and
downright. But his physical disability, by terminating his career as
a law student and inflicting on him the lonely life of an invalid,
hastened his thought to maturity and turned his preferences into
convictions. He knew what he wished to do; and although Dr.
Flaubert fell asleep when Gustave read him the opening of *L'Education sentimentale* and, on being awakened, disparaged the simple
and rather pointless hobby of writing books, it needed far more
than a father's indifference to check him in his course.

In November 1844, however, there was news that upset him
badly: Caroline had become engaged and what was worse, her
fiancé was a certain Emile Hamard, whom he had known in Rouen
and Paris and who, despite pretensions as a poet, struck him as
vulgarity incarnate. 'It is all summed up', he told Chevalier, 'in
the two letters I uttered when I heard the news: AH!' Caroline's
engagement was almost an act of infidelity; she had been as close

to him as a wife. But if she wished to throw herself away, Flaubert could not prevent her, and he found some consolation with Alfred Le Poittevin, who was back in Rouen. Against the touchstone of so keen a mind he could test the durability of his new-found ideas, and for three months the two men were inseparable. Le Poittevin had passed five years in orgies and trivial affairs, which had seriously undermined his health; he was impelled less by viciousness of temperament than by boredom and a desire to prove his cynical theory of love, but although filled with self-disgust after each bout, he could not desist and so developed an extraordinary and quite egotistic faculty of self-criticism. Flaubert, on the other hand, had overcome both the Romanticism of his youth and the mask of worldliness which was only the same thing in a more sophisticated form, and if he had previously undergone Le Poittevin's influence in the field of metaphysical speculation, he now played the dominating role, for he brought Le Poittevin back to literature and tried to calm his distress by inculcating in him the doctrine of objectivity.

On 3rd March 1845 Caroline and Hamard were married, and shortly afterwards Flaubert and his family travelled to Paris for a day or two. One of his first visits was to the Colliers, and he was astonished to find that nothing had changed since he had last entered the house: Henrietta received him exactly as before, with the same voice and the same expression, and while they were talking a barrel-organ struck up beneath their windows just as it had almost two years earlier. The grotesque was remarkably consistent. As they sat together on a sofa, Henrietta took his hand, laced her fingers in his, and gave him a smile that made his blood run cold. At that moment her mother entered the room with a look of conspiratorial pleasure at the choice of a son-in-law. Flaubert, who only a few years previously would have married almost any woman in order to obtain money and independence, left the house feeling like a criminal.[3]

He also called on the Schlésingers, full of high hopes, but was told that Maurice had left the same day for London: it is unlikely that he saw Elisa.

From Paris the family returned to Nogent; and they decided

with rather intrusive solicitude to accompany Hamard and Caroline on their Italian honeymoon. Ever since he had first seen it from the plateau of El Prato, Flaubert had dreamed of visiting Italy; but Italy for him meant the country of Nero and Heliogabalus, not the simpering tour of picture galleries made by bourgeois newly-weds, and he felt no enthusiasm for the journey.

The event proved him right. While Achille stayed at home to mind his father's patients, the rest were packed into Dr. Flaubert's great post-chaise and borne away to Piedmont and Lombardy. They had scarcely left Rouen before Dr. Flaubert was afflicted with an eye-complaint, and when he was not travelling, he stayed indoors and applied leeches to his person; he was bored with the journey and missed his hospital. Meanwhile Gustave resented the speed of their progress and the shallowness of their observation; only at Avignon had he enjoyed himself and that was because of a solitary visit to the Museum and a sight of the bloodstains in the Palace of the Popes. At Marseilles, where he had hoped for another meeting with Mme Foucaud, he walked up the rue de la Darse only to find the Hôtel Richelieu shuttered and apparently empty; after a few desultory inquiries he strolled away, reluctant to open a past in which he now seemed to have been so much happier. By the time they reached Toulon Caroline was complaining of an aching back and general fatigue, and when they came to Italy Mme Flaubert worried increasingly about Caroline and despondent letters arrived from Achille, who was tired and overworked.

But there were compensations. Much as Gustave was irked by the petty restrictions imposed by his mother and by the concessions he had to make to the rest of the party, he was touring Italy for the first time and made the most of his opportunity. As a tourist, he accepted the present as a legacy of the past; whatever attractions it possessed were borrowed from the great events once enacted there, and as he looked at the Mediterranean, he imagined Roman barks gliding over a sea that was already ancient two thousand years before. His sense of history was pictorial and coloured —the history of Michelet and Chéruel—and since he could not be born again in the Rome of the Caesars or the Borgias, he did the next best thing by visiting the museums and art galleries and thinking himself back into crueller and more dramatic periods. The battlefields of Marengo, Novi, and Verceil meant little to him, but Genoa he found a city after his own heart, with its rose-gardens and marble palazzi. He explored its picture galleries, visited its open-air theatre, investigated its churches. He was, he wrote to Le Poittevin, not concerned to make reflections; it was enough to see and drink in what he saw. For although Flaubert sought knowledge, it was knowledge of his emotions, and he was content, when he travelled, to allow sights and sounds to play on his sensibility, leaving the analysis of emotion to a later time. He took copious notes, a habit he had started on his trip to Corsica, but they were essentially reminders, so that when he was home in his room he could rehearse the journey and feel again what he had felt originally. Indeed he was obeying the precept of Jules in *L'Education sentimentale*, reaching out to a more adequate conception of beauty by enlarging his experience of fact; and in the Genoese palazzi he gave his mind free play, seeing pictures dramatically, evocatively, romantically, historically—in short, in any but pictorial terms.

While in Genoa, Dr. Flaubert toyed with the idea of going on to Naples; and at the thought of so beautiful a city being desecrated by the presence of his family in a post-chaise, Gustave experienced as intense an *angoisse* as he had known for months. The project, however, was abandoned, and the return journey commenced, through Turin and Milan. Near the latter Gustave visited the church of Monza and was allowed to handle the comb of Theodolinde, wife of Antaris, king of the Lombards. He had already replaced it when he succumbed to temptation, seized it again, and ran it through his hair, imagining the royal barbarian who had once been its owner.

In Milan, too, he attended a puppet-theatre, and no doubt was reminded of old Legrain and the Foire Saint-Romain. At any rate Legrain was present in his thoughts, for as he left Italy and the Mediterranean and the impressions of his journey gradually clarified themselves in his mind, there was one memory that obtruded till it dominated all the others—a picture by 'Hell' Breughel in the Palazzo Balbi at Genoa, of an old man surrounded by evil and distorted figures, entitled 'The Temptation of Saint Anthony'. To have it, Flaubert told Le Poittevin, he would give a hundred thousand francs.

Notes to Chapter Four

1. The subject is not one for a layman and is in any case too extensive to be treated in a note. But the evidence about Flaubert's malady has been scrupulously examined by Dr. D. Russell-Davis, Reader in Clinical Psychology at Cambridge, who points out the uncertainty of the data. Apart from Flaubert himself none of the witnesses are reliable and many of the so-called facts are second-hand, Du Camp's account of the attack being particularly suspect. Even the word 'epilepsy' lacks precision, for in the middle of the nineteenth century it did not have its present meaning, but was erroneously associated both with degeneracy and intellectual brilliance. Moreover, Charcot and Janet had not described hysteria and its manifestations and in 1888 it was a fresh suggestion that hysteria could occur in men; modern ideas of psychosis had not been introduced by Kahlbaum and the members of the Burghölzli school, and the reports about Flaubert were made long before Kräpelin had systematized psychiatric diagnosis.

There are, however, reasons for questioning the diagnosis of epilepsy. In the first place, the time relations in the attack are unusual for epilepsy and certain characteristic features are absent. Secondly, the recommencement of the attacks in 1871, at a time of distress, suggests hysteria. Thirdly, Flaubert did not possess the so-called epileptic character: he was not markedly egocentric or arrogant; he did not suffer from emotional sterility or sexual impotence in later life; he had no feeling of guilt; he kept his friends; and everything we know about his speech shows that he talked in anything but an epileptic monotone.

Three arguments in favour of the diagnosis of epilepsy can be dismissed: the fact that as a child he fell to the ground while reading proves nothing, for no one asserts that the first attack occurred before 1844; the suggestion that youthful beauty like Flaubert's is characteristic of epilepsy is unfounded; and the cause of his death is irrelevant because he evidently died of some other condition.

But even if Flaubert had epilepsy, it was an incidental and unimportant tendency which could not account for his most important qualities and defects.

2. The book was in fact begun in February 1843, but then dropped till September or October. It was again interrupted by his illness, recommenced in May 1844, and concluded early the next year. In the summer of 1845 he revised it.

3. This episode has sometimes been dated earlier, but the change in Flaubert's attitude to marriage almost certainly places it in March 1845; a plausible alternative is June 1845, after the return from Italy. There is a possible reference to it in the *Notes de voyage*.

Chapter Five

SINNER AND SAINT

'Pour moi, je ne sais pas à quoi peuvent passer leur temps ici les gens qui ne s'occupent pas d'art. La manière dont ils vivent est un problème.' Letter to Louise Colet, 22nd September 1846.

It was characteristic of Flaubert that once he was home at Croisset, his thoughts wandered nostalgically back to Italy and beyond, across the Mediterranean, to Turkey, Egypt, and India. He was like one of his friends who spent years in Calcutta poring over a map of Paris and, when he returned to Paris, bought a map of Calcutta to while away his boredom. Having tasted the South, Flaubert longed to go further, unburdened by his family, to undertake an immense journey in which he could drink deep at the sources of the ancient world. But for the time being he had to remain at Croisset, and he spent a monotonous summer reading, smoking, and sometimes writing. He was allowed to take a boat on the river, but as Mme Flaubert stipulated he should never go alone, he soon tired of his ubiquitous servant and gave up the pastime. Periodically he was visited by Le Poittevin and Du Camp, and he read them *L'Education sentimentale*, which they heard with alternate misgiving and admiration; but now that Caroline and Hamard were setting up house in Paris, the only other regular occupants of Croisset were his father and mother, with neither of whom he felt at his ease.

Like Jules, however, he knew where his energies must be expended; a long apprenticeship lay before him and he read patiently and widely. Voltaire's plays, which he analysed in detail, Shakespeare, who especially delighted him with the brutality of *Timon of*

Athens, and Quintius Curtius, the historian of the Alexandrian Empire, were typical of his interests; he still thought of himself primarily as a dramatist, and when winter came, he and Le Poittevin sketched out endless scenarios together. But work was an escape; even art was only a palliative for life; and Flaubert's solitude was a deliberate withdrawal from emotion and excitement. 'Since what I fear is passion and movement,' he wrote, 'I think that if happiness can be found, it must be in stagnation: ponds have no storms.' But even in the quiet waters of Croisset he was not entirely unmolested; he felt that his father's indifference characterized a universal hatred of literature, and he tended to imagine hostility where there was none. Looking out of the open windows of his room at the great tulip-tree in the garden, he brooded on the disequilibrium in his own nature and wondered how it could be remedied. His health was still uncertain: during the Italian journey he had suffered from two attacks. He may have mentioned them to Pradier on his way home. At all events Pradier gave him some advice which Flaubert could not dismiss entirely from his mind. 'It is what I need', he told Le Poittevin, 'and what I will not do. A conventional, regular, solid and sustained love-affair would take me too much out of myself, would disturb me; I should return to an active life, to physical reality, to "common sense" in fact; and whenever I have tried it, it has harmed me.'

But the calm surface of the pond was suddenly ruffled. On 10th November 1845 Dr. Flaubert fell ill and took to his bed. Achille examined him, discovered a phlegmon on the thigh and operated. But the operation came too late, and the wound continued to suppurate; the patient's condition swiftly deteriorated and on 15th January he died.[1]

Meanwhile Caroline had returned home with Hamard, and six days after Dr. Flaubert's death she gave birth to a daughter. While Achille and Mme Flaubert looked after her, Gustave went to Paris to wind up his father's affairs; but anxious letters reached him from Rouen and he hurried back to find his sister desperately ill. Specialists were summoned; Marjolin and Raspail arrived; but Caroline was beyond help and she died on 20th March.

To his surprise Gustave withstood the shock; in the face of calamity he was hard and unyielding, and yet always ready to perceive the grotesque. When Caroline was buried, the hole dug for the grave was too narrow for the coffin to go in; the men pulled it about, turned it round and manœuvred with spades and crow-bars, till at last the gravedigger, losing patience, put his foot on the coffin just above where the head would be, and forced it down. 'I wanted to tell you this,' Flaubert wrote to Du Camp, 'thinking it would give you pleasure. You are sufficiently intelligent and love me well enough to understand what I mean by "pleasure"— a word that would seem ridiculous to a bourgeois.'

But the full weight of the loss fell on Mme Flaubert, who retired to Croisset with the two-month-old baby and, in her widowhood, assumed once more the part of a mother. Gustave was uneasy about her, fearing that the ultimate reaction would overcome her powers of recovery; but he underestimated her resilience and courage. Meanwhile he meddled in various intrigues which bore fruit in June, when Achille was appointed to his father's post as head of the Hôtel-Dieu.

The change brought about by the deaths of Dr. Flaubert and Caroline was so sudden that Gustave did not at first realize what it meant. To be bereft of Caroline was the heavier blow, for in her he had centred so much of his pride, ambition, and affection; it seemed so pointless and so cruel, and yet part of a general scheme, as though the universe were not merely indifferent but hostile to human beings. Hitherto he had regarded an active life with shrinking and reluctance, but now he feared it. The disaster confirmed his attitude and strengthened its intellectual basis. 'Remain always as you are,' he told Chevalier, 'don't get married, have no children, indulge in as few affections as possible, allow the least hold to the enemy.' Every strong feeling he had ever experienced eventually caused pain, as if it were a loophole in his nature from which he could be sniped at. His love for Elisa reaped only jealousy and disappointment; his awareness of beauty brought a sickening dis-gust with the bourgeois and a profound dissatisfaction with his own work; and now the warmth of his affection for his father and sister was the direct cause for the bitterness of his grief. Like a hedgehog, he curled up and turned his prickles to the world. From this moment he not only despised life, he detested it.

But although he tried to dam his emotions and check the natural play of his temperament, the death of his father hastened him to maturity in another respect; for he became master of the house, with virtually no interference from his mother. She treated him as a delicate child who must be spoilt and humoured; when he woke in the morning, he knocked on the wall for her to come and sit by his bed till he was ready to get up; if he asked for anything, it was usually obtained. The shadow of paternal disapproval had vanished and a career as an author was no longer a furtive and rather indecent prospect to which he owned with a blush, but a legitimate possibility made easier by the annuity that he received under his father's will. In the sheltered ease of Croisset he could explore and experiment with his talent.

Du Camp visited the house frequently and there he met Louis Bouilhet. Bouilhet and Flaubert had been at Rouen *collège* together, though no more than acquaintances; and on leaving, Bouilhet, who wished to become a poet, had been forced by his family to train as a doctor and enter the Hôtel-Dieu. He was a rebellious and unwilling student, and when Dr. Flaubert died, he cut loose and earned a precarious living by teaching Latin and French. What drew him to Flaubert was their common literary ambition, but in other ways they were dissimilar. By contrast to Flaubert's superficial braggadocio, Bouilhet was timid and shy. His ideas on religion, society, and art were fluctuating and uncertain, but he had cast off the Catholicism in which he was brought up, and formed a low opinion of the mob and the bourgeoisie; in literature he had ceased to believe in the social mission of the poet—a mission that was asserted in almost every literary review of the 'forties—and was feeling his way towards a less personal and transient criterion of excellence. As a poet he possessed a fastidious sense of rhythm and an easy command of words, while as a man he could assume a bawdy intolerance which endeared him at once to Flaubert's heart.

Because Bouilhet ultimately arrived at a doctrine completely opposed to the lyrical self-display of Musset or Lamartine, it has sometimes been suggested that he influenced the development of Flaubert's thought. But in fact the roles were reversed. Flaubert was always a move ahead, and two years after their first meeting Bouilhet had still not purged himself of his early surfeit of Romanticism. He was undoubtedly a help to Flaubert, just as any intelligent man can, by his criticism, clarify the ideas of a friend; and when he found himself as a poet and formulated a philosophy of literary detachment, he became almost an echo of Flaubert's artistic conscience. But for the time being he was an acquaintance who possessed undisputed gifts but had yet to prove his worth. If it had not been for his encounter with Flaubert, he might well have sunk to writing facile plays and trivial verse; Du Camp similarly was preserved, at least for some years, from the morass of slick and omniscient journalism.

During the spring and summer of 1846 they all three made excursions to the surrounding country—to Jumièges, Saint-Vaudrille, and La Bouille; and in the church of Caudebec-en-Caux Flaubert was particularly attracted by a little statue of Saint Julian Hospitator. Back at Croisset they worked, translating Plautus and Aristophanes and sketching out plays; and on Flaubert's suggestion they began a mock-classical tragedy entitled *Jenner ou la Decouverte de la vaccine*, in which nature was overwhelmed by artifice and periphrasis was obligatory. *Jenner* was really a dig at the school which considered the proper subject-matter of poetry to be strictly limited, but as it developed, it became increasingly farcical and obscene till Bouilhet and Du Camp wearied of it and only Flaubert was left to bellow out its lines and shout his admiration for its tiresome burlesque.

These, however, were diversions, and for most of the time Flaubert was without his friends. With only his mother to talk to, and the crying of the baby to remind him of Caroline, he realized more than ever the incurable loneliness of suffering, and his sense of abandonment was increased when in July Le Poittevin married a Mlle de Maupassant and went to live in Paris. 'It meant to me', Flaubert said later, 'what the news of a great scandal caused by a bishop would have meant to a believer.' Le Poittevin, the scourge of the bourgeoisie, was compacting with the enemy, and Flaubert remained almost alone to continue the struggle. He, at least, would never recant.

To sustain him, however, he wanted a relic of Caroline, for like all sentimentalists he felt deepest about the past and the future. As she lay on her death-bed he had taken a cast of her hand and features, and in July he was in Paris ordering a bust from Pradier. In the studio, where twenty years before Victor Hugo had met Juliette Drouet, there was a handsome woman with ash-blonde hair—the poetess Louise Colet. Pradier, remembering perhaps his advice of the previous year, introduced Flaubert with the casual remark, 'You see that big fellow. He wants to write. You ought to give him lessons.'

That was on the 29th. Next day they went for a ride by moonlight through the Bois de Boulogne, and on the 31st Louise Colet became Flaubert's mistress.

There was nothing surprising in the immediate physical attraction each felt towards the other, for Louise Colet was famous for her looks and Flaubert still remarkably handsome; but neither had the qualities that might have made the relationship permanent, and there was already a hint of discord in the haste with which Flaubert returned to his mother on 4th August. In a sense, Louise Colet was the last temptation of Romanticism; she embodied everything that Flaubert had once longed for—beauty, fame, and passion—and yet he scarcely hesitated when he felt his art in peril. It was as though his personality were threatened. At first, no doubt, he was flattered and excited; he regretted that he had already learnt the practice of love from more sordid teachers; but his pleasure was at once shot with foreboding when Louise's tears of farewell in Paris were answered by his mother's tears of greeting in Rouen. His experience of life had taught him to beware of happiness as if it always contained the seed of despair; and when happiness was thrust upon him, he was bewildered and embarrassed, unwilling to refuse, yet fearful to accept.

So perverse a psychology was unintelligible to Louise, who was a hot-blooded and petulant child of Provence. She had begun her career as the Muse of the department, and after a brief idyll with a local poet, she married a vain and mediocre music-teacher called

Hippolyte Colet and brought him to Paris, where he intrigued unsuccessfully for Reicha's post at the Conservatoire. Her charms, however, were more considerable than her husband's qualifications, and not only did she persuade literary juries to adjudge substantial rewards for her poems, but, when she had made the conquest of the influential Victor Cousin, Hippolyte was appointed, despite Cherubini's opposition, Professor of Harmony and Counterpoint. Although most contemporary commentators forgot to mention her husband's infidelity, her relations with Cousin were common knowledge; and when in 1840 Alphonse Karr published a transparent reference to the paternity of her unborn child,[2] Louise, who had no sense of the ridiculous, fell on him with a carving knife but was easily disarmed. Karr commemorated the occasion by hanging the weapon on his wall and inscribing beneath it

Presented by Mme Louise Colet . . .
In the back

while Cousin is said to have remarked

Maxime sum mulier, sed sicut vir ago.

Provincial as he was, Flaubert does not seem to have heard of so notorious an episode, which was recounted and embroidered on by every Parisian gossip-writer short of copy; but he already knew some of her poems, for they had been published in *Le Colibri*. As, however, she treated subjects like Poland, the Czar, and the Grand Duke of Tuscany with more political fervour than good taste, he had probably ignored the rest of her productions, feeling that they fell short of his standards. She had a slight talent for versifying, but was incapable of viewing her work dispassionately, and her conception of poetry was of vehement self-expression. If her poems were ill received, she accused the critics of personal animosity, and she had an unfortunate gift for making enemies. Sainte-Beuve detested her because in an unguarded moment she had publicly suggested he would give half his reputation for better looks; and the failure of her comedy on Goethe's youth was all the more dismal because she had tactlessly anticipated the hostility of the reviewers:

SINNER AND SAINT

Le critique, vois-tu, c'est un être impuissant . . .
En face de la gloire, ironique, insensible,
Il souille son foyer qu'il trouve inaccessible.

But Flaubert did not guess all this. For a few weeks he thought
that he had discovered in her a kindred soul with the same disinterested love of art as his own. The sexual relation he regarded as
secondary, but apart from physical pleasure Louise could offer
him only what he possessed or did not want. Life at Croisset with
his mother was more peaceful and congenial than any unstable
arrangement he might make in Paris, while as for love, his heart
was already given to Elisa. On the one hand, his mother was
beginning to feel that any wife or mistress would be her rival; on
the other, as he told the Goncourts, 'all the women he ever possessed were no more than the mattress for another woman he
dreamed of'. Louise was lumped together with the rest, and
although he assured her that she was the first woman who had
really loved him—which was true—she sensed that there was
some memory, some ideal figure, against which his liaison with
her was only a pastime.

It is easy to be unfair to Louise because she usually did herself
less than justice: now she was domineering and violent, now sentimental and wheedling. But Flaubert was the great passion of her
life and her storms of jealousy and reproach were manifestations
of the distress she felt as he slipped away into the arms of literature.
At the time of their meeting she was thirty-six—exactly the same
age as Elisa Schlésinger—and ready for a deeper and more settled
affair than she had yet experienced; in Flaubert, young, handsome,
and warm-hearted, she imagined that she had found at last her true
lover. She asked everything from him—passion, self-sacrifice, fidel-
ity—and might have given the same in return; but they scarcely
knew each other before he escaped from her demands—and his
own temptations—to the seclusion of Croisset.

Once home, he wrote to her almost every day and the inevitable
misunderstandings began. She expected him to love her for ever—
or at least to make the promise—and come back immediately,
while he, obsessed with the suffering implicit in happiness, almost

79

wished they had never met. 'What is the good of growing used to seeing and loving each other? Why luxuriate in affection if thereafter we must live in misery? What is the good? But we can do no other!' As a lover he preserved a Romantic sense of destiny; there remained in him something of René, specially chosen for misfortune. At the praise she bestowed on his work, he was fearful: it might lead him to take himself seriously; while she, the celebrated poetess, was unable to comprehend the immersion of an unknown author in his unspecified writing. Moreover he exhibited a deplorable want of tact. When she asked him for some of his prose, he sent her a passage from *L'Education sentimentale*, welling over with the memory of Elisa. This he followed with a letter to Eulalie Foucaud de Lenglade, which he hoped she would post; and when she reproached him with loving Eulalie, he replied that his passion was purely literary and synthetic and lasted exactly as long as he had a pen in his hand. Try as they might, each exacerbated and alarmed the other till he was perplexed and resentful at her acrimonious tone and she was convinced that he regarded her as little more than a prostitute. Periodically they met, either in Paris or in a hotel at Mantes, and at first these occasions poured balm on their mutual irritation; but their love was at best a precarious excitement, and although they saw one another only six times in two years, their pleasure was soon spoilt by the certainty that it was only a respite before the next bout of reproach and recrimination. Flaubert was forced to speak plainly: 'For me, love is not the first thing in life, but the second. It is a bed where you put your heart to rest it.' And he explained: 'When two people love, they can spend ten years without seeing one another and yet without suffering.' It was too much for Louise. 'What is one to make of this sentence?' she wrote in the margin.

But although she was incapable of giving him the lessons Pradier had referred to, the sheer necessity of explaining himself led Flaubert to organize and formulate his ideas more clearly than hitherto. When Louise declared that she would rather be in love with him than possess all the fame of Corneille, he was shocked by her distorted sense of values; in any case, what did Corneille's fame matter compared to his achievement? 'No one', he wrote, forgetting—or remembering—his correspondent, 'has ever given me a pleasure approaching that I have derived from reading and meditating on the work of a few great men who are dead.' In contrast with her doctrine of personal confession in poetry, he expounded his own policy of self-effacement, and even referred her to Victor Cousin for an adequate exposition of the idea of beauty. Louise's advent in Flaubert's life, with its threat of disturbance and passion, crystallized his theories on art as though he was feeling for a stanchion against misfortune; and in some of the most eloquent and paradoxical letters in the language he clarified his idea of the artist, which he had already adumbrated in the words of Jules, and asserted that objectivity could only be attained by the practice of renunciation and detachment. 'Is it enough to have a feeling in order to express it? Is there a single drinking-song that has been written by a drunk?' The only valid principle was devotion to the ideal of art; for the rest, one needed only to observe and to imagine, dismissing irrelevant considerations of what was pleasant or useful and concentrating on the essential idea, from which the form took shape. Withdrawal from the world, in short, was a necessity, and Croisset, which might have seemed a refuge from emotional stress, became a temple from which ceaseless hymns of adoration rose to the fount of beauty.

During the spring Flaubert had been turning over in his mind the story of Saint Anthony, and in August he at last obtained Callot's engraving of the subject[3] and hung it on the wall of his room. There were several reasons why he should write about the saint. Looking back on his work, he could not take any of it seriously; it all belonged to the period before his self-dedication, and now that the course of his life was determined, he felt a pressing need to prove himself to himself. All his reading—his Homer, his Shakespeare, his Montaigne, Voltaire, and Ronsard—was not only a pleasure but a discipline, intended to sharpen his critical sense, purify his taste, and dissipate those 'Norman mists' which seemed to blur his mind; and when he was not reading he probed cruelly into his own nature, striving to impose some shape on his chaotic emotions. The impact of illness and the reminder, with each new attack, that his mind was an uncharted, uncontrolled domain, strengthened his determination to overcome himself, objectify his terrors, and organize artistically the emanations of his brain.

If, as Goethe said, all good works of art are occasional works, this is especially true of Flaubert; indeed he once declared that no writer chooses his subject, but that the subject insists on being treated. That Saint Anthony should become a symbol for him at this juncture of his life was inevitable: the saint imposed himself on the artist through Legrain, through Breughel, and through Callot, demanding immediate attention; and Flaubert, who later advised Maupassant that the essential for the writer was to acquire and develop an original mode of seeing and feeling, knew that in the figure of Saint Anthony he could convey and explore his own originality—that, in fact, such an exploration was indispensable if he were ever to discover the nature of his talent.

All through the summer of 1846 he worked; and because he was resolved that Saint Anthony should not be a mere replica of himself but a historical figure, he undertook a huge documentation of the East, bathing himself in the literature of colour and light, wandering through the labyrinths of scholastic theology, brooding over the religions of India and China, recreating the life of the ancient world. He promised Du Camp and Bouilhet that they should see the work when it was completed; but until then, he kept his own counsel.

For Flaubert, *La Tentation de saint Antoine* marked the end of youth, and even as he emerged from his former self, the pattern of the future slowly grew apparent. New figures—Bouilhet, Du Camp, Louise Colet—stepped into the foreground of his life, and the old figures either receded or vanished altogether. With the deaths of Dr. Flaubert and Caroline his childhood in the Hôtel-Dieu was pushed back into an unrecapturable past; with Le Poittevin's marriage a chill descended on the fervour of his adolescence; and as the other survivor, Ernest Chevalier, wallowed deeper in conventional success, intimacy between the two men became first hard and then impossible. Elisa Schlésinger, meanwhile, glided out of reach; and when, late in 1846, the Colliers left Paris for England, it seemed that the last actors had gone from the stage. There was only a solitary, unhappy spectator to remember the emotion of the performance.

Notes to Chapter Five

1. A local tradition says that Dr. Flaubert's death was hastened by his worry over Gustave's health.

2. The article, however, was not entitled 'La Piqûre du Cousin' —that was the invention of some later wag.

3. It was *La Tentation de France* (1635). There was not, and there still is not, any reproduction of Breughel's picture.

Chapter Six

AN END AND A
BEGINNING

'Oh! que je donnerais volontiers toutes les femmes de la terre pour avoir la momie de Cléopâtre!' Par les champs et par les grèves, chapter I.

WHILE Du Camp was at Croisset in the autumn, he suggested to Flaubert that they should hike through Brittany together the next spring,[1] and Mme Flaubert, though at first hesitant, gave way when it was agreed that she should follow with Hamard and the child Caroline in a post-chaise. The journey was, in its essentials, to be like the journey to Corsica seven years before: an invigoration after the staleness of Rouen. But Flaubert had changed his conception of travelling; he was no longer content with superficial impressions, and through the winter he prepared himself intellectually by a patient course in Breton history, while Du Camp acquired summary notions of ethnology and archeology.

They gradually collected material necessities: white hats from Avignon, cudgels from Caen, Tyrolese pipes, and Hungarian tobacco-pouches; and on 1st May 1847, gaitered and laden with seal-skin packs, they walked across the Place de la Madeleine to the Gare d'Orléans and took the Paris train to Blois.

On the fourth day, at Tours, Flaubert had an attack, but that was the only event to mar their enjoyment. It was in fact the high summer of their friendship; each was delighted with his companion and the country and the people. On the way they passed through Chenonceaux and Flaubert saw with an itching curiosity the great canopy-bed of Diane de Poitiers; relics of the past stirred up unanswerable questions in his mind so that he yearned for an intimate knowledge of the thoughts and habits of remote generations. A person who had died centuries before was thereby infused with a pathos and poetry beyond the reach of any contemporary, as though the fact of death shed a sombre and ironic beauty over the life that preceded it. The *châteaux* of the Loire were full of tantalizing survivals from the Middle Ages: beds, tables, tapestries, swords, and seals; and kings, lords, and bishops lingering in effigy on the walls.

But although learning and imagination could not restore that medieval world, Du Camp and Flaubert found, by the time they reached Carnac, that a new contemporary world was opening before them. For Brittany—at any rate 'la Bretagne bretonnante'—was at that date a primitive region, cut off from the rest of France and possessed of a unique culture and history. Apart from the main military highway, there were only hollow lanes between high hedges, and the peasants spoke Celtic and nothing else. Travellers were few and tourists virtually unknown. When Flaubert and Du Camp showed their passports on which they were designated merely as *rentiers*, customs officials were usually suspicious and often frankly incredulous: one, at least, took them for Bourbon emissaries. But as strangers, foreigners even, they enjoyed a flattering prestige, and farmers surrounded them in the villages, asking through an interpreter if Louis Philippe were still alive and how often they dined with him.

Flaubert took trouble over his notes, going into lengthy detail about church interiors and ancient monuments. But although his preliminary documentation gave him eyes for the dolmen and the logan-stone, his main interest lay in the people and their customs. A fisherman's wife at Carnac, weeping over her husband who had been washed up on the shore; folk-dancing at Finistère to the tune of the bagpipes; a brothel in Brest; a quarrel between two women at Pont l'Abbé, during which both were seriously wounded; and a circus-fight between a bear, an ass, and some dogs—these caught his attention; while at a fair at Guérande his tireless search for the grotesque was rewarded by the discovery of the 'young phenomenon'—a sheep with a turned-up tail and five legs.[2] He took the owner out to dinner and made him horribly drunk; he met him again in Brest, again took him out to dinner and again made him horribly drunk; and he christened Du Camp 'the young phenomenon' and chortled for weeks about the happy encounter.

But there was a darker side to Breton life. Travelling as they did, sleeping now in a first-class hotel, now in a prison, now in a monastery, now in an inn and now in a slum, Du Camp and Flaubert rubbed shoulders with poverty and disease. There was little to eat but eggs and bread, and not everyone could afford even the latter; meat was a rare luxury; at Quiberon one of the hotels was kept by Rohan Belle-Isle, a noble of ancient lineage, who padded about barefoot;[3] and often they were surrounded by ragged beggars who poured out long, plaintive, and incomprehensible stories.

Perhaps the most moving experience, however, occurred at Combourg. On the islet of the Grand Bey, just off Saint Malo, they had seen the empty tomb which Chateaubriand, with a flamboyant gesture, had prepared for himself, and now in the *château* of Combourg they visited the scene of his youth. The rotting wood and crumbling stone filled them with a delicious melancholy; that evening they read *René* again together; and half-way through the night Flaubert got up and brooded over the great master of prose whose seductive rhythms had soothed his unhappiness in the dormitory of Rouen *collège*. It was a last tribute to the great word-charmer from a disciple who was beginning to feel the need for a more critical sensibility. Flaubert had lived out and exhausted the emotions of René, but to read the book again called forth echoes of what he had once felt, and he surveyed with a detached curiosity the mechanism of his enthusiasm and despair.

The trip to Brittany took just over three months, blithe and carefree months of unclouded friendship and uninhibited pleasure. For once in his life Flaubert managed to enjoy himself in the present, without regrets for the past and fears for the future. Liberated from Rouen and the sepulchral atmosphere of Croisset, he could rant and dilate and enthuse to his heart's content with a companion who shared all his fervour and most of his prejudices. The brisk open air blew away his worries and gave him new spirit.

But when he returned to Croisset his problems crowded back on him. He and Du Camp had decided to write up their holiday, composing the chapters alternately; and as he began the work, Flaubert felt for the first time the effect of his reading: he had developed a benumbing faculty of self-criticism, and words which once flowed almost without effort from his pen were now checked, scrutinized, and often rejected. His conscience no longer allowed phrases that almost, but not quite, conveyed his thought, and he groped patiently for the precise and harmonious expression. Not that *Par les champs et par les grèves* is a work of art: indeed much of it is clumsy and uneven. But Flaubert was undergoing the discipline of fact, subduing the personality of the narrator and forswearing the self-revelation that characterized *L'Education sentimentale*. From a journey of three months he could hardly hope to bring back new modes of sentiment or to enlarge his experience as Jules required; but Brittany offered fresh sights and different types of humanity, and he tried to record them—people, landscapes, customs, buildings—in a way to satisfy his own canons. As he wrote, he fused together description and judgement so that the observer only became apparent in the thing observed; and he worked his erudition into the text till it was subordinate to the crisp and detailed evocation of life. Learning for its own sake he despised, but he used it as a means to create colour through exotic detail and to build up character through personal anecdote. Everywhere his historical imagination was awake. But though he wrote for his own pleasure and benefit, there was a moment of weakness, months after the book was completed, when he wished fervently that publication were possible.

Meanwhile, he learnt that another loss was imminent. In the autumn he and Du Camp visited Le Poittevin at Neuville Chant-d'Oisel and were shocked to find him depressed and emaciated. The ravages of an *angoisse* that was as much metaphysical as personal in origin had driven Le Poittevin to a hopeless dissipation, and this in turn had broken down his health. He was too honest to deceive himself and he hurried to complete a book containing the pith of his despairing thought. To the end he remained lucid, observing the approach of death with a steady eye and remarking that

Saint-Simon was wrong to call it terrible. At his request Du Camp sent him a complete edition of Spinoza from Paris and he read passages daily till his death on 3rd April.

Flaubert watched for two nights over Le Poittevin's body, and, as was his custom, allowed his mind to stray back over the life that was ended. After Caroline's death he had reopened his letters from Eulalie Foucaud de Lenglade, as though his sister were part of the fabric of his youth; and after Le Poittevin's he reread the two books that symbolized the intensest moments of their friendship: Hugo's *Feuilles d'automne* and Creuzer's *Religions de l'antiquité*. The glow of excitement when he first intoned the poems in the little room at Fécamp and the sense of revelation when he was first transported to the ancient world, were debts which could never be redeemed; as he washed the putrescent body and prepared it for the coffin, he draped a shroud over all the enthusiasms of his virgin intellect.

Private grief, however, could not shield him from public calamity; indeed he welcomed the distraction of political upheaval. Late in the afternoon of 23rd February Du Camp, returning to his rooms after a day in the Paris streets, had found Flaubert and Bouilhet awaiting him, newly arrived from Rouen to observe the insurrection 'from an artistic standpoint'. But in a tour of the neighbourhood they saw nothing more exciting than two or three companies of the National Guard and some troops of the lines blocking the Boulevard des Capucines; and after dinner, rather disappointed, they walked back to Du Camp's rooms. As they opened the door there was a heavy explosion. 'Platoon-firing', said Flaubert with interest. 'Children with fireworks', said Du Camp, leading the way upstairs. They spent the rest of the evening discussing the first canto of Bouilhet's *Melaenis*, while only a few hundred yards away troops had opened fire on demonstrators and sealed the fate of Louis Philippe's regime.

The following morning the revolt had begun in earnest. They ran into a barricade on the corner of the rue du Helder and street-fighting near the Place du Palais-Royal. Bouilhet, who was separated from his companions in the crowd, was forced to help in barricade-building till he disabled himself by dropping a paving-stone onto his foot. In the meantime Flaubert and Du Camp, hearing rumours that Louis Philippe had abdicated, joined the stream heading for the Tuileries and found the palace open to all. People wandered through the royal apartments with respectful curiosity; not till later, with the arrival of the insurrectionists proper, did the destruction begin. But when Flaubert and Du Camp returned with Bouilhet the same evening, looting and burning were in full swing, while outside the Tuileries the ex-king's servants were ripping up their livery and trampling on it, to the approving roar of the mob.

Flaubert's principal reaction to the February Revolution was one of pleasure that so many of the ignoble ambitions associated with the July Monarchy should have been frustrated; he could hardly mourn a regime that was morally, aesthetically, and politically bourgeois. But at times of crisis he rediscovered his solidarity with his own class, at least in so far as the bourgeois feared disorder, and he joined the Rouen National Guard and attended, with some reluctance, a typical ceremony for the planting of a tree of liberty. For a moment, caught up in the universal excitement, he contemplated applying for a diplomatic post in the Near East, and there is evidence that when a recently appointed prefect was unmasked as an ex-convict, he threatened to take over the post himself if a suitable candidate was not found within twenty-four hours. He seems to have been in Paris for the Days of June and to have helped to restore order with a fowling-piece. Because of family business he was unable to remain in the capital or see Du Camp, who had been wounded in the fighting. But a month later he returned and seized the chance to visit the fairs near his hotel. Du Camp was lying in bed one morning when Flaubert burst in, flushed with excitement, and promised a surprise. Some hours later Du Camp was disturbed by an uproar in a distant part of the building: loud voices, the stamping of iron-studded boots, and a quavering note of complaint. The door opened dramatically and the five-legged sheep of Guérande hurtled into the room. It trotted round, bleating and fouling the carpet, while Flaubert boomed out his admiration and the showman, bowing tipsily to the company, emptied a large bottle of wine.

The episode enraptured Flaubert so that he never forgot it; it appealed to his sense of the abnormal and excessive, one of the most uncompromising aspects of what Louise Colet called his 'monstrous personality'. She, meantime, had found him more and more intractable, while after seven months' acquaintance he had already concluded that their natures were essentially incompatible. Every device a woman can use to retain a lover, she had used: she had sent him presents and written him verse; she had tried to make him jealous; she had shown him her letters from Victor Cousin, mocked his subservience to his mother, and sought to work on him through Du Camp. While he was quite content with their rare meetings, she wanted to possess him entirely, and the suspicion, amounting soon to a conviction, that he dismissed any idea of habitual contiguity, put her in a fury of resentment and unfulfilled desire. Moreover, he seemed to despise her: not only did love come after art, but it came after friendship; if he could spend three months with Du Camp, why should he not spend three months with her? She was merely a convenience in his life, and she felt that Du Camp connived at her humiliation.

Although their liaison was several times near breaking-point, it somehow dragged on into a second year. When Flaubert asked Louise if she wished to give him up, she shrank from the decision, intolerable as she found the present arrangement. He, on the other hand, was not in love, if he ever had been. Why then did he continue a relationship that was a source of persistent annoyance? In the first place, he seems to have been genuinely fond of her and to have enjoyed her company when it did not encroach too far on his life at Croisset; provided she kept her distance and ministered to his emotions instead of exacerbating them, he was satisfied; indeed he needed some confidant to whom he could reveal as much as he dared of himself. Secondly, he was not inclined to mortify the flesh any more than the practice of art demanded, and a mistress so beautiful and famous could not be found elsewhere, certainly not in Rouen. But above all, he was coming to regard her as a document, an object worthy of study; and although she failed to see his motive, he urged her to confide in him, to describe her daily life, her feelings and desires. What principally irritated him was her hypocrisy, her habit of exalting love as something divine and referring to the senses as beneath contempt; for when she was hypocritical, she lost her documentary value. But however important she was to Flaubert the artist, she was only an expedient to Flaubert the man. Because he wrote her such long and revealing letters which occupy so great a space in the collected edition of his correspondence, it is easy to infer that her role in his life was cardinal; but in fact his feelings for her were superficial and impermanent. René Dumesnil has suggested that the passage in *L'Education sentimentale* of 1869 where Frédéric Moreau, sick with love for Mme Arnoux, takes Rosanette to the room he has prepared for the other, and lies alongside her, weeping over what might have been, has its origin in reality; that, in fact, Flaubert enacted this scene with Louise Colet, weeping over the memory of Elisa.[4] It is certainly true that for Flaubert possession intensified the sense of loss; his gaze shifted from what he had gained to what he desired; and it is likely that his conquest of Louise Colet was no exception.

As, however, the makeshift became less and less suitable and deteriorated into a chronic irritant, the inconvenience of prolonging the relationship exceeded the advantages. The outlook, which had once been fair, declined to stormy. While Louise nagged, carped, and sulked, Flaubert grew increasingly restless beneath her criticism. Talking about her to his friends, he did not hide his true feelings, and in May 1848 he told Du Camp with some amusement that she now hoped to rent a small farm from him while he would continue to live in his country house nearby.[5] How the break came, we do not know, nor even who was primarily responsible. Probably Flaubert engineered it, but as he was the only one capable of lucid calculation, he may have manœuvred Louise into making the decision. In June she had given birth to a child, which died; and the fact that Colet was its father may have precipitated the quarrel. By the end of August they ceased to write to each other.

Meanwhile *La Tentation de saint Antoine* was under way. Partly out of nervousness, partly out of a desire to be thorough, Flaubert had postponed the writing till he had accumulated more facts than he would ever need; 'better not write at all than set to work only half-prepared', he had told Louise; but eventually he had to begin and the labour proved far greater than he had imagined. Troublesome though it was, *Par les champs et par les grèves* had taken only a few months, and he probably expected to devote about as long to the new book; in fact, it kept him busy for a year and a half. But he steadfastly refused to hurry, and his refusal was in the face of severe temptation; for not only was he anxious to have the measure of his talent now that he felt mature, but as soon as the book was finished, he was to realize one of his dreams.

After recovering from the wound he had received in the June fighting, Du Camp went for a holiday to Algeria. He was planning a long journey to the Near East in 1849, and in February of that year he stayed for a few days at Croisset speaking both of his past travels and his future projects. Flaubert sighed with envy; and acting on the spur of the moment, Du Camp discussed the matter with Achille, who agreed to approach Mme Flaubert. The suggestion fortunately coincided with a letter from Dr. Cloquet, who urged that Gustave's health would benefit from a long journey in a warm climate; and what with Achille's representations and Cloquet's advice, Mme Flaubert reluctantly gave her consent for Gustave to accompany Du Camp. Du Camp, however, was hardly back in Paris before she visited him; although she was prepared for her son to be away for two years, she regarded the proposed itinerary as unduly exhausting and dangerous, and suggested instead a stay in Madeira. To his great credit, Du Camp put his foot down, declaring that the journey was indispensable to his studies. Mme Flaubert did not insist, but left with a sense of grievance.

The idea of travelling to the Levant, to Africa and Asia, was so much part of Flaubert's youth that he contemplated with some apprehension its descent into reality. In 1846, shortly after Du Camp's return from Constantinople, they had spent three days over a map, planning in the minutest detail a journey that would take six years and cost over three and a half million francs; and although they now hoped to cross Persia to the Caspian and to see the Caucasus and Georgia, Flaubert still clung to the dreams that would not be fulfilled and longed to bathe in the Ganges and wander through Ceylon—or the Taprobane of the ancients, as he preferred to call it.

The proposed journey, however, was a chance that might never recur. Because of his nervous complaint, Flaubert could not think of such an undertaking on his own; but with Du Camp at his side he had little to fear, and he knew from their preliminary canter in Brittany what pleasure was to be derived from a companion of the same age and with the same interests. Moreover, Croisset, despite its beauty, was full of unhappy associations; Mme Flaubert brooded over the empty places at the family table, communicating her grief to those around, and to escape from the atmosphere of mourning would in itself be refreshing. It would also be a liberation; for although Flaubert pictured himself as a solitary devoted to the pursuit of art, his hermit-life was dominated by his mother, and indulgent as she was, she imposed her will by over-solicitude. Out of reach of her worry, he could give himself free rein.

He insisted, however, on *La Tentation* being finished before he left, and not till 12th September did he write the last word and summon Du Camp and Bouilhet to judge the work. 'If you don't shout with enthusiasm,' he cried, brandishing the manuscript over his head, 'then nothing can move you.' The reading took four days, eight hours a day, and Mme Flaubert hovered anxiously near, waiting for the verdict. When he ended, he turned to his friends: 'Now tell me your frank opinion.' Bouilhet, who had conferred privately with Du Camp, delivered judgement. 'We think', he said, 'that you must throw it in the fire and never speak of it again.'

How the blow stunned Flaubert is only intelligible when one remembers all the book represented for him; he had cherished it for more than three years, working himself into frenzies of delight over its passionate rhetoric, and he was sure that it vindicated his renunciation of society and retirement into solitude. To tell him that it was worthless was to annihilate all his efforts, his grappling with the problem of style and heroic recreation of antiquity, and, going beyond the book itself, to shake his whole conception of life and subvert his confidence in his ability and taste. But he trusted his friends; he believed in their loyalty and relied on their decision; and for twelve hours he argued with them, yielding ground inch by inch and finally conceding the position. He recognized that he had humoured his own weakness, that he had been led astray by the enchantments of lyricism and that in the person of Saint Anthony he had succumbed to temptations of his own devising.

The opinion of Bouilhet and Du Camp may seem harsh, but it is just. If they had accepted the *Tentation*, Flaubert would certainly have developed one-sidedly and might have become unreadable. Indulgence would have been justified only had he possessed less talent.

In the light of his later work it is tempting to read promise into the book and to magnify its qualities, but when judged by the standards he had already formulated, it is inadequate. It is amorphous and it lacks objectivity. When he reread it three years later, he remarked that all unawares he had himself been Saint Anthony. It is perhaps truer to say that he used the temptation as a pretext and that the saint was only the helpless observer of what it pleased the author to evoke. Far from depicting himself as Saint Anthony, Flaubert turned the central character into a lifeless puppet, the vehicle of strong, alternating, but purely nominal emotions; it was twenty years before he dared to analyse part of his own nature in Frédéric Moreau. But having created an artificial link between the scenes, he proceeded to conjure up every vision that seemed to him attractive; and the so-called temptation is in fact a cavalcade of all the daydreams which had beguiled his leisure since he first escaped from reality into a world of fantasy. Women, riches, power are only the more obvious enticements in a catalogue that includes necrophily and sadism; and not content with ransacking his imagination for fierce and illicit pleasures, he piled on references culled from his reading till the book foundered beneath the weight of his erudition. In fact, *La Tentation* of 1849, if it does not describe Flaubert, expresses his temperament. In no other of his works is he more completely himself, and for that reason it is, with its successors of 1856 and 1874, the hardest of approach for readers with a different cast of mind.[6]

Despite, therefore, its iridescent prose and splendid rhythms, Du Camp and Bouilhet condemned it; to persevere in that vein would be fatal to Flaubert, and they suggested that he should tackle a subject which was foreign to his nature and afforded no scope for oratorical development—a subject, in short, like *La Cousine Bette* or *Le Cousin Pons*. According to Du Camp, Bouilhet even mentioned Delamare, a local doctor, as a possible point of departure. But for the moment Flaubert was too sick at heart to contemplate anything new; he pushed *La Tentation* into a drawer and prepared himself for his journey.

Du Camp immediately returned to Paris and with his customary dispatch secured for them both an official mission. Since there was no salary attached, the concession was not significant, but it meant a number of useful introductions. As a result, he himself had to send memoranda to the Ministry of Education, while Flaubert, by some malignant irony, was to collect information about ports, caravan-routes, and business centres for ultimate transmission to French Chambers of Commerce.

On 22nd October Flaubert left Croisset with his family. Passing through Paris, he seized the chance of calling on Maurice Schlé-singer; after an evening together at the opera, they said goodbye beneath the arches of the Rue de Rivoli, and the scene remained in Flaubert's memory as though it held some latent symbol.

From then on, preparations for departure took up his time. There was a swift visit to Nogent, where he took a brusque but anguished farewell of his mother; a last dinner with friends in Paris; and on 29th October he and Du Camp climbed into a coach and began the first stage of their journey to Marseilles.

Notes to Chapter Six

1. Du Camp's testimony has long been recognized to be unreliable, but it has not been certain whether his distortions were deliberate or accidental. Conclusive evidence is now available. In

his *Souvenirs littéraires* Du Camp writes, apropos of the Brittany trip: 'Il fallait obtenir l'assentiment de Mme Flaubert, assez jalouse de son fils, et toujours inquiète dès qu'elle ne l'avait plus sous les yeux. Je me chargeai de la négociation, qui fut moins difficile que nous ne l'avions redouté' (vol. i, p. 331). Auriant has recently published, in his *Lettres inédites de Gustave Flaubert* (1948), some of the correspondence that was available to Du Camp as he was writing the *Souvenirs littéraires*, and there is a letter, half-destroyed, in which Flaubert tells Du Camp: 'Tantôt ma mère et moi nous avons parlé de voyage—et d'un voyage comme je veux en faire avec toi, notre voyage à pied, en Bretagne. Elle a approuvé ce projet. Elle t'aime' (p. 24). Du Camp's bad faith is proved.

2. This, at least, is Du Camp's account. Flaubert speaks rather mysteriously of *two* 'young phenomena', 'porteurs d'un bras, quatre épaules', and says they had an arm in the middle of the back.

3. At any rate, Flaubert thought he was of noble blood. But the inevitable researchers, checking every detail of the journey, have concluded that he was probably a peasant and that his fathers had borrowed the name from their masters.

4. The suggestion is strengthened by the fact of his impotence on the first night he spent with Louise Colet. Moreover, in *L'Education sentimentale* Frédéric takes Rosanette to the bed he has prepared for Mme Arnoux, and the whole passage looks like a transposition of Flaubert's psychological relations onto the plane of concrete reality. It is even possible that he hoped to prevail on Mme Schlésinger in that summer of 1846 when he first met Louise Colet, and that, like Mme Arnoux, she was protected by solicitude for her child. Her son Adolphe had been born on 1st January 1842.

5. This letter was first published in its entirety by Auriant, op. cit., pp. 29-32.

6. The Conard edition is even more formidable than it need be: it prints every word of Flaubert's manuscript and gives no indication of what he had crossed out.

Chapter Seven

THE LEVANT

'Ce vieil Orient, pays des religions et des vastes costumes.'
Letter to Mme Flaubert, 5th January 1850.

When Flaubert travelled, he took his past experience with him—and not as a vague background of recollection, but as a corpus of emotions which he continually stirred up and re-examined. He was like a man always looking back over his shoulder to see how far he had come. In Marseilles, for instance, his mind was not set on Egypt, Nubia, and Palestine; instead, he recalled his trip to Corsica and his meeting with Eulalie Foucaud; and without any hope of seeing her again, he stole away to the rue de la Darse and gazed at the shuttered windows of the Hôtel Richelieu, relishing the memory of passion.

During the ten-day voyage across the Mediterranean, the boat ran into rough seas, and while Du Camp, bereft of his usual self-assurance, spent much of his time below, Flaubert brooded fixedly on Le Poittevin, to whom the journey would have meant so much. His melancholy remained with him till 15th November when land came in sight; as they drew into Alexandria, he stood in the bows and made out the black dome of Mehemet Ali's seraglio glittering in the sun.

Although Egypt was not yet a centre of tourist traffic, it was quite usual for two Europeans to go up country together; Englishmen were particularly in evidence and two years later Dickens described in *Bleak House* the emptiness of the law-courts in the long vacation, when 'dispersed fragments are to be found on the canals of Venice, at the second cataract of the Nile . . .' Flaubert and Du Camp, however, could boast special recommendations, and they enjoyed a princely reception from both Soliman Pasha, the terror of Constantinople, and Hartim Bey, his Foreign Minister. They had brought with them Du Camp's valet, an artful and ingenious Corsican called Sassetti, and although he had visited Egypt before, he had never known such hospitality. 'Whatever happens,' he exclaimed periodically, 'I can say that once in my life I've had ten slaves to attend me and one to chase away the flies.'

Always possessing an eye for novelty, Du Camp had travelled from France heavily laden with photographic apparatus: phials, flasks, basins, chemicals, and an unwieldy camera. A minimum exposure of two minutes was necessary, and as he and Flaubert wandered through the streets of Alexandria looking for suitable subjects, they were accompanied by a band of soldiers who beat back the crowd with sticks and held them off till the exposure time had elapsed.

Du Camp, indeed, was thinking of the prestige he could derive from his journey, for an illustrated account would make his name. But Flaubert was unconcerned about success or the future; he was still living in a torpor induced by the condemnation of his book, and to the people and landscapes of the country his attitude was that of a perceptive but slightly bored observer. 'I am', he said, 'getting a bellyful of colour, just as a donkey takes its fill of oats.' Crossing Lake Edku in a ferry, he noticed some rotting hulks along the shore—all that was left of Nelson's Battle of the Nile; but during the first weeks he absorbed the atmosphere and watched the people instead of pursuing relics of history. When he reached Cairo, he discarded conventional European dress, had his head shaved bare except for a lock behind, and donned cloth trousers, a long white Nubian smock with tassels, a rough cravat, and a heavy red tarboosh. Had it not been for the exceptional treatment accorded to Europeans, he would have adopted the local costume altogether; as it was, he promised himself that pleasure later in his journey and found consolation in the smoking of a chibouk. Mosques, bazaars, and camels all attracted him, but his chief delight sprang from an unexpected discovery: that in Egypt just as in France the grotesque was supreme. He had first noticed it on disembarking, for when the ship drew in, a battery of sticks descended on the heads massed by the quay-side; and as he came to know the country he realized that lavish distribution of corporal punishment was characteristic of the native temperament. This, however, was only a superficial manifestation, on a level with the camels who occasionally peeped through the tent-holes of the bazaars and gazed round in bewilderment. Far more delightful was the inscription painted on Pompey's column in black letters three feet high: THOMPSON OF SUNDERLAND. And the quintessence of the grotesque was embodied in a certain Chamas, a French dabbler in medicine who was helping to organize a health service in the Egyptian Army and lived in an obscure house with a dirty negro. His hobby was writing verse, which he declaimed to anyone showing the slightest interest, and at Flaubert's instigation he was induced to read long passages from his works. Among them was a poem that had been addressed to Lamartine in 1848 and ended

Vive à jamais le Gouvernement provisoire!

But his crowning effort was a five-act tragedy entitled *Abd-el-Kader*. Reaching the line

C'est de là, par Allah! qu'Abd' Allah s'en alla

Chamas stopped and gravely explained that it was an experiment in what the ancients had called imitative harmony. Flaubert beat the air with his hands and cried 'C'est énorme'.

The most important of their excursions outside Cairo was to the Pyramids, which they reached in the evening. It was one of those episodes in Flaubert's life so charged with emotion that he remained silent; the Sphinx, the Father of Fear, red in the sunset, filled him with solemn dread, while Du Camp, pale with excitement, intoned a passage from *La Tentation de saint Antoine*. They camped nearby and in the small hours they began the ascent of Cheops, the Great Pyramid. On the summit they waited for the winter dawn to invade the valley of the Nile, and as light fell on the Pyramid it disclosed a label attached to the side: *Humbert, floor-polisher.*

They employed a certain Khalil Effendi to come every evening

and instruct them in the customs and tenets of Mohammedanism;
he translated songs and stories, and they both took copious notes,
Flaubert meditating on a work about the Orient, Du Camp amassing material for a factual description of Moslem life. Flaubert
also obtained an interview with the Coptic bishop, a white-bearded
old man who received him kindly; and presuming on the out-of-
the-way knowledge he had acquired at Croisset, he put searching
questions about the essential Christian dogmas and probed the
doctrines of one of the most ancient of all Christian sects.

Altogether they spent two months in Cairo; but they were
anxious to continue their journey, and in February, accompanied
by ten sailors and Joseph, a particularly roguish dragoman, they
entered their *cangia* (or river-craft) and began the long trip up the
Nile. But although they visited temples, explored ancient sites,
and filled notebooks with picturesque descriptions, they did not
forget France and its people: Flaubert, in particular, was constantly harking back to Le Poittevin, recalling Bouilhet's verse,
comparing the Nile with the Seine, and thinking of the white house
at Croisset. He was often bored and perhaps he was homesick; at
any rate a well-known figure suddenly reappeared on board the
cangia, a figure who had hitherto seemed typical of the French provinces and unsuitable for export: *Le Garçon*. In this incarnation he
was known as a sheik and represented by Flaubert (Quarafon) and
Du Camp (Etienne). They asked each other imbecile questions
about travelling and received imbecile answers. Did, for instance,
the trains shake unduly and was good wine obtainable? Were the
ladies attractive and did shop-girls parade their love of luxury? It
was to be hoped, at least, that socialism had not spread into those
parts. And when they had come to the end of their repertory, the
two sheiks quavered off into an endless catalogue of their culinary
preferences and physical infirmities.

Sometimes, however, while the boat moved on upstream, with
a high white cliff to port marking the edge of the Arabian plateau,
the beauty of the country and its history burst upon the travellers
and overwhelmed them. Such an experience came upon Flaubert
at Thebes. They passed before the ancient city to the music of the
tarabook and flute and to the clattering of crotals; and he was so

moved that, forgetting his animus against the church and his deep-rooted scepticism, he offered thanks to God that such joy should be possible.

According to Henry James, indeed, it was during his Eastern Journey that Flaubert received the disclosure essential to every artist—the revelation of beauty that was to sustain his courage and sharpen his purpose for the rest of his life. But James knew nothing of Flaubert's youth, of his palpitating discovery of *Faust*, his passion for Elisa, his inspiring conversations with Le Poittevin, his experience of pantheistic unity with nature. By the time he finished *L'Education sentimentale*, Flaubert was already converted to his religion as an artist, and nothing that happened after that could much alter his knowledge of beauty and his dedication to a perfect ideal; he had been vouchsafed a particle of the truth and he was resolved to preserve and perhaps increase it, but however far he travelled, however many countries he traversed, he already possessed what he was seeking, and even in the East, on which he had lavished such fervent hopes and such gorgeous dreams, he was visited by no new afflatus. In some ways he was even disappointed; the temples of Egypt quickly palled despite the warmth of his curiosity, and although he wrote long and enthusiastic letters home, his travel-notes show that he was far from recapturing the excitement he had known in Brittany. Egypt, indeed, appeared to him as a land he had visited before in his imagination; but now its dim contours grew precise and clear. 'Anyone', he said, 'who looks at things with some care finds them for the second rather than for the first time.' If he was surprised, it was not at the nature but at the extent of this world observed: he had not foreseen its scope and variety. But even in looking at it, he remembered his literature and history, and whenever he was deeply stirred, it was not at some purely human situation or some purely natural landscape but always at a sight whose significance was enhanced by the shadow of past civilizations and the echo of ancient writers. In lesser matters, however, his originality was more evident—an originality intrinsic to his temperament—and instead of Byron's delight in passionate colour and excess, he was drawn to the 'harmony of dissimilar things. I remember', he remarked, 'a bather who had on his left arm a silver bracelet and on his other a cyst. That is the true and therefore the poetical East.' The 'therefore' is characteristic.

When they reached any substantial town, he and Du Camp usually sampled the local love-making, partly from curiosity, partly from pleasure, and partly from hostility to conventional morals. At Isna, in particular, they were conducted on landing to the house of Kuchiuk Hanem, an *almeh* or dancing-girl from Cairo, who had once been the idol of great pashas and who now, in exile, catered for rich travellers and helped to give Isna its prosperity. She was a splendid creature, whiter than an Arab, and she possessed a servant, who also danced, and a tame lamb, spotted all over with henna, and muzzled in black velvet. Flaubert stayed for a single night, but although the episode seemed trivial, it exercised an unusual compulsion on him. After Kuchiuk had fallen asleep, he remained awake, contemplating her still body and calling up, with the utmost intensity of which he was capable, all his memories of pleasure in Paris, all his old desires for love; he explored the necropolis in his own heart, pausing to reconsider each buried affection, relating it to the present in which he lay with an Egyptian dancing-girl near the banks of the Middle Nile. In spite of herself, Kuchiuk had aroused him as Louise Colet never could—had opened his nature to emotions which he thought had dried up long ago; and he tried to grasp the experience in its entirety and to hold it in his mind, so that it took root in his tenderest recollections.[1]

Above Isna lay the Coptic convent of Gebel el Tayr. As soon as a boat came into sight, the monks used to swarm down a tunnel leading to the water's edge, swim out, stark naked, and clamber aboard, begging for alms. They were on this occasion beaten off with sticks by the Mohammedan crew of the *cangia*.

Still further upstream, beyond Korosko, Du Camp and Flaubert met two Arab boats conveying slaves to Cairo; they were mostly women who had been stolen from the territory of the Gallas, and the Arabs introduced among them a few old negresses to act as interpreters and proffer some consolation. The two travellers went aboard and stayed as long as they could, haggling over ostrich feathers and an Abyssinian girl. Their purpose, said Flaubert, was to enjoy the *chic* of the spectacle, just as three months earlier he had visited the slave-market in Cairo and noted without displeasure the prevailing scorn for mankind. In a way, he was affected; but his pity always tended to be more sentimental than genuine, and when he could not identify himself with the suffering of the individual, he was even gratified by human distress, as though it invalidated the doctrine and practice of philanthropy. In fact, his dislike of cant and detestation of the bourgeoisie led him to reject the bourgeois virtues as well as the vices, and betrayed him into a defect of sensibility that was also a flaw of character. He had so revised his scale of values that the sight of a slave-boat filled him not with compassion or anger but with a dark satisfaction at the sad epitome of human life.[2]

During the first weeks on the Nile, he had hoped to write up the journey as he went, but he soon realized that it was too exacting a task, and so he contented himself with making short but detailed notes. For the rest he became an observer, storing up impressions against his return; but he still felt incapable of another book and undecided about what to tackle. His head was just empty.[3] What was worse, as they reached Wadi Halfa, the farthest point in their itinerary, and turned back, the old ennui, which had never been far removed, descended on him once more and he regarded with a positive dislike the temples that they visited almost daily. He assured his mother that he had already begun the journey home, though by a circuitous route; and no doubt the assurance was not for her only, but for himself.

At Isna they visited Kuchiuk again, but she seemed tired and her pet lamb had died; for Flaubert the encounter was yet another taste of the bitter cup, and a welcome taste at that. At Luxor they stayed for a fortnight, and Du Camp suddenly became a keen swimmer with a reckless contempt for crocodiles. At Thebes they spent three days, after which they camped beneath the Colossus.

On the whole, however, the return journey afforded none of the pleasure and novelty they had enjoyed on the way upstream, and the only important variation was a detour from Qena to Quseir. It was in May and so hot that when Du Camp grasped the barrel

of his gun, it scorched off the skin of his hand. After four days'
riding, they reached the Red Sea and bathed in the waters that had
swallowed up Pharaoh; but they only regained Qena after a gruelling passage across the desert, during which the dragoman was
delirious with fever and Du Camp, for one, was convinced that
they would die of thirst.[4]

In his letters Flaubert often referred affectionately to Du Camp,
so attentive and fraternal. 'He's an awfully good chap', he told his
mother. But he grew tired of this man perpetually at his elbow,
pulling his arm to show him something else. Living with Du Camp
for months on end, discussing with him everything from Egyptian
temples to dancing girls and Homeric literature, Flaubert gradually realized that their minds worked on different planes and in
different ways. Whereas he himself was concerned with daily life,
whether ancient or modern, and the secret passions consuming
people of every kind, and whereas he completely neglected his
official mission, which would have meant tedious inquiries about
supply and demand, crops, ships, and caravans, Du Camp, on the
other hand, made the most of his position as a Government emis-
sary, frequenting men of power and fame and establishing an
influential network of acquaintance that would further his ambitions on his return to France. He entered readily into Flaubert's
mockery of the bourgeoisie, but it was precisely in bourgeois
society that he was determined to rise; and as he seems already to
have rid himself of the dangerous delusion that he was a genius,
the means by which he attained eminence would not be originality or outstanding brilliance, but the more orthodox ones of application, soliciting, and self-advertisement. Unfortunately, however,
he assumed that his aims and methods were universal; and when
Flaubert, who had been thinking hard about his own projects,
declared that his one intention was to lead a solitary life at Croisset and that he did not feel he had either sufficient talent to write
or sufficient nervous strength to publish, Du Camp was shocked—
genuinely shocked out of altruistic affection—and pressed his
friend to change his mind and embrace a more active and purpose-
ful career in Paris.

But although Flaubert did not own to any certain plans, his

slow ruminations were pointing to another end. It was still uncertain and undefined, and he did not admit it even to Bouilhet. But he confided that at last the wound inflicted by the failure of *La Tentation* had begun to heal; and the trend of his thought is evident from the books he read during the journey. He still indeed devoured Greek classics, but he also asked for modern French works, and they were neither plays nor verse but novels: inferior and even trashy novels like *La Maîtresse anonyme* by Scribe, *Gerfaut* by Charles Bernard, *Le Solitaire* by the Vicomte d'Arlincourt, and Sue's *Arthur*.[5] They convinced him that modern French literature was almost incurably sick; but if Du Camp had been less ready to jump to conclusions, he might have discovered in such a course of reading more than either bad taste or helpless nostalgia.

They took a boat from Alexandria to Beirut, sailing with two or three Christian merchants who came from Syria. One of them had a negress slave, a girl of ten or twelve, who spent the journey in a corner, crying. When her owner wished to clean her, she was stood naked in water and rubbed down with sand till the blood came. Even the sailors were sorry for her.

In Beirut the postmaster was Camille Rogier, a painter who had taken Gautier's Orientalism seriously enough to leave France altogether; and he and the French consul were excellent company. Flaubert and Du Camp, however, were anxious to travel south into Palestine, and, getting together a small caravan of four mules and five horses, they continued their route parallel to the mountains of Lebanon, amid country that delighted them by its colour and contrasts after the monotonous glare of the Egyptian landscape.

Coming up the long hill into Jerusalem, Flaubert was at a high pitch of excitement, but it collapsed quickly enough when he arrived. The city had a sad charm, with its heaps of dung and ruins and the occasional black-bearded Polish Jew, capped in foxskin, gliding along the walls. But to obtain the keys to the Holy Sepulchre, application had to be made to the Turkish *pasha*, for the Christian sects would have come to blows. And when Flaubert did at last enter, devoid of any emotion but a receptive piety, and peered through the holes cut in the door, the first object that became visible overwhelmed him with its complete incongruity—

a full-length portrait of Louis Philippe. In the tomb of Jesus the grotesque had achieved its noblest triumph; and Flaubert left, coldly ironical, fatigued, and disgusted by the pretentious dishonesty with which the churches had sullied the Holy Places. The whole atmosphere was meretricious, and back in his hotel, he reread the four gospels to soothe his bitterness.[6]

The Basilica of the Nativity in Bethlehem caused him the same disappointment, though he had to tear himself away from the Chapel of the Manger; and when he returned to the Holy Sepulchre and was led into the second room and offered a rose which the priest had blessed before his eyes, he felt a stab of bitter regret: the moment would have been so precious to a believer! The reflection was perhaps not unusual, but it was symptomatic of Flaubert; for despite a logical ability abnormally powerful in an imaginative writer and a formidable capacity for perceiving and unmasking cant and humbug, his fundamental criterion was emotional. If an event or a scene failed to move him, he either dismissed it as inadequate or deplored his own feeble response. Apparently it did not occur to him that intellectual perception was enough in itself; and though he was never specific on the point, he always implied that experience, to be truly known, must be deeply felt. The idea was so common, especially to those bred in Romantic ways of thought, that its effects were not analysed or appreciated, but it involved cardinal principles governing the conduct of life and set up intensity of feeling as a standard and guide in matters of religion, love, and personal morality. In particular it entailed a choice of subject for Flaubert the writer; for if the stuff of literature was experience and if the most suitable experience was that which had been most deeply felt, it meant that as he grew older he would continue to hark back to the intellectual and emotional patterns of his youth, which, by constant recollection and recreation, had been gouged in his mind.

Meanwhile, however, he felt distressingly barren in spirit, and the moments of exaltation that overtook him as he rode to the Dead Sea and then turned north again for Damascus, did not dispel the pall of ennui. The country was infested with brigands, and travelling, which was dangerous at the best of times, had to be

carried out at night. To make matters worse, the dragoman fell
ill at Baalbek, and while Du Camp took him back to Beirut, Flaubert and Sassetti pursued their way over the chain of Lebanon.
The rigours of the journey and the bitter cold on the heights now
began to exhaust Sassetti: he chattered with fever and rolled in his
saddle, and Flaubert barely managed to get him as far as Eden.
There they were joined by Du Camp, appalled at the rumour running round the villages that one of the foreigners was on the point
of death. He feared it might be Flaubert. Thanks, however, to
heroic doses of quinine and the devoted care of a Carmelite monk,
Sassetti rallied sufficiently to be escorted to Tripolis; and they
made the journey with Amaya, a Spanish Lazarist of high integrity
and noble intelligence, who diminished, if he could not destroy,
the impression of corruption and hypocrisy they had received at
Jerusalem.

The original plan had been to cross the Syrian desert after a
rest at Beirut and pass through Bagdad and Basra on the way to
the Caspian, making for Constantinople via the Caucasus and the
ancient Greek colonies on the Black Sea. But the itinerary was
altered—Du Camp says because of interference from Mme Flaubert, who could not bear the thought of Gustave beyond the
Euphrates; Flaubert says simply because of lack of money.[7] It is
clear, at any rate, that Du Camp acquiesced with some unwillingness, but that Flaubert was already hankering after France and
Croisset. What was true of Schubert's wanderer was also true of
him:

Dort wo du nicht bist, dort ist das Glück.

At Beirut they embarked for Rhodes, and after ten days on the
island, during which they discovered the inevitable Englishman
carving inscriptions in a church, they crossed to the mainland. But
Flaubert was too preoccupied with his return to derive consistent
pleasure from the country or the people; there were sudden peaks
of emotion—a mountain torrent by the ancient road to Ephesus
and a sunset seen from Mount Pagus—but for the most part he
lived among the grey lowland of tedium and satiety. One door
after another slammed behind him. Smyrna, the Golden Horn,

Constantinople were all visited and disposed of, and on 18th December 1850 he and Du Camp arrived off the Piraeus and were promptly fumigated, sulphurated, and quarantined for five days.

Since money and time were running short, there was no hope of seeing Greece at leisure; but though his attitude was often that of an Alexandrian Hellene, Flaubert responded whole-heartedly to the Acropolis. He and Du Camp preserved their Eastern costume, even to the tarbooshes, and gave the Greek Queen a graceful Turkish salute as she drove past one day in her coach. Even if he failed to deceive her, Flaubert made a great impression on a band of English naval apprentices, who, buried in uniforms several times too large, arrived in his hotel, eager to speak with him about his native Turkey.

As they pushed on to Corinth, they took the track between Megara and Kineta—scarcely wide enough for a horse, winding up and down the hillside between scrubby pines, with a sheer drop to the sea on the left. It was a landscape of such inexplicable beauty that Flaubert felt like weeping or rolling on the ground or offering up a prayer. Words were inadequate to recall, much more to describe, a moment so irradiated with joy.

He was, however, an alarming figure and peasants looked on him with misgiving. The sun had tanned him a handsome brown, and he had put on weight. During the journey his hair had begun to fall out, but he compensated for that with a huge beard fit for either a *pasha* or a bandit. His shirts were in rags, his socks worn through, and his shoes mended times without number; he wore a large goatskin coat patched with fox-tails, and to complete the portrait of menacing eccentricity, he exasperated Du Camp by taking lessons as a howling dervish and practising on the most inconvenient occasions.

When he reached Naples, he reluctantly shaved off his beard and adopted a more conventional dress. The city and its museums delighted him just as Rome and Venice were to do a few months later; and although, striking the flagstones of the Via Sacra with his stick and longing to see Titus's triumphal procession, he characteristically denounced the shroud of Christianity that had descended on the haunts of the Caesars, he could not refuse his admiration to Michelangelo, and his heart so went out to Titian and Veronese that was afraid of falling in love with the Virgin. During his stay in Rome he visited San Paolo fuori le Mura, and coming out of the church, he noticed a woman in a red bodice leaning on the arm of an old companion. She was short and rather squarely built, and walked with a slight swing of the body. With her pale face, black eyebrows, and the red ribbon tied to her chignon, she was almost the double of Elisa Schlésinger, and for a moment Flaubert felt a tigerish desire to spring on her. Neither Kuchiuk Hanem nor the courtesans of Egypt, Turkey, and Italy had been able to efface his conception of the perfect woman, fixed for ever at Trouville.

In Rome he met his mother, and she found that he had changed, had taken on a tinge of brutality. The journey to the East had, in fact, hardened him and confirmed his outlook on life. But brutality is hardly the right word for a kind of open-eyed cynicism that was always groping for a sharper emotional perception of reality. He returned home, he said, the same as he left, only with less hair on top and more landscapes inside. But when he set out, he thought of himself as exploring the sites of ancient civilizations, gazing at exotic scenes, evoking the shadows of the past, and emptying, in short, a great cornucopia of colour and history. What he did not foresee was the human revelation that broke upon him: it is not too much to say that in the East Flaubert discovered humanity. His writing had hitherto been palely inadequate as soon as he dealt with characters who were not close to his own nature, and his method of observation, even in Brittany, had been too superficial and anecdotal to overcome the defect. But in Egypt, in Syria, in Turkey, he was fascinated, willy-nilly, by the people, and while Du Camp courted the famous and influential, Flaubert had striven with all the intensity of his imagination to understand the existence of the seething masses. The merchants in the Cairo bazaars, with whom he haggled for hours at a time; the Beduins with whom he spent ten days in the desert; the Coptic priests who expounded to him their faith; the *almehs*; the sailors on the *cangia*; the slaves; the Jews who wept on the ruins of their temple in Jerusalem; the Syrian *moucres* who prayed devoutly for protection against bandits;

the sheiks of Lebanon; the French *déclassés* who trafficked in opium between Marmarice and Smyrna; the eunuchs and dervishes of Constantinople; the wandering musicians of Greece; the brazen prostitutes of Naples—they all fitted into a vast tapestry that he glimpsed for the first time. Despite all the differences of creed, costume, and manners, he realized that these people were essentially the same, linked by an eternal, inescapable baseness—*cette vieille canaillerie immuable et inébranlable*. Everything he saw confirmed the opinion he had reached at Croisset, that humanity was odious and incurable; often pathetic, but always ignorant, presumptuous, hypocritical, and selfish. He felt a withering scorn for its pullulating vileness, and a fierce contempt for any philanthrope or socialist who intended to reform its incorrigible vices or to heal its hopeless disorders.

But although he detested humanity, he did not recoil from it, but drew nearer with an almost prurient curiosity, attempting to see deeper into its leprous nature; and by the time he had reached Rome and France was only a few weeks away, he was longing to return to Egypt, to penetrate to the Sudan and meet the Tooaregs, who veiled their faces like women—to hunt negresses and elephants, to cross the Sahara, and to find his way at last into the golden land of India.

Notes to Chapter Seven

1. Flaubert described the episode to Bouilhet, who made out of a poem entitled 'Kuchiuk-Hanem' in *Festons et Astragales*.

2. In Du Camp, on the other hand, the journey developed a vague socialism; after his return he wrote a book of humanitarian verse. The inevitable effect of the Levant on Flaubert was the wished-for effect.

3. Du Camp relates that as they stood on the peak of Djebel Aboukir, looking down onto the second cataract of the Nile, Flaubert suddenly cried 'I have it! Eureka! Eureka! I'll call her

Emma Bovary!' All the evidence of Flaubert's letters and travel-notes conflicts with this story.

4. In the *Souvenirs littéraires* there is a long and amusing story of Flaubert crossing the desert and rhapsodizing on Tortoni's lemon ices till Du Camp, with thoughts of murder rising in his mind, avoided temptation by falling back so that Flaubert was out of gunshot. The story is not true.

5. When he reached Alexandria, he spent an afternoon in his hotel reading *Valentine* and *Indiana* (George Sand), *Thadéus le ressuscité* (Masson and Luchet), *La Guerre du Nizam* and *Une Veuve inconsolable* (Méry).

6. The larger dome of the Sepulchre was not there in Flaubert's time: it was set up under Russian auspices in 1868. The other dome formed part of the Crusade building and after the earthquake of 1927 it had to be taken down and re-erected. The gallery round the dome, like the steps leading to the Chapels of Golgotha, was divided into two so that there should be no undesirable co-operation between Romans and Greeks or Romans and Armenians.

7. In a subsequent reference Flaubert also adduces the massacres at Aleppo and the insurrection of Bagdad province; in fact, he gives so many reasons that Du Camp's account may well be correct.

Chapter Eight

EMMA BOVARY

*'N'importe, bien ou mal, c'est une délicieuse chose que d'écrire,
que de ne plus être soi, mais de circuler dans toute la création
dont on parle.'* Letter to Louise Colet, 23rd December 1853.

When he reached Croisset in the early summer, he took
stock. The journey had given body and life to his picture
of the East and superseded the uncertain fumblings of
his imagination. Whether or not he was to visit India, Persia, and
China, he had already glimpsed the relation between illusion and
reality and acquired a sense of fact that would constantly check his
intellectual extravagances. More perhaps than he knew, the journey
represented a peak of experience. Till now he had been unable to
interrelate and interpret the components of his life and even when
they seemed clear in outline they did not fit together. But from his
new point of vantage he could survey the pattern of his youth and
retrace each circumstance of emotion. Henceforward his task was
to extract and refine his experience till it transcended his personal
limitations and conveyed a wider truth; his sensibility was no
longer exposed to the world, but turned inwards to art. In fact,
despite the thirty years of writing that lay before him, there
is scarcely a page of deeply felt emotion in his subsequent work
that does not have its origin in his life before 1851.

But although he concentrated his sensibility on art, he was painfully hesitant about his next undertaking. In 1850 he had written
to Bouilhet that he would only go into print if the literary climate
became exceptionally favourable; and the decision expressed both
his loathing for most contemporary work and his conviction that
his own writing was of value solely to himself. His talent was

still unproved, though all his friends conceded him promise; and now that he had cast the mould for his future, his courage and self-respect could hardly afford another fiasco like *La Tentation de saint Antoine*. He copied out his travel-notes, visited London to see the Great Exhibition and brought back a governess for his niece. But he always carried with him a doubt about his true propensity and a paralysing irresolution. When Du Camp suggested that he should write an account of their journey, he dismissed the idea scornfully: travel-books were rubbishy literature. But he listened more readily to the proposal that he should make selections from *La Tentation* for the *Revue de Paris*, whose editorial staff Du Camp had recently joined. While Du Camp pushed him on and Bouilhet held him back, Flaubert could not make up his mind: one night he was intoxicated with his own lyricism, and the next morning he repudiated it entirely. In November he came to Paris to ask Gautier's opinion, but the visit was not satisfactory. He was caught in the street-fighting that marked the *coup d'état* of 2nd December and almost lost his life; and Gautier, on being consulted, expounded so cynical a view of literature and literary success that Flaubert hurried home and put *La Tentation* back in its drawer.

Several ideas had taken root in his mind. For some time he had been meditating on Don Juan, jotting down fragments as they occurred to him, yet fearing to lapse into convention. And then there was *La Spirale*, a novel based on his own hallucinations. It was to deal with an artist who acquired the hashish habit in the East and lived almost entirely in a world of fantasy, seeing the woman he loved as an odalisque and her husband as a sultan. But the subject was not without its dangers, especially for a man so suggestible as Flaubert; it threatened a return of nightmarish obsessions, and he postponed its execution till he was farther removed from his own nervous disorders.[1]

It was probably in December that he made his vital decision—to continue *Madame Bovary*, which he had begun two months before. And from that moment till April 1856 he did not flinch from a labour that demanded from him huge and unpredictable powers of endurance and concentration.[2]

With the writing of *Bovary* Flaubert suddenly reaches his full
stature as a man and an artist, as though responding to a secret
stimulus: he becomes the Flaubert that the Goncourts described,
Henry James knew, Barbey d'Aurevilly hated, and George Sand
admired—the Flaubert in whose likeness the ideal figure of the
novelist has been fashioned and whose shadow threatens with
opprobrium every writer who sends out for publication a page he
knows could be improved. And yet there is no point at which one
can say: here the old Flaubert ends and the new one begins, here
maturity is attained. There are not even differences, contrasts or
modified ideas. It is simply that he had found himself, accepted
his own nature, and ceased to pursue other men's qualities; and as
he became truer to his essence he was purified and strengthened.
From this point more than ever, his concern was not to imitate
but to emulate.

But he was no nearer solving his own problem and indeed he
had decided that it was insoluble. In the East he had seen the life
of the masses, a grotesque amalgam of suffering and futility; and
he had concluded that his own predicament was not a private
visitation of injustice, but part of the universal human destiny. By
assenting to his personal constraint, he acquired the liberty to
move at will within its limits, to know it absolutely; his acute
sensitivity to pain, insuperable as it was, clarified and illuminated
for him the unhappiness of other people so that he could perceive
motives and velleities they never suspected. The predicament of
the man was therefore the gain of the artist. But the artist was
trapped in his own predicament; for Flaubert combined with his
emotional affectibility an ideal of artistic perfection to which no
one could attain, an overwhelming awareness of beauty, and an
excruciating critical sense of what was pompous, foolish, preten-
tions, and inane. As a writer, he knew that he could never reach
the standard he had set himself and that the public, if they read
his work at all, would do so for the wrong reasons, missing his
faint and subtle overtones and discovering instead implications
that were entirely foreign to his art and nature. Not that he was
unduly perturbed at the prospect of being misunderstood: he
expected falsification, however much it wounded him. But his

problem was the eternal one of the adequate communication of a vision, and the vision was so sharp in outline and so rich in colour that he despaired of finding words, rhythms, images, and symbols that would not completely distort and dispel it. And whereas he grew reconciled to his situation as a man, he could never accept this ineluctable dispensation according to which the artist, struggle as he might, was ultimately defeated in his search for words and had to be content with the best obtainable instead of the absolute best.

Flaubert was beset with the familiar weakness of those who feel strongly: a fundamental instability of temperament, as a result of which he was now on the pinnacle of delight and now in the abyss of despair. His long periods of brooding and melancholy compensated for his moments of glowing enjoyment and were a condition for them; he reacted with painful rapidity to circumstances, whether good or bad; but he knew that without his distressing ennui and acedia he would not experience the beauty that alone gave meaning and direction to his life. If he could not and would not dismiss this alternation of mood, he was at least able to exploit it artistically; and the right method lay in uncovering truth, in exposing and discarding the illusions and misconceptions in which it was veiled.

The writing of *Madame Bovary* belonged to this process, for the book, just as much as *La Tentation*, was a stage in Flaubert's development. The time had come for him to analyse in detail the Romantic world-picture, which in his formative years he had accepted as true, and to follow out its effect on personal relations. In Emma Bovary he took a farmer's daughter, not particularly intelligent, but ambitious and vaguely literary, and observed the gradual corruption of mind and character that ensued when her poetical fancies were stifled and checked by a prosaic marriage with a prosaic husband in a prosaic Norman village. Emma's adulteries were an attempt to impose illusion on reality, and it was by probing and depicting them that Flaubert was himself able to impose reality on illusion.

But *Bovary*, of course, is much more than that; and even in the context of Flaubert's life it had other functions. It drained away,

for instance, some of the contempt he felt for the provincial bourgeoisie, and in the person of Homais he organized and compressed
the ignoble, stupid, and unreflecting opinions that so infuriated him
on the lips of his countrymen. But instead of being a mere carica-
ture of imbecility, a figure designed only to amuse and shock,
Homais springs into vibrant life and becomes indeed the most
forceful character in the book.

Putting the scene of *Bovary* in 'Yonville' (or Ry) and Rouen,
Flaubert chose with his eyes open, but he did not realize how long
he would have to spend with odious people in an uncongenial
environment. The eternal company of a vaporous woman, an incompetent doctor, a rakish nobleman, a dingy clerk, a humdrum
apothecary, a dull-witted priest, and an unscrupulous usurer exhausted and repelled him; but to write as he wished, he had not
only to examine and describe them but enter into their minds and
identify himself with their feelings. Persevere though he did, the
task became daily more irksome and rebarbative; and the greater
his dislike, the more remote became the end of his labour.
Wrestling with his bourgeois subject, adapting the commonplace
material to an adequate form, he expended an infinitude of
pains on every paragraph; passages were recast three and four or
more times, and often he worked for almost a week before he was
content with the final state of a page.[3] Compared to this drudgery,
the writing of *Par les champs* or even of *La Tentation* had been a
mere pastime, if not a self-indulgence.

Flaubert's attitude and aims were quite unintelligible to Du
Camp, who had settled in Paris and was bent on making his name.
Apart from his post on the *Revue de Paris*, he was working on an
inferior novel and a book about the Nile, and in January 1852 he
was made an Officer of the Legion of Honour for his perfunctory
explorations in Nubia. To think of Flaubert leading a life of self-
imposed solitude at Croisset aroused his sympathy and pity. That
anyone should renounce celebrity and power amazed him: the
reason evidently lay in some defect of character. But it still was not
too late for Flaubert to change his mind, and so with the utmost
goodwill and the least possible tact Du Camp wrote him a letter of
advice, the kind of avuncular advice that is often inflicted on the

unambitious, urging him to leave Normandy and join the literary circles of Paris, where he would at least find an atmosphere conducive to work, and friends who would be glad to press his claims. Flaubert replied with a strong negative, which he considered adequate. When Du Camp returned to the attack with further importunities, there was a roar of anger, of outraged independence, and Flaubert set down with a cruel insistence the contrast in their characters. 'We are no longer going the same way or travelling in the same boat. May God lead us to our different ends! For myself, I do not seek port, but the high seas. If I am shipwrecked, you need shed no tears.'

There was, however, no break between the two men. Flaubert's letter showed that further remonstrance was pointless and Du Camp acquiesced with good-natured regret. They continued to be on amicable terms, though intimacy was interrupted, and despite Flaubert's rawness and irritation, which lasted for years, he could not obliterate the memory of Brittany and the East, or their common friendship with Le Poittevin. Du Camp, with his fluent promises and ready wit, his mercurial personality and effervescent schemes of self-advancement, was too deeply embedded in Flaubert's life to be easily extirpated: he maintained his position by what he had once been rather than by what he had since become.

Flaubert's life, however, was not exclusively concentrated on his book: in fact, *Bovary* occupied only part of a long day. He never gave up his Greek and English, acquiring some of the facility he might have possessed at school, and in addition he became a self-appointed tutor to his niece. Flaubert as a tutor is perhaps rather a contradictory figure, tactfully gliding over the despised conventions and nonplussed when Caroline asked apropos of Alcibiades, Cambyses or Alexander: 'Was he a good man?' He took the task with becoming gravity, and every afternoon he retired to his study with his niece, settling into an armchair with a pipe and a nail-file, and catechizing her on the rudiments of history and geography. He seems to have been an efficient teacher with a scorn for book-learning, and one has a glimpse of him descending into the garden with a spade and a bucket of water and demonstrating the difference between an island and a peninsula. As she grew up he launched on subjects that interested him more deeply, and while she took notes he descanted on the history of French literature. Probably he enjoyed the opportunity of talking without being challenged or interrupted, and of watching the gradual unfolding of Caroline's mind. At all events, he kept up his lessons for thirteen years, till the eve of her marriage.

Except when he overworked and worried, his health was good. His nervous attacks had been almost eliminated by eighteen months in the open air, and although he scarcely took any exercise, he could rely on a constitution that was naturally robust. His mother, however, was frail and unhappy; she fretted over her dead husband and daughter and nursed a secret anxiety about Caroline's physique. As a result, she slept badly, increasing her depression and irritability. Since she was often unable to go out, it fell to Flaubert to accompany Caroline on her walks and even to take her to church on Sundays; and he complied without a murmur, accepting the social obligations of a bourgeois *rentier* and quelling his scorn of the conventions as soon as it was no longer a matter of shocking other bourgeois but of pleasing the women in his family.

He was, in fact, following his own advice that the artist should live like a bourgeois and think like a demi-god, and the placid routine of his life at Croisset was a necessary condition for bringing forth works of art. As far as possible he fled distraction, disturbance, and emotional distress, and turned the sharp edge of his sensibility to literature; for writing in itself seemed to him an entirely adequate and sufficient mode of feeling, and whatever he felt outside his work involved to some extent a dispersal of nervous energy. How far this attitude was justified, how far it was a rationalisation, is perhaps impossible to judge; Flaubert himself did not know; but although he never abandoned his belief that art was a channel for the sensibility and one of its many forms of expression, he came to the conclusion that his youth had been an evasion, that he had turned away from the demands made upon him. 'I was cowardly in my youth,' he told George Sand, perhaps with less than justice to himself, 'I was afraid of life.'[4]

Almost the only company he regularly enjoyed outside his

family was that of Bouilhet, who visited Croisset every Sunday. They criticized each other's work with great zeal and acuity, and although Mme Flaubert suspected Bouilhet, like Du Camp, of envy and therefore injustice, Flaubert knew that Bouilhet at least was not moved, even unconsciously, by anything but a desire for perfection. So to Bouilhet he submitted the plan of *Bovary* and the chapters as they were written, and while each encouragement gave him new heart, each objection distressed him by its fairness and accuracy. Bouilhet became indeed an embodiment of Flaubert's own scruples, assimilating, and applying a standard of judgement before which the mildest assonance, the slightest incongruity, the palest recollection, the least illogicality, stood condemned.

Bouilhet, however, could not save him from himself, from the incurable loneliness of his own soul; and his melancholy was deepened by the knowledge that Elisa Schlésinger was no longer in Paris. Her husband, who cheated and defrauded composers with cheerful impunity, discovered that some of his other creditors were less easily put off; and in spite of his wriggling attempts at evasion, he was caught in the net of his own intrigues and lifted out of his element into the cold atmosphere of justice. He had to sell his business and he took his wife and family to Prussia. But even there his ill luck did not abandon him; for he was overheard proclaiming republican doctrines in the inn at Kösen, arrested, and sentenced to three months' imprisonment. On his release, he settled in Baden, and although Flaubert received occasional invitations, Baden was too far from Croisset for him even to consider accepting them.

When, therefore, almost immediately after his return from the East, Louise Colet made overtures to him, he did not discourage her. They met in July 1851, as she was passing through Rouen on her way to London, and the liaison was renewed shortly afterwards. Considering that their relationship had previously deteriorated from the excitement of novelty to the mutual irritation of two incompatible personalities, it is perhaps surprising that Flaubert should have recommenced an experiment that was bound to fail. But in his hesitant and distorted way he was fond of Louise and probably did not admit to himself the gulf that divided them.

In spite of their estrangement nothing had been said that could not be mended, and he may even have contemplated asking her to accompany him on the Eastern Journey.[5] At any rate he was fairly certain that she offered him the possibility of happiness, especially now that he had few illusions about her. Indeed for Flaubert, who had renounced marriage and avoided the company of women because they might distract him from his art, the liaison with Louise Colet was the one and only possibility of happiness, and if that failed, he would have to admit his total unsuitability for the most intense relationship in the average man's life. But his interest in Louise was also professional, for she had not ceased to be a first-hand document, especially for a novelist with a Romantic heroine. And his attitude was further complicated by his notion of a hermaphroditic communion between two artists, who could discuss and criticize their work and help each other on to new achievements: a notion that was both suggested and invalidated by his gross overrating of her poetry.

Since their quarrel in 1848, however, her situation had altered. She was growing older, uglier, and more vexatious. In 1850 she had been involved in a protracted and notorious lawsuit for publishing the intimate letters of Benjamin Constant to Mme Récamier, and although she was cleared of the charges of captation and fraud, her reputation was not enhanced. The next year her husband died and this event must have made her all the more anxious to see Flaubert again. Colet's death removed the main obstacle to a public liaison, perhaps even to a permanent one, and she was poor, with a daughter to maintain and educate. But Flaubert, who was so clear-sighted about some facets of personality, seems to have been quite unaware of her ultimate aim and to have assumed that the occasional meeting in Paris or Mantes would satisfy her. He examined and amended her work line by line and gave her a bottle of sandalwood oil he had brought back from his journey; but of any closer relationship there was no mention, and while Louise continued to weave her net, he perversely ignored it.

But Flaubert felt grateful for the help she had given to Bouilhet by introducing him to men of note and arranging a soirée in his honour; and when in November 1853 Bouilhet left Rouen for

Paris ostensibly in pursuit of a more resounding success than he could obtain in the provinces, she was doubtless pleased; for Bouilhet wooed her friend, Mme Roger des Genettes, with even greater ardour than he wooed fame, and his presence in her salon was a convenient link with his best friend.

Bouilhet's departure wounded Flaubert, whose isolation became almost absolute—wounded him with a strange severity. His personal emotions ran deepest round his friends, whereas for women, apart from Elisa, he felt mere prickings of desire or flushes of passion. There is no suggestion of homosexuality in his nature, but only with men could he find the true intimacy in which character is revealed; and because he demanded so much, he was consistently disappointed. He expected his friends to yield entirely to him, to strip off the mask that confronted society and be unrestrainedly themselves; and when they were lured away by ambition or love, he was bewildered and aggrieved. He preserved this naïvety to the end and never ceased to look for a frankness in others which they did not even wish to possess.

At Croisset habits became tyrants. He got up late, read his letters, lunched and gave Caroline her lesson. Apart from a stroll up the garden after lunch and, in summer, a talk on the balcony after dinner, he scarcely stirred from his room. Walking, he asserted, was harmful—so harmful that when he grew older it even annoyed him to see his friends indulging in so unwise a practice; and he remained for most of the day in his high-backed oak-chair, smoking interminable pipes, glowering at his stubborn pages, loudly intoning his sentences as they were written, and muttering with irritation while the steamboats puffed up and down the river with an odd grating of their chains. Sometimes, when the phrase simply would not come, he slumped onto his divan in a mood of hopeless depression. Most of his writing was done at night, and about three or four in the morning, when he had exhausted himself on *Bovary*, his private emotions, so long constrained, clamoured for expression; he pulled out his writing-paper, scribbled his letters—amorous, exasperated, argumentative, and expansive—to Louise Colet, Bouilhet and Du Camp, and finally tumbled into bed for six hours' sleep just as the servants began to move at dawn.

But even if Croisset became as much of an ivory tower as he could make it, it also cloaked political intrigue, and thanks to Louise Colet Flaubert found himself a go-between for the voluminous and inflammatory correspondence of Victor Hugo. Hugo was in exile in Jersey, trying to unseat Napoleon III from his throne with vast tornadoes of abuse, and kept in close touch with the secret opposition in France. Louise Colet had republican sympathies, and at her suggestion Hugo sent his letters to an address in London, from which they were posted to Croisset and so to Paris. At first, indeed, Hugo seems to have imagined that Gustave Flaubert was an ingenious pseudonym devised by Louis Colet, and Flaubert had to remind him of their meeting in Pradier's salon before he was disabused. But then he recalled the occasion most distinctly (for Hugo overflowed with indiscriminate benevolence) and after that he often included tracts and manifestoes for the ardent revolutionary he conceived of at Croisset.

Meanwhile, as she tried to tighten her hold, Louise pressed to meet Mme Flaubert, who had been informed of the liaison. Perhaps she hoped to release Flaubert from his mother's apron-strings; at least she would be able to form an opinion of the woman who was her principal rival. For the figures of his past seemed to be fading away, abandoning the struggle. In the summer of 1853 Flaubert had spent some weeks at Trouville, and when Louise reproached him with pursuing the phantoms of the place, he denied the accusation; it was rather that he evoked his memories in order to exorcize them. 'I have brooded a good deal on this theatre of my passions', he told Bouilhet. 'I am taking leave of them—I hope, for ever. I am half-way through life. It is time to say farewell to the vexations of youth.' And as he at last vanquished the haunting picture of Elisa, he dismissed also the lingering desire to write his memoirs, which had periodically exercised his mind, and sheared away the remnants of a personal, relative approach to art.

Although he seldom visited Paris, Bouilhet and Du Camp were there continually, and Louise Colet plagued them with requests and suggestions. To Du Camp she wrote three hundred letters, apparently unaware that he had lost his influence: she regarded him as a substitute for her lover, and when he yielded to expressions of resentment and irritation against Flaubert, she was glad, for they confirmed her own view of Flaubert's personality as morbid and arbitrary. On Bouilhet she made less impression, for in spite of the encouragement she had given him, he had no wish to become a tool in her hands. Indeed he avoided her. 'I agree with what you say about the Muse', he wrote to Flaubert shortly after his arrival. 'It is an attachment that will come loose on its own, without sharp jerks.' Flaubert evidently saw that the relationship must end; but although he did not blame himself, he felt that Louise was also in the right. 'Whose fault is it? Destiny's. As to my part in the whole business, I feel my conscience quite at ease and consider I have nothing to reproach myself with. Anyone else in her place would be tired too. I am not in the least *lovable*, and I use the word in its deep meaning. She is the only woman who has loved me. Is it a curse the heavens have sent her? If she dared, she would say I do not love her. Yet she is wrong.'

Their relations again became bitter and tense. 'One day I find you pleased with me', Flaubert told her; 'the next, you are quite different. But I think I am always the same.' And again: 'Muse! Muse! What is wrong? What caprice is running through your head? What disturbs you so violently? Why? What has changed between us?' Louise took objection even to Flaubert's words of endearment and when he tried to defend himself, he increased her irritation. She followed him in Paris, waited outside the houses he visited. Once she burst into a private room in the Trois frères provençaux, ready to kill her rival, and found Flaubert peacefully dining with three of his friends. She was insanely jealous; and imagining that his jealousy was equal to hers, she deliberately provoked it. In 1852 she had indulged in a brief affair with Musset, a pathetic attempt by two middle-aged people to warm up stale Romantic passion. She failed miserably to cure Musset of the absinthe habit and the episode filled her with a virulent animosity which she vented in *La Servante*. But when she showed the poem to Flaubert, he was not gratified. He had warned her that 'alcohol doesn't preserve the intellect as it preserves a foetus . . . Musset is more a poet than an artist, and nowadays much more a man than a poet—and a poor sort of a man.' But he criticized the poem severely and advised her against publication: 'I find the work ill-intentioned, wicked, and badly written.' She could not learn from her mistakes, however, and early in 1853 she was for a short time the mistress of Alfred de Vigny, with whom she had had an affair six years before. Her first motive was perhaps to increase her chances for the poetry prize offered by the Academy; but she also used Vigny as a goad to Flaubert.

In the summer of 1854 Flaubert visited Paris for a few days and was so exasperated by her constant nagging and reproaches that he came close to killing her. Perhaps it was at the same time that she followed him into the station waiting-room and created such an uproar that she was ejected by the railway staff. At all events he pulled down the blinds of his coach as he travelled about the city, afraid that she would recognize and pursue him.

For some months they had ceased to write to each other and Louise's only method of communication was through Bouilhet, who made occasional trips to Croisset. Presuming too far on his pliability, she urged him to test Flaubert by mentioning Vigny; and Bouilhet, who evidently concocted his letter with Flaubert's assistance, informed her that the name had no effect. He was himself convinced that she hoped to become Flaubert's wife, and the suggestion appalled him. Meanwhile Cousin had reappeared, wishing, it seems, to assure the future of his daughter, and it is probable that he made an offer of marriage.[6] This she turned into a bargaining weapon, with disastrous results; for Cousin, hearing what she was about, immediately withdrew, and Flaubert, wearied and disgusted with her machinations, refused to see her again. Did she storm into his house at Croisset and was she brutally shown out by Flaubert? She says so and the story is plausible. At any rate, early in 1855 Flaubert sent her a curt and emphatic note which terminated their liaison.

The resounding failure of her great passion disrupted Louise Colet's life. Her health, already uncertain, deteriorated and her emotional instability was enhanced. Because of her folly and selfishness she had alienated her best friends and destroyed her chances of financial security; but she kept some shreds of pride, and when Hugo offered to mediate between her and Flaubert, she prevented him, feeling that any attempt at reconciliation was futile and humiliating. If, however, she had lost a lover, she could at least enjoy a revenge; and in 1856 she sold to the *Moniteur universel* a novel entitled *Une histoire de soldat*, in which she described herself as the angelic Caroline and Flaubert appeared as the odious Léonce. Even this did not satisfy her, and three years later she produced *Lui*, which mingled attacks on Flaubert with vituperation of any who had incurred her dislike, including George Sand, Liszt, Sainte-Beuve and Villemain.

Meanwhile Flaubert continued to labour at *Bovary*, now groaning over the difficulties of the subject, now sighing with pleasure at the completion of a phrase. 'Since style was invented, I don't think anyone has taken such trouble as I. . . . I am wearier than if I were heaving mountains about. . . . Do you know how I spent my afternoon the day before yesterday? Looking at the countryside through coloured glasses; I need it for a page in *Bovary*. . . . As I write this book, I am like a man playing the piano with lumps of lead on each finger. . . . My head reels and throat aches with chasing after, slogging over, delving into, turning round, groping after, and bellowing, in a hundred thousand different ways, a sentence that I've at last finished. It's good, I warrant you. . . .' The thought of echoing Balzac or copying Hugo threw him into a frenzied agitation; and when he discovered that *Le Journal de Rouen* would have to be altered because there was an actual paper of that name, he worried for weeks. To put *Le Progressif de Rouen*, as Bouilhet suggested, would spoil all his sentence-rhythms, and the dilemma was only solved when he fixed on *Le Fanal de Rouen*.

In April 1856, however, the book was finished and he was content. Were it not for his friends, he might never have published it, for to his mind producing a work of value was enough, whether others read it or not. But Du Camp pressed the claims of the *Revue de Paris*; and urged on by Bouilhet, Gautier, and his mother, Flaubert gave way. His reluctance was genuine, but so was his desire for recognition, and once he had decided to release his book to the world, he was as impatient as anyone else to see it on the market. He revised and amended the text, had it copied, and late in May he posted it to Paris.

While waiting for its appearance, he could not remain idle and he took *La Tentation* out of its drawer and began to recast it. The fruit of so much labour was still dear to him for its own sake and for its associations, and with *Bovary* disposed of, he felt he could present the saint in a guise that would disarm criticism. He did not rewrite the book, but pruned it of half its length, sacrificing all the passages, long or short, that seemed irrelevant and unnecessary. The task took him six months and his immediate aim was to prepare extracts for Gautier's paper, *L'Artiste*. That he hoped to publish the whole work shortly afterwards is probable; but as he copied it out, he realized that much more was lacking: there was no plan and Saint Anthony was devoid of character. In any case, by the autumn the storm had broken over *Bovary*.

Almost as soon as they received the text of the novel, Du Camp and Laurent-Pichat, joint editors of the *Revue de Paris*, demanded cuts, for fear of prosecution. The *Revue* was connected with *la bohème* and the so-called realist school, and for the Government of the Second Empire realism meant socialism and socialism meant revolution. Any occasion would be welcome of following the several warnings the *Revue* had already received with a final suppression, and Du Camp and Laurent-Pichat meticulously scrutinized their pages for anything that might be seized on as a pretext. When, therefore, Flaubert burdened them with a novel in which there was no attempt to glamorize adultery, they were naturally apprehensive; distortion and humbug were the essential ingredients for popular success and official favour, and Flaubert, realizing that his honesty had done them a disservice, agreed to several omissions. But he soon grew impatient. Publication, which they had originally planned for August, was postponed, and in July Du Camp, fortifying his objections of inexpediency with those of incompetence, coolly wrote to Flaubert: 'Leave us in charge of your novel so that we can print it in the *Revue*. We shall make the cuts we think indispensable. . . . You have buried your book under a mass of redundancies. . . . It must be disencumbered. The job is easy. We will have it done before our eyes by an able and experienced person.' Flaubert read the letter with disgust, scrawled 'Colossal' on the back, and sent no reply. It is almost certain that the endless criticisms with which he was assailed were a device to defer publication, and Flaubert, who probably suspected this, reluctantly conceded some further changes, but insisted that the delay should end. Accordingly, on 1st August the *Revue* announced that in September the first number of *Mme Bovary* would appear; but always on the lookout for an evil omen, Flaubert observed with a pang that the author was named as Gustave Faubert—a grocer of his acquaintance.

More anxiety, temporizing, and procrastination held up the appearance of the novel till 1st October, but after that the numbers followed one another regularly. Although Flaubert discovered in them only misprints, repetitions, and jingling *qui*'s and *que*'s, they were well received by discriminating readers and he could claim a moderate success. Disquieting rumours, however, soon began to circulate, and Du Camp and Laurent-Pichat took fright. Since Flaubert answered with a blunt refusal all their requests to tamper further with the text, they acted on their own: the number of 1st December announced that the editors had been obliged to omit certain passages out of keeping with the *Revue*, and a fortnight later the author publicly repudiated their policy and asked that *Bovary* should not be regarded as a whole. A crisis was obviously impending and before the end of the month proceedings were instituted against Flaubert as author, Laurent-Pichat as publisher, and Pillet as printer. The charge was of offending public morality and religion.

For Flaubert, who wrote essentially for his own pleasure, cared nothing for worldly success, and published *Bovary* only under pressure, the notoriety of the courts was an enormous evil. But it was not without its amusing side that the apostle of art for art's sake should be arraigned for pornography and become famous on the criminal benches; and in spite of his anxiety and perturbation, he did not fail to appreciate a pleasant manifestation of the grotesque when it appeared that the *juge d'instruction*, who examined him about his scene of extreme unction, was a Jew. But as soon as the prosecution was announced, Flaubert furiously exploited every possible resource to avoid it: he pulled strings, hatched plots, importuned his acquaintances, and badgered his friends; he even got Achille to stress the serious political unrest that would ensue in Rouen if M. Gustave Flaubert were found guilty. And for a moment it looked as though his intrigues would be successful and the case would be dropped. But he reckoned without the Empress. For it seems that from friendship for Octave Feuillet, the insipid novelist of anaemic heroines, she ignored all other representations and insisted personally that the prosecution should go forward.

The Government's policy was short-sighted: although papers might be suppressed and writers intimidated and silenced, the effect of such measures was to turn the literary world into an opposition stronghold, and even to the most superficial observer the hypocrisy of the charges was manifest. To prosecute Flaubert, who was on any showing a serious, deliberate writer, and to ignore Scribe, Paul deKock, and Ponson du Terrail was so flagrant an injustice that as soon as the indictment was announced he had the mass of authors behind him. In spite of himself he was a martyr, the representative of every anxious editor who sucked his pen and wondered how to disguise an innuendo, and of every harassed novelist who chose his subjects with an apprehensive side-glance at the police-station.

The hearing took place on 31st June 1857. Pinard, the Imperial advocate, delivered a severe attack on the book and singled out passages for particular blame; but he was unskilful in his methods, denouncing parts that had not been published and going astray in his references; and he concluded with magnificent illogic: 'Without control art ceases to be art; it is like a woman who takes off all her garments.'

For the defence Sénard excelled. Himself a Rouennais, he stressed the eminence of Flaubert's family and the earnestness of his character. Turning to the incriminated passages, he read extracts from Mérimée, Chénier, and even Bossuet and Massillon to show that *Bovary* did not treat love or religion with such crudity as the acknowledged classics. He quoted the *Lettres persanes*, which were given as a school prize, to prove the relative mildness of Flaubert's descriptions. And finally, while Pinard squirmed in his seat, he pulled out a Catholic Ritual and read the passages which Flaubert had toned down to use at Emma's death.

Judgement was postponed for a week, but there was no serious doubt about its tenor. President Dubarle, who was known to be an Orleanist, had smiled openly at some of Sénard's thrusts and once, during the reading of a passage from *Bovary*, was seen to whisper 'Delightful'. By the sentence of the court the book was severely censured, but its merits were recognized and all three defendants acquitted. Possibly Dubarle intended the court's censure as a crumb of solace to the Government and therefore a guarantee against further prosecution. At any rate a Belgian journalist reported: 'I will only remark, with, I believe, the agreement of the judges, who took great interest in the incriminated novel, that it reveals a talent of the highest order.'[7]

The French public delivered an even more generous verdict than its magistrature and Flaubert had to endure an unsought-for fame. The *cause célèbre* shed its celebrity onto the book, and when, yielding to the instances of his mother and Bouilhet, he agreed to the publication of *Bovary* in volume-form, success was immediate and overwhelming. No doubt many of its purchasers hoped for the kind of work that ought to be circulated *sub rosa*, and were disappointed at its propriety and lack of illustrations. Others bought it merely to know what everybody was talking about. But the fact remains that *Bovary*, which might have taken years to establish itself, became famous all over the country in the space of a few months and that by the end of the year Emma had made her bow in vaudeville and music-hall. As for the profits from such extensive sales, they were quietly absorbed by the publisher, Michel Lévy.

The critics, however, were less ecstatic than the public; in fact they were bewildered. Their preferences lay with straightforward novels in which heroes and villains were sharply contradistinguished, and they were as perplexed as the casual visitor to a botanical garden would be if all the labels had been removed from the plants. Even the dullest of them realized that the style was careful and rhythmical, but they reproached Flaubert with not writing the sort of book they expected. Some pronounced his work crude, some heartless, some false; since realism had been mentioned, Flaubert was alternately told that he must write like Champfleury and like Balzac. Sainte-Beuve gave him uncertain praise, placing him among the heads of his generation and by that meaning that he could rank with Champfleury and Murger. 'Immoral', 'brutal', 'the morbid exaltation of the senses and imagination', 'laborious, vulgar, and blameworthy', 'a pamphlet against humanity', 'a huge heap of dung'—the denunciations tumbled out one after the other, and although they were interspersed with cries of enthusiastic admiration, Flaubert disliked almost all the criticisms of his book: they were either narrow-minded and stupid or fulsome and inexact. He was grateful for a mediocre article by Baudelaire, but the man who understood his art—Barbey d'Aurevilly—was regarded by Flaubert as an enemy because he had ventured to attack Bouilhet.

Perhaps the most irritating commentators were those who thought they had discovered the origin of *Bovary* in the history of Delamare; for Flaubert had borrowed the entire skeleton of the book from a notorious case at Ry, and for fifty years and more researchers were to exhaust their ingenuity in identifying and tracking down the minor characters and inviting their recollections about the heroine. But whenever he was asked for the name of his model, Flaubert was categorical; there was none. And his meaning was clear; for *Bovary* aimed at a far wider generality than the trivial boredom of a doctor's wife in a small Norman village, and Emma transcended the provincial limitations of Delphine Delamare.

Publication brought Flaubert a heavy correspondence in which he was accused of describing people he had never heard of. In particular, a man from Reims thanked him for avenging the infidelity of a wife; and almost every chemist in the Seine-Inférieure, discovering his own portrait in Homais, thirsted for the author's blood. To such reactions Flaubert was not indifferent: they confirmed his belief in the supreme truthfulness of good art. But the most exquisite news came five years later, when he discovered that there was in Africa the coquettish and Romantic wife of an Army doctor and that her name was Mme Bovaries.

Though it is doubtful if he ever knew Delphine Delamare, he certainly profited from his liaison with Louise Colet; with a cold-blooded tenacity he had encouraged her confidences and observed the morphology of her emotions. He even attributed to Emma the signet Louise had sent him, inscribed *Amor nel cor*.

But ultimately his knowledge of Emma, her illusions and temptations, was self-knowledge; and the writing of *Bovary* was a prolonged autopsy, an excision of the Romantic cancer. In an environment which he knew by heart, Flaubert followed out the widening gulf between illusion and reality and by sacrificing Emma he saved himself. It was not a coincidence that in 1852, when *Bovary* was well under way, he visited Trouville, and determined to cast out the fantasies of his youth; the rehearsal of his own dreams was essential to the portrayal of Emma's. But although he discarded the immature Romanticism which, in his view, culminated in unhappiness and disaster, he preserved those elements in the Romantic tradition which seemed beautiful and true: the love of fine language, for example, and the use of irony. Above all, he retained the conception of fate, bringing about Emma's downfall by a series of events and circumstances which might have been harmless in themselves, but in conjunction formed a rigorous chain of calamity. Charles's pathetic cry 'It's the fault of destiny!' and Homais's decoration with the Legion of Honour represent Flaubert's attitude when he was writing *Bovary*: a distrust of life, a belief in the hostility of the world, and a biting scorn for the qualifications of success. While his scepticism had hardened, his sense of destiny had grown deeper and he was convinced that there was no solution to the human problem. Even to use the word 'problem' was presumptuous; things had to be accepted as they were.

But however hopeless was Flaubert's metaphysical outlook, he had reached his first goal as an artist; he had satisfied himself of his own talent, and though *Bovary* seemed to him riddled with faults, the acclamation of discriminating friends and his own sense of achievement dispelled his doubts and convinced him that the failure of *La Tentation* had been redeemed. As for technical competence, the virtues of *Bovary* were apparent to the most careless eye; but he knew that he had not only eclipsed the professional novelists in form and structure, but that he had found words, images, and symbols to convey a fragment of his vision.

Nowhere more than in *Bovary* did he express his sense of the grotesque, for the juxtaposition of sentimental vapourings and hard-headed realism was the supreme method of showing up the inadequacy of the Romantic ideal. The grotesque, however, dominated life at all places and all times, offering some comfort for the boredom and misery of existence, and Flaubert was the first to admit that in reality enormous ironies, denied to the artist, were discoverable every day. Of such ironies he was a connoisseur, and he may even have felt that his prosecution was worth while when, twenty years later, he heard that Pinard, the representative of law and order, who had thundered against the scandal of *Bovary* and the immorality of *Les Fleurs du mal*, was the secret author and circulator of a slim volume of lewd verse.

Notes to Chapter Eight

1. The exact date of these plans is uncertain. Flaubert was certainly thinking about *Don Juan* on his way back through Greece and Italy. *La Spirale* is first mentioned in March 1853, but its origin may be considerably earlier.

2. *Madame Bovary* therefore took four and a half years to write, not six as is often stated.

3. Flaubert's average, however, was about three pages a week. He was naturally inclined to talk about his most gruelling passages, but some came much easier to him.

4. If Freud is right about slips of the pen, there is a significant mistake in Flaubert's advice to Henri Brainne (Letter of 30th December 1874): 'Pense à ta santé. Fais tout ce qu'il faut pour devenir un gaillard robuste. Les lettres exigent un tempérament de forgeron. N'oublie pas ce prétexte [i.e. précepte], mon bonhomme, et embrasse-moi.'

5. The evidence for this is uncertain and cryptic. At Debout, on the journey down the Nile, Flaubert met a negro fortune-teller and was struck by the truth of his assertions. 'He declares', run the *Notes de voyage*, 'that I shall receive two letters at Assuan, that there is an old lady who thinks much about me, that I intended to bring my wife on my journey, but that, all things considered, I left on my own; that I wish simultaneously to travel and be home, that there is in my part of the world a very powerful man who wishes me well, and that when I am back in my country, honours will be showered upon me.' One can neglect the predictions (in any case, the letters at Assuan were for Du Camp and Sassetti), but if the fortune-teller had been wrong about the past and in particular about his intentions as regards his 'wife', would Flaubert have bothered to take down what he said?

6. It has been stated, on inadequate grounds, that in 1854 Cousin again became her lover.

7. By law the French Press was not allowed to report cases in which immorality was alleged.

Chapter Nine

THE ARTIST

'Le génie, c'est Dieu qui le donne; mais le talent nous regarde.'
Letter to Louise Colet, 23rd February 1853.

Flaubert's writing was his life-blood: by its pulsation he survived. Devotion to art was a law of his nature and therefore binding and absolute; he was persuaded, as Martin Luther had been persuaded in a different cause, that any disloyalty, any betrayal would so destroy him as to be unthinkable. 'I feel, in my conscience, that I am doing my duty, obeying a superior destiny, doing good and acting rightly.'

The history of his life till the writing of *Bovary* is the gradual recognition of this compulsion, the history of not only his self-abandonment to it, but his discovery of its terrifying power and breadth. As he realized the ideal for which he stood and the fragility of his talent, so the problem of his life was starkly posed: how to mediate between the absolute and the relative, between art and the world. That he had reached his position by a not always creditable route, that he had sometimes treated art more as a refuge than a mission and shrunk from a distasteful reality, was of little importance once he had perceived his predicament and duty; for the purpose and conduct of life were enriched and transmuted.

With his fondness for *boutades* Flaubert sometimes declared that art surpassed in value and pleasure the sorry business of living and that dead authors meant more to him than his contemporaries. As he grew older, however, he grew more sceptical. 'Art, in the last analysis, is perhaps no more serious than skittles', runs a letter as early as 1851, and he later told George Sand with some indignation: 'I'm not such a pedant as to prefer phrases to people.'

The figure of Flaubert is so well known that it is nowadays almost impossible to realize how original, even revolutionary, his attitude was. To most of his poet-contemporaries, literature was a pursuit that was naturally combined with a more orthodox profession. Few of them were so wealthy that they had no living to earn and almost all indulged in some kind of public activity. Many, like Lamartine and Hugo, were drawn to politics; indeed for Lamartine the writing of poetry was a peripheral and subordinate occupation. Others, like Sainte-Beuve and Gautier, subsisted by weekly journalism; and those, like Musset, who were largely indifferent to politics and could escape the drudgery of reviews and articles, were familiar stars in the social life of Paris.

The prose-writer, unless of course he were a Chateaubriand, had less of a *cachet* than the poet, but he, similarly, treated his art as secondary, often using it as a lever to fame and advancement. Chateaubriand himself, like Benjamin Constant, was a politician, while Stendhal was a diplomat, Mérimée a civil servant, and Fromentin a painter. But novelists were hardly regarded as purveyors of serious literature, and men like Eugène Sue and Dumas, however famous and successful, could not claim to be anything but merchants of melodrama. As for Balzac, although he was admitted to spend all his energies on his craft, his social position was equivocal and in any case he was spurred on as much by fear of his creditors as by disinterested love of beauty.

Flaubert, on the other hand, was a bourgeois, born of a respectable and honoured family and endowed with a comfortable annuity; no economic necessity impelled him to write, and if he wished, he could subsist in utter idleness. When, therefore, he chose to devote himself heart and soul to literature—and not even to poetry but to the despised novel—he was consciously and deliberately flouting the conventions of both the bourgeois and literary world; only a man like Baudelaire could understand his motives, and the pained reproaches of Du Camp were natural, friendly, and quite irrelevant.

The artist in his eyes was a being apart from other men, a 'monstrosity', as he said, 'something outside nature'. 'If you want happiness and beauty at the same time,' he wrote, 'you will attain neither, for the second is only born of sacrifice. Art, like the Hebrew God, feeds on holocausts. Come! lacerate and whip yourself, roll in ashes, abase the flesh, spit on your body, tear out your heart!'

But art was not an escape from life. Writing might be a refuge, but art was a representation; and he stressed above all the need of observing accurately. By that he meant an intense apprenticeship to the object described, whatever its kind. 'You have only to look at a thing long enough and it becomes interesting.' Originality was to be found by seeing clearly, for each man's temperament would inevitably modify and individualize his vision; but it was important for the artist to discover where he was most himself and thus most original, and to explore and extend this domain by all the intellectual and emotional resources at his command.

Flaubert's prescripts for the artist's life flow naturally from his idea of art. Writing of Balzac, he once remarked that he must have been a good man because he was a good observer; for it was only possible to observe clearly when the mind was free of prejudices and passions. To achieve such a mind, lucid, impartial, unattached, full of sympathy yet bereft of pity, he banished himself to the solitude of Croisset, leading a life from which the traditional disturbers of repose were rigorously excluded. Gautier, seeing him repulse a woman who had been attracted by his fame and person, asked why he was so hard on the poor creature. 'Because', said Flaubert, 'she might come into my study.'

His serenity was easily interrupted, and once that had happened, writing was impossible. He was tyrannically tidy, with books, paper, and quills each in its proper place; if a penknife was mislaid he seethed with fury, and the visit of a friend or a trip to Paris or Trouville so disorganized him that it might be days or even weeks before he could recapture his mood and train of thought. However cordial he was in Paris, he snarled hatred at the casual intruder in his lair. Prolonged solitude was an essential condition for the functioning of his mind, and one of the reasons he worked at night may have been that in a sleeping world his brooding sense of detachment and independence was enhanced. The pilots of Rouen knew the lamp in his window and used it as a beacon.

It was indeed a beacon in a darkened world; by withdrawal and renunciation he had solved his own problem as an artist, lighting the path of a few navigators in quiet and lonely waters, but appearing as no more than an obscure eccentric to the mass of his compatriots. The general problem of the artist in society, however, was further than ever from being settled; indeed Flaubert's example merely sharpened it by showing the huge discrepancy between the artistic ideal and everyday practice. He was one of the last writers of high rank to enjoy sufficient wealth and leisure to pursue their aims without privation and penury; and his figure implicitly and triumphantly condemned the intellectual and economic conditions that were engulfing his contemporaries in the morass of self-advertisement and journalism. Living in the brief bourgeois interregnum between domination by the aristocracy and domination by the managerial class, he incarnated the bourgeois artist, economically independent of both patronage and State aid, but free to emit anarchic and subversive doctrines about the basis of his own position. He set an example of devotion and self-sacrifice which his successors had neither the desire nor the physical ability to follow; and glimpsing in his last years the *muflisme*, the new vulgarianism that seemed to be overtaking and swamping humanity, he turned away in disgust, relieved that he at least would not be alive to see the new world that was in the making.

To many of his readers, however, he seemed all too deeply embedded in contemporary reality, and they did not hesitate to attach to him the convenient label of 'realist'. The word itself meant little: its primary association was with the group of artists and writers who had centred round Courbet, Champfleury, and Duranty in the late 'forties; and because they were tainted with social and political unorthodoxy, 'realism' had become a useful weapon for conservative critics wishing to cast a veneer of impropriety on any author or work. To its adherents it denoted a contemporary theme, an honest approach, and no limitation in subject-matter; to its opponents it described almost any unconventional characteristic that failed to receive approval at the bar of the popular Press.

Flaubert had read Champfleury and been interested, though not impressed; he accepted Balzac and Dickens as his contemporaries and the implied duty of factual accuracy; but he flatly refused to be known as a realist and docketed and imprisoned in a school. It seemed to him a naïve illusion to imagine that reality could be adequately perceived merely by looking at it. Four years before he died, he was still affirming his scorn for labels. 'How can people be taken in by words empty of meaning like "Naturalism"? Why have they abandoned the good Champfleury with his "Realism", which is an ineptitude of the same order, or rather the same ineptitude? Henry Monnier is no more true than Racine.' And though Champfleury wrote him letters of cautious praise, *Le Réalisme*, which was Duranty's paper, castigated *Bovary* as 'calculated, overworked, all right-angled and, in short, arid and dry'.

But to call Flaubert a realist is, on the face of it, plausible. No doubt he used physical reality as an anchor against the shifting tides of imagination, just as he developed irony to check his headlong enthusiasms; and in *Bovary* he ridiculed Romantic illusions far more profoundly and incisively than Champfleury had succeeded in doing in, for instance, *Chien-Caillou*. Moreover, the gruesome death of Emma by arsenical poisoning broke away sharply from the colourless tradition of the average novel, as exemplified by the heroine of even Duranty's *Le Malheur d'Henriette Gérard* (1861), who drowned herself on her wedding day; by Mélie in Murger's *Le Sabot rouge* (1860), who died of a broken heart; and by Gastonne in Louise Gagneur's *Une Femme hors ligne* (1862), who threw herself into Vesuvius. Even if heroines died dramatically, they did so in a very literary way, and it was a normal practice for novelists to execute their characters off stage and to infect their superfluous women with an unspecified wasting disease.

But there is so much more in Flaubert's work than the mere notation of physical detail that his similarities with Champfleury, Monnier, and the rest are superficial and unimportant. The Realists were indifferent and indeed opposed to his whole conception of literature and had no time for either his stylistic scruples or his concern with transcendent beauty.[1] He was therefore much further removed from their ideals than he was from those, say, of Chateaubriand or Gautier.

His period was one in which science was acquiring enormous prestige. In 1846 Le Verrier had located Neptune by mathematical means, and the impact of a new and apparently infallible form of knowledge was soon reinforced by the activities of such men as Claude Bernard, the physiologist, Deville, the discoverer of aluminium, and Berthelot, the chemist. Flaubert was impressed; and although he had little time for the dogmatic pedantry of Taine, he felt that the artist could in some ways learn from the scientist—could become, like him, impartial and clear-minded, content to observe and correlate without hurrying to form a conclusion. He admired the patient accumulation of facts that was the essence of scientific method, and in all spheres outside that of art he seems to have accepted scientific orthodoxy, though less credulously than Zola, as a sufficient basis for judgements of value. It is possible that the mounting wave of positivist thought even penetrated his sanctum and contributed something to the rigorously tight structure of *Bovary*.

In general, however, he avoided conclusions of any kind, scientific or not, and his reluctance to pass judgement derived from two sources: his reading of literature, which showed him that geniuses like Homer and Shakespeare never revealed their real opinions, and his philosophic scepticism, which he had learnt from Spinoza and confirmed by observing the endless variety of intellectual dogma. 'In order to live', he told one of his correspondents, 'one must give up having downright ideas about anything. *Humanity is as it is*; our job is not to change it but to know it. . . . Throw away all hope of an explanation. The explanation lies with God; He alone possesses it and He doesn't pass it on.' This hesitation to pronounce an ultimate opinion was linked with his belief in the moral virtues of dispassionate observation and crystallized in his doctrine of impersonality. Perhaps impersonality[2] was an unfortunate word to choose: all too often it has been taken first by his correspondents and then by his critics to mean an inhuman detachment from every emotion, painful or pleasant, whereas Flaubert intended it to convey a rejection of the personal only so far as the personal distorted and vitiated art. If an author expressed his own opinions, the effect was to limit the operations of his characters, to hamper them with an irrelevant intrusion and destroy the general truth by reducing it to individual prejudice. '*The less one feels a thing, the more suited one is to express it as it is* (as it is *always* in itself, in its generality, stripped of all its ephemeral contingents). But one must have the faculty of *making oneself feel it.*' Flaubert did not rule out moral judgement, but he wished it to be implicit in the facts rather than suggested by the text. 'If', he said, 'the reader doesn't deduce from a book its inevitable moral, the reason must be that the reader is a fool or the book is *false* as to exactitude. For as soon as a thing is true, it is good. Even obscene books are only immoral because they lack truth. Life just isn't like that.'

Flaubert once told George Sand that he wrote for the pleasure of ten or a dozen people, and in fact he expected the reader to imitate his own detachment. He conceived of his public as a handful of Flauberts, contemplating with a melancholy enjoyment the pathetic story of humanity and listening with pure delight to the music of good prose. Just as he regarded any attempt to draw conclusions about life as a manifestation of hubris, a foolish challenge to divine omniscience, so he would have looked on the conventional happy ending as a wilful and wicked tampering with the fabric of life. The novel, being a representation, had to tell the truth, however unpalatable, and the only domain in which the novelist might legitimately satisfy his longings was style—style, that is, covering not only the choice of words and images and the balancing of sentences and paragraphs, but the whole conception of narrative, with its architectural structure, calculated parallels, and hidden symbolism.

Flaubert's toil has become legendary and it was indeed stupendous. But the slowness with which he produced a finished page did not derive from any lack of fluency. His earliest works were composed without difficulty, and the mass of his published correspondence—which represents only a part of all his letters—is enough to show that when he wished he could write fast and yet admirably. If he spent years over his books, it was rather that he refused to abandon any passage that was still capable of improvement. As a result his method of work was laborious. He began by jotting down the general idea of a paragraph with perhaps a few metaphors he hoped to work in; and once its contours were clear, he wrote out a preliminary draft, which he then tested for sound and lucidity. He continued to write and rewrite the passage, introducing new images and scrapping old ones, till he was at last sure that it was luminous in conception and unified in mood. In this way he accumulated acres of documents. The final version of *Bovary*, for instance—and it was only a fraction of his labour—was written on 1788 leaves, numbered, because of repetition, from 1 to 505; and *L'Education sentimentale* of 1869 was represented by 2355 leaves, 72 of which, dealing with the Forest of Fontainebleau, were reduced to 4 in the final text.[3] When Flaubert mentioned in his letters that he had spent a week over two or three pages, he meant, of course, two or three pages in their final condition, and he may in fact have covered ten, twenty or even thirty before arriving at a satisfactory version. But there was nothing essentially new in his methods: good writing has always been hard and careful stylists have always polished and repolished their work till it acquires a uniform brilliance. Quite apart from the arduous practice of the ancients and the Horatian prescript of year-long elaboration and maturation, there is a lively tradition in France according to which strong and supple prose is the fruit of careful and self-effacing labour.[4] Flaubert was doing what Boileau, La Bruyère, Montesquieu, and Chateaubriand had done before him: what even Balzac, so often reproached for his solecisms, had tried to do within the time at his disposal. Flaubert's task was increased by the clotted richness of his imagination and the acuity of his self-criticism; but if he is to be regarded as the supreme figure of the novelist, it must be less for his huge exertions than for his high conception of his art and for his actual achievement.

Grammar he acknowledged and respected: it was a necessary convention. But he declared that no grammarian had ever been able to write, and when academic correctness involved ugliness of sound, he rode rough-shod over the rules. He was responsible for a number of syntactical innovations which were plundered and overworked by the Naturalists, but for the most part he did not stretch the limits of the existing language. He took it over in its completeness, regarding with horror the neo-barbarian notion that men should only write as they spoke; but he avoided technical terms except for some special purpose. Even in *Salammbô* he was careful to use unfamiliar words only where their meaning could be guessed or had no importance. His conception of the *mot juste*, therefore, was not of pedantic accuracy but of suitability in a context: its associations, factual and metaphorical, had to fit in with the passage, and his final test was to chant his prose in a high, incisive voice, listening intently for echoes, assonances, and repeated rhythms. No phrase was allowed till it had endured the *gueuloir*, and his friends who heard him read his work say that he distorted vowels and indulged in strange intonations as though to enhance the sonority of the language. It distressed him to notice how men like Goncourt and Zola, whom he respected, remained indifferent to words and phrases that transported him with delight; and Du Camp describes his rapture at the name of 'Taprobane' and his reluctant admission that Racine, tiresome classic though he was, had written the loveliest line in French poetry:

La fille de Minos et de Pasiphaé!

He had no ear for music: on the rare occasions when it pleased him, it was because of its extramusical associations. And despite his perception of delicate shades of colour he was short-sighted, unable to distinguish the sharp outline of distant objects and therefore regarding them as masses rather than shapes. As for nature, his attitude varied. When he was young he tended to see it with the eyes of Chateaubriand, looking in it for consolation and sympathy, and once at least he was swept away by the feeling of pantheistic unity. But in his maturity he was more indifferent, more easily bored, and more suspicious of its hostility. 'Nature,' he wrote, 'far from strengthening, exhausts me. When I lie on the grass, I feel I am already under the ground and lettuces are growing out of my belly.' As he aged, however, he reverted to his earlier attitude, and a few years before his death he told his niece: 'You can't imagine what a "lover of nature" I am becoming. I look at the sky, the trees and the greenery with a pleasure I've never enjoyed. I'd like to be a cow so as to eat grass.'

But his only sustained pleasure was writing, despite all its trials. By his art he managed to dominate life and there is in his search for the *mot juste* an element of magic. Savage tribes believe that words have in themselves a special power over the objects they refer to, and that once a thing has been named, its strength is impaired. Certain neurotics similarly hesitate to write down their names for fear of giving away some part of their personality, and the same vague belief is found in children. To pursue and capture the exact word wherever it may be hiding is therefore one way of mastering life. In an adult the nature of the satisfaction is unconscious, but it persists. The function of meticulous accuracy, however, goes much further, for thought is inseparable from language and an idea can only be realized when it has been expressed in adequate symbols. Literary composition is thus a form of discovery, and Flaubert, as much as any other writer, was struggling towards a precise formulation of what had hitherto lurked in the tangled mass of his experience.

'A book', he once told a friend, 'has never been anything to me but the means of living in a particular environment.' He observed the environment, absorbed it, re-created, and controlled it. As he wrote, his mind drifted away down long and delightful perspectives from which he returned unwillingly to his text. But although the world of imagination seems often to have been as vivid as the real world, he would not admit that his condition when writing was remotely pathological. 'In the hallucination proper, there is always terror; you feel that your personality is slipping away from you, that you are going to die. In the poetic vision, on the other hand, there is joy; it is something entering into you. All the same you don't know where you are. . . . Often the vision grows slowly, piecemeal, like different bits of scenery being set up; but often, too, it is sudden and fleeting like hypnagogic hallucinations. Something passes in front of your eyes, and you must seize on it greedily.' Like Balzac, Flaubert was embarrassed by the exhaustive details furnished by his imagination: they had to be shorn away till the picture was of manageable simplicity.

Composition affected him physically. When he was describing
Emma's death, he had the taste of arsenic in his mouth and was
sick twice running; and at the moment of stopping work he often
had an irrational fear that there was someone standing behind
him. But however much he girded at his task, the dominant
emotion was pleasure, which sometimes became much more.
'Last Wednesday', he wrote on 24th April 1852, 'I had to get up
to find my handkerchief; tears were running down my face. I
had affected myself as I wrote, I was savouring a delicious enjoyment both at the emotion of my idea and at the phrase which conveyed it and at the satisfaction of finding the phrase.' This confession could be matched by several more, in which Flaubert
actually uses the language of devotion; and François Mauriac has
used these passages to bring a grave reproach against Flaubert:
not only was he, like all novelists, an ape of the Creator, but he so
completely upturned moral values that he replaced religion by
art and theology by aesthetics, illicitly enjoying the beatitude
of the mystics while indulging in an unworthy and idolatrous
adoration. There is certainly a taint of scandal in his attitude:
it is more than selfishness or escapism and borders on blas-
phemy. But most people will prefer to abstain from judgement
and contemplate an excess which, even if sinful, was heroic and
unique.

Flaubert, however, did not exalt himself; he was far too per-
spicacious to indulge in Hugo's pride or Tennyson's ambition
and his aim was perfection of writing rather than greatness or
eminence. He gave vent to his ideas with thundering emphasis and
allowed himself exaggerations and sallies that have been taken
with portentous solemnity by his more hasty critics. The voice
that reaches us through the letters is often almost a loudspeaker,
amplified till its natural tone is perilously distorted; he puffs up
his preoccupation with style till he threatens to write a book
without a subject at all; he reverts so often to the pains of letters
that they seem to swamp the pleasures; he condemns the vice of
subjectivism so roundly that he is considered a monument of
frigid impassibility. And in private life he infuriates Goncourt by
always talking as though his personal emotions are more pro-

found and acute than anyone else's. But the one subject on which
he preserves invariable moderation is his own achievement and
when he does speak it is to criticize his admirers. Before great men
he feels annihilated. 'I think that if I saw Shakespeare in the flesh
I should die of fear.' And in 1876 he writes about an article comparing him with Molière and Cervantes: 'I am not modest, but
though alone in the silence of my study, I blushed for shame.
Stupidity cannot be more revolting.' Indeed he avowed that the
greatest writers—men like Homer, Shakespeare, Rabelais, and even
Goethe, who carried all before them—were not stylists and often
wrote badly; and that the art of composition was best studied in
their inferiors, Horace and La Bruyère. As for his French contemporaries, the only one he regarded as a genius was Hugo,
whose merits outweighed his platitudinous mind and leaden ponti-
fications.

His modesty did not prevent his art from conveying much of his
character. His novels are themselves part of the fabric of his life,
and their technique is also a personal documentation. From *Bovary*
to *Bouvard et Pécuchet* he places his words, scenes, and events so
that their intrinsic significance is enhanced by symbolic implications, and these are so frequent that it is hard to tell whether Flaubert intended all of them or not. The part of the world he describes
becomes a microcosm of universal destinies; petty adventures seem
the shadow of vaster conflicts; and life in his eyes takes on the
ambiguity of hallucination—the kind of hallucination to which he
was a prey, simulating reality and enriching it. Moreover his
picture of reality, whether in Yonville, Carthage, Paris, Nogent or
Chavignolles, is heavily scored by a corrosive irony; it pervades
his writing like a hair in his pen; and his sense of the grotesque,
never more awake than at the crises of deep emotion, discovers
settings like the *Comices agricoles* in which it can be permanently
enshrined. He carried over into his art his hatred of stupidity, the
mechanical repetition of commonplaces as a substitute for conversation and thought, and this is nowhere more apparent than in
Bovary, where the ideas, feelings, and actions of his characters are
constructed on the pattern of unreflecting normality, and the catalogue of suffering and failure is inevitable because of the absence

of anyone sufficiently independent to break the chain of intellectual and moral conditioning.

As an artist he exploited his natural tendency to intellectualize emotion. It was almost impossible for him to be totally immersed in any experience whatever; on the brink of self-abandonment he would be held back by a detached observer inside himself, looking on with caustic contempt; and this faculty, destructive though it was of the usual means of happiness, was of cardinal value to him as a writer. It enabled him to grip the sinews of emotion, to study them as they tensed and slackened; and he deepened his knowledge by the systematic recapitulation of the past and the deliberate stirring-up of nostalgic memories so that they could be fastened on and described. The effect he aspired to on the reader was essentially illusion—the illusion, that is, of Flaubert's private reality; and in attaining it his Balzacian power of detailed imagination was reinforced by an exceptionally accurate memory, which applied not only to facts, dates, and passages of literature but to the evocation of scenes witnessed years before. It seems that his memory was almost exclusively visual, and no doubt its natural excellence was magnified by his conscious, earnest contemplation of the physical world. 'Sometimes by looking at a stone, an animal or a picture,' he said, 'I have felt myself entering it. Communications between human beings are no more intense.'

But the secret part of Flaubert's personality, the part he showed only to his most intimate friends, is withheld from the novels. The reader can divine some of the trends in his character but nothing at all about his private life: the personal implication of the author is not permitted to cloud his eyes and vitiate his descriptions. Yet we know that Flaubert was continually unhappy, dissatisfied with his work, his environment, his acquaintances, and above all himself. The stupid face that leered at him daily in the shaving-mirror, the imbecile called Gustave Flaubert, filled him with disgust. Among his notebooks Louis Bertrand has discovered a passage about his friendships:

'The first (Alfred) left me for a woman; the second (Bouilhet) for a woman; the third (Du Camp) was going to leave me for a woman. All of them.

Am I then a monster?

"The absurd man is he who never changes."

I am the absurd man.

Poor old fool preserving at fifty the devotion they had (perhaps) at eighteen.'

But Flaubert's absurdity, his unchanging, unflinching integrity, is his essence; the poor old fool who never came to terms with humbug and place-seeking is less foolish than the knowledgeable people who did. The man, in fact, is as important as his work. He himself knew that he had only stressed a fraction of his personality in his novels and right up to his death he was feeling his way towards a subject that should be absolutely suited to him. But even if he had found it, we may doubt whether he would have conveyed anything but a fragment of his nature; and since he did not find it, many people who seek in literature the expression of character rather than artistic achievement prefer the correspon- dence to the novels because in his letters they can meet the man who retires so tantalizingly from the rest of his work. In Flaubert they have someone alive to every moment of his age; its tensions are focused onto his anguished sensibility and his personal disequi- librium incarnates and condenses the general disequilibrium about him. At the same time he masters his sensibility and interprets it as an artist; and he formulates his own canons and obeys them with such unswerving rectitude that he becomes a symbolic figure, the patriarch of fiction, the prototype of the stylist.

Notes to Chapter Nine

1. When accused of solecisms, Champfleury is credibly re- ported to have answered: 'C'est l'affaire du prote qui corrige mes épreuves' (Hippolyte Babou, *La Vérité sur le cas de M. Champ- fleury* (1857), p. 17).

2. Coleridge makes the same observation as Flaubert about Shakespeare, though he does not systematize it, and he experiences

the same difficulty in finding a suitable word. 'Shakespeare's poetry is characterless, that is, it does not reflect the individual Shakespeare' (*Table Talk*, 12th May 1830).

3. Flaubert was still not content even when his books had been published, and continued to make changes in subsequent editions. Unfortunately it is often the text of the first edition that is reprinted in popular collections.

4. In so far as Flaubert's labour was not self-effacing, it is at least arguable that he was a less consummate stylist than some of his predecessors. The effort of his prose is almost always palpable.

Chapter Ten

CARTHAGE

'A moi, puissances de l'émotion plastique! résurrection du passé, à moi! à moi! Il faut faire, à travers le Beau, vivant et vrai quand même. Pitié pour ma volonté, Dieu des âmes! donne-moi la Force—et l'Espoir! . . .' Notes de voyage, 12th–13th June 1858.

The prosecution of *Bovary* confirmed Flaubert's idea of society; nothing could have been better calculated to foster his suspicions and inflame his anxious sense of detachment. Though the book had been successful, it was for the wrong reasons, and its success counted for nothing against the hostility it aroused in officialdom. There was evidently a universal, deeply rooted 'hatred for literature', and this hatred not only showed up the hypocrisy of a society which demonstrated its sense of values by prosecuting its artists, but it also sounded a warning for the future. Flaubert's summons to the criminal benches left a permanent scar on his mind; to be met with incomprehension and obloquy when he faced the public for the first time, after an apprenticeship of some twenty years, was so flagrant an injustice that he might have renounced publication altogether. It was only under pressure that he had given *Bovary* to the *Revue de Paris* and he regretted the decision ever after. But however sincere his shrinking from notoriety, there was a certain pleasure in having a book on the market, reaching unknown readers and being understood perhaps by people in other countries—a pleasure that Flaubert may not have entirely admitted to himself—and he did not propose to remain utterly silent. At one time he had hoped to follow *Bovary* with *La Tentation*, extracts of which had appeared in

L'Artiste; but he was still not satisfied with it, the extracts had aroused little enthusiasm, and the moment was inopportune. 'I must deny myself that pleasure,' he wrote in February 1857, 'for it would take me straight to the Assizes.'

The public expected him to repeat *Bovary*, for the average novelist who had struck a successful vein mined it for the rest of his life till it was exhausted. But the conditions that forced Flaubert to deal with his bourgeois subject had altered: he had worked the Bovaresque element out of his system and no longer needed the discipline of a modern theme. While he was writing it, the flatness of *Bovary* had irked him, and he broke into periodic expressions of disgust. 'It's essentially a work of criticism, or rather of anatomy. By another side of my nature I am drawn to write huge, gorgeous things, battles, sieges, descriptions of the ancient, fabulous East.' And with *Bovary* out of the way and a firm self-confidence in his powers, he was ready to confront the flamboyant luxury of a dreamed-of past and to re-create it in every particular.

The subject that occurred to Flaubert (he seems to have hit on it spontaneously early in 1857[1]) was the war between the Mercenaries and the Carthaginians, fought out two hundred years before Christ in a country of ruins and monsters—the war of a now vanished people. But in 1857 standards of accuracy about the past were far higher than when Hugo had written *Notre-Dame de Paris* and Vigny, *Cinq-Mars*. There had been an uninterrupted stream of scholarly works on the ancient world, and Creuzer's monumental study was flanked with important volumes by Thalès Bernard, Jacobi and Alfred Maury. Moreover, archeology had invaded poetry, particularly in the erudite verse of Louis Ménard, and Bouilhet himself had published *Melaenis* (1851), a tale of the ancient world from which he was persuaded only with difficulty to omit a tangle of justificative documentation. Gautier, with whom Flaubert was becoming increasingly intimate, was bringing out his *Roman de la momie* in *Le Moniteur universel*; and through Gautier Flaubert had just met Feydeau, an archeologist turning novelist, whose exhaustive work, *Histoire générale des usages funèbres et des sépultures des peuples anciens*, was even then in course of publication.

These were not sufficient influences to determine Flaubert's choice of a subject. He picked on the war of the Mercenaries simply because it pleased him, and if there was any book that turned his mind to Carthage, it was Michelet's *Histoire romaine,* which he had studied under Chéruel and reread in 1846. But once he had selected his theme, so vast in its scope, gaudy in its detail, and challenging in its obscurity, he accepted the scruples of his period; he would only begin writing when he had mastered all the known facts. It was a stupendous enterprise, far more ambitious in conception than *Bovary,* and even to contemplate it argued a detachment from the contemporary world that would be out of the question in the twentieth century.

He began his researches in March 1857, while he was still in Paris, haunting the great libraries of the capital and amassing dossiers of relevant material. Back in Croisset, he piled his table high with books and multiplied his notes. Because there were cypresses in the court of Astarte's temple, he hurried through a 400-page memorandum on the pyramidal cypress, and this represented only one of the fifty-three volumes he had demolished by May. But already he was complaining: 'I am sated with books. I belch folios.' Selden and Braunius on Phoenician religion, Isidore of Seville's *Origins* and Cahen's translation of the Bible, *L'Encyclopédie catholique,* Silius Italicus, Pliny, Plutarch, Xenophon, Athenaeus, and the monographs of the Académie des Inscriptions—they were all obtained, surveyed, and epitomized. But as his information accumulated, Flaubert realized increasingly that it was not knowledge—not, at least, the knowledge he desired, for it was not felt. His mind was stocked with facts about Romans, Carthaginians, Greeks, and Jews, but the subject itself escaped him. The cardinal faculty of 'making oneself feel' was slow to be aroused; he was dealing with names instead of people, words instead of pictures.

Still, on 1st September he began to write, and after two months of labour and self-questioning, with the recurrent fear of being now trite and now melodramatic, he completed his first chapter in November. Chapter II was even harder: the language rebelled against his attempt to control it, the right tone was lost and not recaptured, and the psychology of the characters was patently inadequate. In December, with a third of the chapter finished, he stopped altogether; Bouilhet arrived in Croisset for consultations; and a few weeks later Flaubert announced his intention of leaving for Africa.

Although he was away from France only two months, two months were sufficient: they enabled him to cast off his contemporary preoccupations which persisted from *Bovary*, and to think back into a crude, uncivilized era in which passions were fierce and uninhibited. He wanted to strip his mind of all that was French, European, and Christian, and to imagine, if only for a moment, the barbarian compulsions that pressed upon his characters. He was seeking stimulus rather than information, and he found it.

His journey took him to Marseilles, and Marseilles was heavy with memories. In helpless pursuit of melancholy, of sentimental nostalgia, he sought out the Hôtel Richelieu. 'Everything has changed!' he told Bouilhet with gloomy satisfaction. 'The ground floor, which was a lounge, is now a bazaar, and on the first there is a barber's. I went there twice to be shaved. I spare you my commentary, my Chateaubrianesque reflections on the passage of time, the falling of leaves and the falling of hair. No matter: it was long since I had thought or felt so deeply.'

Though his new heroine could never mean so much to him as Eulalie, the Algerian desert and the thought of the scenes once enacted there swept him up to sudden peaks of enthusiasm. Near Constantine he experienced a delirious joy in his freedom—'in which I came to shouting aloud, drunk with the blue sky, solitude and empty spaces'. No wonder the French consul at Tunis noted prudently: 'Flaubert is an excellent man, possessed of much wit and learning, but he is an artist in the fullest sense, with an artist's erroneous ideas and characteristic bearing.'

He spent several days on the site of Carthage, snatching greedily at authentic details. A significant note runs: 'A dromedary on a terrace, working a well: *that must have happened at Carthage.*' He carried on a broken conversation with an English minister who was conducting excavations; tried to locate the ancient position of Bizerta; rode overland through the deserted

and lion-infested country between Tunis and Constantine; and
before he left could say: 'I now know Carthage and its environs by
heart.'

But Flaubert, for all his scrupulous documentation, laid little
stress on local colour; it was of secondary importance and belonged to the trappings of a novel. His mind sought out generalities, particularly generalities about *cette vieille canaillerie immuable et
inébranlable*, and he was alert to seize on the parallel that linked
remote and contrasted customs. The effect was to give to local
tradition a universal application. In Bizerta, for instance, he noted
in connexion with the hand-kissing ceremony: 'Bigotry is the
same everywhere: the intolerance of Ramadan reminds me of the
intolerance of Catholic Lent.' His journey to the Middle East in
1849–51 had convinced him of the permanence of social and intellectual habits and his opinion was confirmed by his visit to
Tunisia: in a coach outside Constantine he encountered an Italian
and three Maltese who perpetuated in an even grosser form the
obscenities of Plautus, and all round him he discovered types who
had peopled the African coastline long before there had been
historians to describe them.

So when he returned to Croisset and, after obtaining Bouilhet's
approval, began his novel again from the first page, he had no
hesitation in drawing on his memories of Egypt and Syria and,
when he lacked details, supplying them from the historical books
of the Bible. In particular, his new heroine, Salammbô,[2] was not
merely a Carthaginian: she was a sister of Kuchiuk Hanem and a
cousin of Elisa Schlésinger.

Flaubert's great authority was Polybius,[3] the Greek historian
who accompanied Scipio at the taking of Carthage, but he supple-
mented Polybius with every available monograph remotely connected with his subject. By the time *Salammbô* was finished, he had
made himself familiar with virtually all the relevant scholarship of
his time. He asked Feydeau for a photo of Medragen, the burial-
place of the Numidian kings; he called on the Goncourts because
he heard that they had seen somewhere in Paris a mace which
looked vaguely Carthaginian; and to describe the Mercenaries'
slow death from hunger in the Defile of the Axe, he not only

studied first-hand accounts of the wreck of *La Méduse*, but he visited his brother in the Hôtel-Dieu, cross-questioned him and his *chef de clinique* about the effects of hunger, and carried away twenty volumes from the library.

Since his return from Tunisia, he was confident in the rightness of his method. The visit had fulfilled its purpose, and the doubts that constantly assailed him were due to the obstinacy of the material rather than to any inadequacy in his conception of it. But the writing of *Salammbô* posed new problems. Apart from the description of Emma's death, which, in its accuracy and ordonnance, was a *tour de force*, *Madame Bovary* had not necessitated prolonged research: Flaubert knew his background and his task had been to assimilate the knowledge emotionally. But for *Salammbô* he set to work in relative ignorance, and he added to the huge labours of writing the not inconsiderable labours of documentation. Moreover, he preserved absolute intellectual integrity: he invented only when he must. No doubt he was not as accurate as a modern researcher is supposed to be and his methods were open to criticism: he made errors in arithmetic, confused people and places, and misread some of his authorities. And he sometimes used his documentation as an excuse to postpone writing. But he did what no novelist had hitherto tried to do: he re-created an ancient civilization that had perished over two thousand years before, leaving only random traces and oblique references, and he presented it with sufficient accuracy to be plausible, and sufficient distortion to be acceptable, to the nineteenth-century mind.

The difficulties inherent in the material involved him in a change of method that was to become habitual: while still working on one chapter, he collected data and prepared plans for the next, and as the book proceeded, his impatience to be done with it was fostered by his familiarity with what was to come, till his tedium was magnified and his speed of writing unduly accelerated.

But Flaubert never wavered in his direction: in spite of the prosecution of *Bovary* he did not even consider forsaking his duty as a writer, and in spite of its success he was not tempted to leave Croisset for Paris. During the winter he spent three or four months in the capital, but the rest of the year he remained contentedly

in the provinces, visited occasionally by friends and relations, but
for the most part free to pursue and express his own peculiar kind
of knowledge. His freedom entailed solitude, and his solitude a
temperamental variation so acute as to be almost intolerable.
Ennui still mastered and exhausted him, but it was different from
the pretentious disgust for life he had expressed in *Les Memories
d'un fou* and *Novembre*. That was Romantic ennui, a bitter feeling
for the discrepancy between reality and the ideal, but still not
hopeless, because of the inadequate experience on which it was
based. Now, however, he was mature: as an artist, he felt that
his experience was complete, that he had explored the emotional
possibilities of his own nature and that wherever he went, however
he lived, there was no valid pleasure still to be discovered. His
mature ennui was, in the first instance, the savourless satiety of a
personality that fed upon itself, the tedious repetition of Gustave
Flaubert, 'the absurd man'. In this ennui, unlike Romantic ennui,
there was no room for self-deception; Flaubert knew all of the
world that he could know, and in so far as rebellion was useless,
he accepted the world factually, even aesthetically. But his discontent festered, and to assuage it he still toyed with desires—
desires which took no cognizance of physical difficulties, desires
which he saw to be unrealizable and which nevertheless afforded
him a despairing compensation. His ennui was a sharp focus of the
movements of his time: it was created partly by the Romantic perception of other-worldly beauty, partly by the Industrial Revolution, partly by the cruel and clear-minded positivism that set the
other two elements in irreconcilable conflict. Flaubert, for his part,
was aware of the abnormal acuity of his response and welcomed
the evidence of other men in similar case. 'Ah!' he wrote to
Baudelaire after reading *Les Fleurs du mal*, '*you* understand what
a bore [*embêtement*] life is! You can boast of that without arro-
gance.' And *Salammbô* was born of his ennui and gave him temporary refreshment. 'Few people', he said, 'will guess how sad one
has to be to undertake the resuscitation of Carthage! It is a Thebaid
to which I have been driven by disgust for modern life.' A Thebaid, too, which, with the reading of Creuzer, must often have
reminded him of Alfred Le Poittevin. And there were still

moments when he thought that to escape from Europe would bring relief, that the East would attain his expectations. Late in 1859 he owned himself 'a little unsettled by the idea of a journey to China. It would be *easy* for me to leave with the French expedition. And I will not deny that I should abandon my book and my labours without hesitation if I had not an ageing mother to whom my departure would be fatal.'

This was a period of repose in his life. Apart from Bouilhet he had no intimates and few friends. He remained in touch with Ernest Chevalier, but although he had overcome his savage resentment at Chevalier's progress in bourgeois society, it was quite impossible to discuss with the man any matter involving the high seriousness of art: Chevalier, with his rank of Imperial attorney, was a successful and undistinguished friend who had renounced his exuberance but was prepared to recall it if requested. Flaubert kept a tender spot in his heart for Chevalier because with him he could conjure up and sentimentalize over his years at the *collège*, his conversations with Le Poittevin, his visits to Les Andelys. But Chevalier afforded him no chance to be properly himself, and after his break with Louise Colet there was no one, apart from Bouilhet, who provoked a genuine expansion of his nature.

So far as the physical relationship was concerned, Louise Colet had her successors: there were, among others, probably Jeanne de Tourbey, a provincial girl who had set up a Parisian salon under Sainte-Beuve's tuition, and possibly Juliet Herbert, Caroline's English governess.[4] But in spite of his rough gallantry Flaubert treated them as pretexts, and sex was emptied of emotion and became the mere occasion of physical hygiene. He had failed completely to make a reality of the fantasies he wove as a schoolboy; what with the natural rigidity of his temperament, his devotion to art, and the passionate fixation he had centred on Elisa Schlésinger, he had blundered into an unfortunate liaison, misunderstood and exasperated his mistress, and concluded, rather fearfully, that such an experiment was not to be attempted again. His attitude was ambiguous: on the one hand he regarded woman as an 'ogive pointing to the infinite'; on the other, he turned fornication into an infrequent and trivial pastime for which he found

occasion when he happened to be in Paris. At Croisset, especially
when he was left alone with his mother, he excluded distraction
and made emotional abstention part of his artistic credo. No doubt
it was partly a rationalization of his failure, but it also expressed
a kind of scrupulous timidity. Flaubert was never a man to intrude
deliberately on another person's life: he made the most exacting
demands on his friends, but only because he felt he was thereby
respecting them. When he approached women, he hesitated, and
his hesitation, though not really moral, was the counterpole of
his generosity: he felt that he had nothing to offer. Louis Bertrand
has printed a characteristic jotting found among Flaubert's notebooks:

'The least love-affair may cost a woman, however low, her
position, her fortune, even her life.

Conclusion: it is for the ladies to make advances to *us*.'

The remark illuminates retrospectively his meeting with Eulalie
Foucaud and his liaison with Louise Colet.

But in a nature so rich and complex as Flaubert's it is inevitable
that the sexual impulse, largely denied its physical expression,
should be widely diffused and discover many outlets. In theory he
rejected the traditional social inhibitions, and his natural extravagance of language, coupled with his addiction to *delectatio morosa*
has led those so minded to attribute to him a scarifying catalogue of
perversions. His work, particularly *La Tentation de saint Antoine*, is
fair game, and there is no difficulty in making out a specious case
for half-a-dozen accusations. All his life, for instance, he remained
a reader of the Marquis de Sade; *ergo*, he was a sadist. But although
he was drawn to all the manifestations of human psychology,
particularly to those which were base or inept, and although he
felt answering echoes within himself, there is no scrap of evidence
that he ever fell a victim to such powerful disintegrators of the
personality as sadism, fetishism, and the like; indeed the suggestion is at utter variance with the habitual temper of Flaubert's
mind and is as sensible as the argument that the student of crime,
because of his intellectual propensities, must be a criminal.

His happiest relations with women, however, were when gallantry was restricted to conventional phrases or was entirely

absent. He despised the endless intrigues of Parisian salons and condemned literati who held their favourite audiences in the alcove: life, and therefore art, should rise above such trivialities. In Amélie Bosquet, a Rouen teacher who gave lessons to Caroline, he discovered a woman who was prepared to meet him on equal terms. But she was determined to make her way in the world by writing inferior novels, and they broke for good when she, imagining that La Vatnaz of *L'Education sentimentale* was her portrait, published a hostile review of the book. He derived more pleasure from the company of Mme Sabatier, Baudelaire's Egeria, for as a hostess she made little attempt to curb his freedom of expression; 'an excellent and, above all, healthy creature', he gratefully called her. But the woman whose friendship broke down the customary barriers was Mlle Leroyer de Chantepie, a spinster living at Angers. Moved to tears by *Bovary*, she had written him a letter of admiration, and Flaubert replied with a hint of coquetry. She sensed his tone and revealed her age—fifty-seven. He, in turn, was moved by the honesty and intensity of her character and pitied her sense of loneliness. 'You cannot believe', he told her somewhat later, 'the emotional revelation your first letters caused me. Because of you and thanks to you, I felt better and more intelligent.' She unfolded to him her religious doubts, her hesitations to attend confession, treating him as her spiritual director; and he, glimpsing in her a rare depth of sensitivity and suffering, accepted the role thrust upon him, urging her to give up the practice of religion if she had already lost her faith, advising her to read Spinoza and Montaigne, beseeching her to leave behind the petty worries and intrigues of provincial life and to travel. She dabbled in literature in an unhappy, ineffective way; and just as Flaubert found it hard to place her novels, so he found it impossible to convince her of his own mystique of art. She hovered on the brink of decisions and entangled herself in endless subtleties; she asked for advice and would not take it. When Flaubert returned from Algeria, she implored him to console her; but by this time he had come to the conclusion that her ultimate failing was a lack of will-power, and the kernel of his reply was brief—*Voulez*. The correspondence continued spasmodically and indecisively over a period of twenty years, with

long silences and sudden confessions; and Mlle Leroyer de Chantepie lived on at Angers in perpetual metaphysical malaise, unsuccessfully seeking relief in music, plays, painting, and gardening,
and, after years of spiritual independence, finally revoking her
order not to admit the priest and dying in complete submission
to the Church. Her wavering, helpless entreaties revealed Flaubert
at his most intimate—a tender, unpretentious soul with a deep
reservoir of pity and understanding.

Meanwhile, his withdrawal to Croisset could not check his
growing fame. When he dined with the Director of the Post Office
at Constantine and three of his friends, Flaubert was astonished to
find that they knew *Bovary*; even if he expected to be read, he had
not imagined the effect—had not realized that utter strangers
would penetrate his mind. But while he was meditating on the
subject and structure of *Salammbô*, *Bovary* was gradually imposing
itself on his contemporaries; and though he might protest as indignantly as he liked, he could not prevent the slow but sweeping
change that was to carry the French novel from Champfleury to
Zola. At first, indeed, he did not realize himself what he had done,
and neither did such productive and fashionable figures as Feuillet,
who continued to enjoy universal success with his pallid romances,
or Feydeau, who had made a scabrous and triumphant début with
Daniel in 1859. But serious writers of the calibre of the Goncourts
did not ignore the challenge: *Bovary* showed up the fiction of the
Second Empire, almost without exception, as unreal, unoriginal,
and inartistic; Champfleury, Dumas *fils*, Feuillet, Amédée Achard
were doomed, and henceforward any novel worthy of the name
must be both a repository of truth and an achievement of beauty.
The name Flaubert was the criterion of an unsparing excellence.

One thing only drew Flaubert away from *Salammbô*, and that
was the production of Bouilhet's plays. Since 1857 Bouilhet had
been living in Mantes, but his resources were inadequate and he
pinned his hopes to theatrical success. While *Bovary* was coming
out in 1856, Flaubert had bestirred himself for the rehearsals of
Madame de Montarcy, and in November 1858 he arrived mena-
cingly in Paris for *Hélène Peyron*. If Bouilhet was too timid to
interfere, Flaubert had no such inhibitions. He took complete

charge, enforcing his own interpretation, instructing and bullying the actors, tyrannizing over the stage-hands, and *tu*'ing everybody indiscriminately. In his dealings with critics, reviewers, and editors he displayed an unexpected sinuosity, and on the first night he was aggressively in attendance, a formidable encouragement to the paid *claque*.

Unlike Bouilhet, he grew more and more disgusted with his contemporaries. 'The bourgeois is becoming *physically* intolerable to me. I shall shout with pain.' He asserted that the study of the ancient world inclined one to indulgence towards the modern one, but the one effect of writing *Salammbô* was to intensify his nausea. At the same time he was bored with his book and longed to describe again the contemporary scene that was so antipathetic to him. Caught between his satiety with the imagined world and his detestation of the actual one, he persevered grimly, blindly. One of his visitors thought he was going insane when he talked to her eloquently and incomprehensibly about a seraglio of birds.

He had no illusions about the appeal of his book. '*Salammbô* will (i) annoy the bourgeois, that is to say everybody; (ii) unnerve and shock sensitive people; (iii) anger the archeologists; (iv) be unintelligible to the ladies; (v) earn me the reputation of a pederast and a cannibal. Let's hope so!' But his ferocious grapplings with style and subject at last came to an end, and in September 1862 the contract was signed, the grotesque idea of illustrations was eliminated, and the last touches were made to the text. By November *Salammbô* was on sale.

Three editions were exhausted in two months, but the critics were uniformly hostile. They attacked Flaubert because they knew next to nothing of the history of Carthage and were therefore not interested in his subject. They also attacked him because, in spite of their avowed ignorance, they suspected him of tampering with the established archeological facts. They found the book boring, ferocious, and unclean. Two priests denounced Flaubert from the pulpit for wishing to bring back paganism to France; Sainte-Beuve demanded a dictionary, accused him of childishness, and discovered a 'sanguinary imagination', a 'bizarre sensuality', and a touch of sadism. Mérimée apologized for his moment of weakness:

'If I had been anywhere else with a *Household Cookery* to read, I should not have opened the volume.' Even the Goncourts felt that *Salammbô* was not worthy of its author.

Only George Sand and Cuvillier-Fleury had the courage to declare that art was independent of archeological exactitude. As for the handful of friends who enjoyed and appreciated the work, their voices were drowned in the storm of indignation and they expressed their opinions in private letters. 'A fine book, full of faults', Baudelaire wrote to Poulet-Malassis, his publisher and friend. ' . . . What Flaubert has done, he alone could do.' And the feeling was echoed by Hugo, Michelet, Leconte de Lisle, and Berlioz.[5]

Salammbô was relished by two groups: Romantics of the old school who delighted in its colour, and Parnassians like Leconte de Lisle who appreciated the firmness and clarity of its construction. But most readers judged it as a historical novel, and in historical novels like *Cinq-Mars* they were accustomed to see the familiar figures of the past intimately and informally portrayed. *Salammbô* was not written with this intention, but Flaubert encouraged the misunderstanding when, out of all the criticisms made of his book, he selected only one for a public reply: an article in the *Revue Contemporaine* by the professional archeologist, Froehner. He resented Froehner's allegations of incompetence and inaccuracy and answered them systematically and caustically. Flaubert's letter is, in fact, a model of successful polemic: it is tense, downright, and supported by obscure references. If, however, one turns to Froehner's article, it is clear that Flaubert ignores all the points on which he has been proved wrong, and concentrates on those details where he thinks a devastating reply can be made. Some of his references are erroneous, and if Froehner had been more cautious in his first charges and more persistent in following them up, Flaubert would have extricated himself only with difficulty. He also replied, though privately, to Sainte-Beuve, and since Sainte-Beuve, with a rather self-conscious erudition, had ventured to take exception to certain 'invented' details, Flaubert demonstrated with alacrity that they came from such respectable sources as Theophrastus and the Bible.

L

But he did not succeed in imposing the book on the critics. *Bovary*, which had caught them at a disadvantage, had been met first with bewilderment and then with respect; but *Salammbô*, though it was equally new in conception and treatment, was sufficiently like the novels they were familiar with to be judged by ready-made standards and to be found wanting. Flaubert's readers imagined that his accuracy of documentation was an end in itself, whereas it was subservient to his main purpose. 'As for archeology,' he told Feydeau before he began the writing, 'it will be "probable". That is all. Provided no one can *prove* I have talked nonsense, I ask no more.' And twenty years later he said more specifically: 'Heaven only knows how far I carry my scruples in the matter of documents, books, information, journeys, and so on. Well, I regard all that as very secondary and inferior. Material truth (or what passes under that name) should only be a springboard to reach something higher. Do you think me simple enough to believe that in *Salammbô* I have given a true reproduction of Carthage? . . . Ah no! But I am sure that I have expressed the *ideal* picture we have of it today.'

Salammbô is precisely a nineteenth-century picture of Carthage, rendered in that narrow gap of time when science had achieved its huge prestige but impartiality had not been recognized to be the crudest of prejudices. Flaubert, like his contemporaries, would not concede that the person of the experimenter was part of the experiment. But he outstripped them in his acute feeling for the impermanence of his objectivity; he thought to escape the idiosyncrasies of his person but not those of his time; he knew that *Salammbô* was a modern work, rooted in 1862. His idea of history, his selection of significant material, his sense of beauty were all poised on the brittle moment; their conjunction was unique and unrepeatable both in the span of the century and in the span of his life. Desiring to resuscitate an ancient civilization, he found an intellectual climate in which knowledge was available and detachment of the mind could be attained. For all its faults, *Salammbô* is an isolated monument. As Baudelaire said, what Flaubert did, he alone could do.

Notes to Chapter Ten

1. Arsène Houssaye (*Les Confessions* (1885–91), vi, 96) says that Gautier proposed the subject while Flaubert was thinking of another book about Rouen. But Flaubert was sated with Rouen, and there is no independent support for the story.

2. In the first drafts she appeared as Pyrra. In October he referred to the provisional title as *Salammbô, roman carthaginois*, but till 1862 he also called it *Carthage*.

3. There is, however, no evidence that Flaubert read Polybius in Greek.

4. M. Edmond Ledoux, of Rouen, has seen the copy of *La Tentation de saint Antoine* which Flaubert sent to Juliet Herbert. It was inscribed 'Premier exemplaire' (like many others) and 'A ma fiancée'.

5. The explorer Stanley, who at least knew his Africa, was a great admirer of *Salammbô* and it was one of the last books before Shakespeare and the Bible that he threw away to lighten his pack.

Chapter Eleven

THE TESTAMENT OF FAILURE

'J'aime à user les choses. Or tout s'use; je n'ai pas eu un sentiment que je n'aie essayé d'en finir avec lui.' Letter to Louise Colet, 31st December 1851.

Salammbô was no more a Romantic work than *Madame Bovary*. In writing it Flaubert was tied willy-nilly to the critical standards of his own day, and despite his longing to luxuriate in the imagined fulfilment of desire he was checked by his own artistic scruples: fact, even the invented and merely probable fact, controlled fancy. He left the book, therefore, with a feeling of relief and fatigue—relief at the end of constraint, and fatigue at the imposition of it. But although it was six years since the completion of *Bovary*, he was still as disgusted with the modern world as he was wearied of the ancient one; in neither had he found release, and the predicament of his temperament and vocation was unalleviated. Carthage was only an extension of his study at Croisset, and he thirsted for real journeys, bright fresh lands, new people: 'If I were ten years younger (and rather more wealthy),' he told a correspondent in July 1862, 'I would go to Persia or India, overland, to write the history of Cambyses or even Alexander.' If . . . the word recurred daily in Flaubert's thought, and his suppositions were always just out of reach. But in his irritated, chafing mood he turned away from the novel and listened to a temptation that had never been entirely mastered since the days of the billiard-room theatre and the inspired buffoonery of *Le Garçon*: he would make his début as a playwright.

He hit on the *féerie*, or fairy-play, as his genre, immediately devouring thirty-three *féeries* in order to grasp the method of construction. Even then he did not feel confident in his knowledge but called in the Comte d'Osmoy, an experienced practitioner, to give him advice; Flaubert was ruthlessly importunate, and once, at least, d'Osmoy arrived for a consultation with his head swathed in bandages and invented acute toothache to escape for the rest of the day.

Flaubert intended to use the *féerie*, with its tableaux and fantastic atmosphere, as a vehicle for moral satire—to ironize visually over the bourgeois. He called his experiment *Le Château des cœurs*. Sometimes, as the characters speak, their ideas materialize: a servant expresses a wish for a fur and it appears on the bed beside him; a bourgeois praises a clean-shaven face and his beard vanishes. And Flaubert, conscious of these and other innovations, developed complex theories about the *féerie* as an art-form, and planned to embody them in a preface. Although d'Osmoy was unable to give him much help because of the illness of his wife, Flaubert, working spasmodically at the idea, finished the play in October 1863; he was proud of the construction and had no doubt of success. But then he struck a rock: no producer would co-operate. Marc Fournier of the Porte Saint-Martin praised the idea and execution, but felt that the work was not quite suitable; Hostein of the Châtelet kept the manuscript six months and then politely refused it. And for sixteen years it passed to and fro, from one theatre manager to another, with periods of intermission during which it reposed at Croisset, until at last, a few months before Flaubert's death, after being turned down by Dumaine, Raphaël Félix, Noriac, Peragallo, Weinschenk, and Carvalho, it was accepted for publication by *La Vie moderne*.

Theatrical success was a dream of Flaubert's, and to achieve it he was prepared to relax the high standards he set for the novel. 'The theatre isn't an art,' he told the Goncourts, 'it's a secret.' A secret, apparently, to be discovered by stealth. He haunted the little theatres in Paris, chatting to the actors, welcoming the indiscretions of the actresses; he wanted to incorporate this hidden comedy of manners in a novel, a successor to *Gil-Blas*. Anything to do with the stage excited him and, apparently at Gautier's suggestion, he prepared an operatic scenario from *Salammbô*, for which Gautier was to write the libretto and Verdi the music. It is a monstrous travesty of the book—*Salammbô* raddled for the footlights.[1]

Theatricality was, in fact, part of Flaubert's nature: he performed well in front of an appreciative audience. *Bovary* and *Salammbô* had made him a public figure and after his long reticence at Croisset he felt the need for expansion; so when, in 1862, Gavarni, the caricaturist, founded a fortnightly dinner, which was soon transferred to the Restaurant Magny and christened the Dîner Magny, Flaubert was a welcome and delighted guest. There was an understanding that anything could be said and nothing would be repeated. Dramatic critics were barred, and so was the facile Edmond About because of his unguarded tongue; and the only woman admitted was George Sand, who came as a guest of Flaubert's. In time the noise became so intolerable that Gavarni stayed away.

Flaubert took the stage aggressively. He roared out his paradoxes with resonant enthusiasm while the Goncourts treacherously noted them for the *Journal*. He ranged over the whole field of literature and quarrelled with Sainte-Beuve, who sat in a black silk skullcap, sipping rum and curaçao and softly demolishing reputations. He united with Gautier in terrible denunciations of the bourgeois and, in tenderer moods, sentimentalized over love, dwelling in veiled language on his passion for Mme Schlésinger and describing his encounter with Eulalie Foucaud. He vented every prejudice and exaggerated every sentiment of which he was capable. Brandishing his arms and bellowing 'C'est hhhénaurme!' (the *h*'s are to taste), he abandoned himself whole-heartedly to the spirit of the occasion.

Despite his moods of depression and occasional minor ailments, Flaubert's health was good—as good, indeed, as it had been for twenty years. His nervous attacks had ended and he thought himself cured. Moreover, he looked well. He was plump and square-shouldered, with a patchy red complexion and a rough drooping moustache, and he made a picturesque, imposing figure. There was nothing but his own inclination that prevented him from enjoying the homage his contemporaries wished to pay him; and he yielded more to himself, especially to the buffoon in his nature. He polished up his technique as a howling dervish and became an expert in popular pantaloonery. His masterpiece he considered to be *Le Pas du créancier*. He taught it to Gautier and they danced it together at Neuilly, competing as contortionists. 'That's what I call theatre,' Flaubert shouted as he subsided onto a divan, '*real* theatre!'

His social life was largely restricted to the winter months, which he spent in Paris. Mme Flaubert and he had taken flats, one above the other, in the Boulevard du Temple, and on Sundays he kept open house. 'They are conversations', wrote the Goncourts, 'that leap from peak to peak, returning to the beginning of the world, prying into religions, surveying ideas and men, passing from Eastern legends to Hugo's lyricism, from Buddha to Goethe.' At Croisset, by contrast, he was entirely alone, apart from his mother and niece. But he now began to entertain his friends, and in 1863 he invited Taine and the Goncourts down to his solitude. For Taine he had great respect, coupled with a suspicion that a mind of such lucid dogmatism, closed to powerful emotions, was over-liable to explain and codify. For the Goncourts he felt a warm sympathy, no doubt encouraged by the admiration they professed, especially at this period, for his work. He read them *Novembre* and his travel-notes; and, since he was embarked on a journey into the past, he dressed up in his Turkish outfit, including the tarboosh, and displayed with a sigh the old skin breeches that had taken him so many miles on camel, mule, and horse.

As he was looking for *Novembre*, he chanced on a collection of oddments: the autograph confession of the pederast and murderer, Chollet; a letter to a pimp from a girl in a brothel; and the autobiography of a man who, at the age of three, grew humps on his back and chest, then became scurfy, then lame, and finally lost both his legs. They are documents of bitter significance; they flash light on the mental attitude behind *Bovary* and *Salammbô*.

Greedy as he was of fact, Flaubert did not keep them for their novelistic value, nor again as a guarantee against facile optimism. He needed no reminder of the desperate misery and baseness of much of the human race. If he stored documents of this kind, it was to gloat over them; he derived a savage pleasure in the contemplation of pain and vileness, provided they were sufficiently generalized. The grotesque—sorrow lurking in pleasure, ugliness in beauty, the worm at the heart of the rose—gave him as sharp an excitement now as it had done twenty years before. In its literary expression it was perhaps a partial evolvement of his own temperamental variation, except that the gap of time separating his moods was annihilated and they became simultaneous. It was also a means of forcing into the frame of a single picture the immensely contrasting opposites that made up life, a means of grasping and juxtaposing extremes so that in a tiny space they summarized the scope of nature. But it is hard not to feel that the grotesque, in Flaubert's case at least, was a deviation of the sense of beauty, and the response that should have been given to beauty itself was diffused over the whole range of aesthetic emotion, pleasant and painful, till ugliness, cruelty, and suffering delighted him as much as beauty, love, and happiness. Perhaps they sometimes delighted him more.

In any account of Flaubert's character it must become plain that he was a victim of his sense of the grotesque. Whatever the obscure mechanisms by which it came to blur his judgement of values, it was evidently an affliction, not an achievement. In so far as he fostered it, was proud of it, and regarded it as an originality to be cultivated, he revealed a dangerous lack of self-knowledge, a lack that is apparent elsewhere. Even at this stage of his life he seems to have kept a fragmentary sense of personal destiny reminiscent of *René*. Not, that is, a sense of his own legitimate standing as artist and stylist, but an exaggerated feeling of his selection by fate. He treats himself as capable of abnormal emotions of unique intensity; he annoys Edmond de Goncourt by the aggrandizement of his personal experience; he approximates secretly to the *homme fatal*. When Baudelaire sends him *Les Fleurs du mal*, one of the poems he singles out for praise is 'L'Albatros', and one suspects that his admiration is not merely for the structure and expression of the piece, eminently suited for anthologies as it is, but for the sentiment in its ending:

> *Le Poëte est semblable au prince des nuées*
> *Qui hante la tempête et se rit de l'archer;*
> *Exilé sur le sol au milieu des huées,*
> *Ses ailes de géant l'empêchent de marcher.*

Exactly such affirmations occur in Flaubert's earliest work and loom indistinctly in his letters: the poet, the artist, is a giant in stature, with stronger feelings than the rest of the world. But these are hesitant avowals that he would like to believe in but cannot entirely. He wavers according to the mood of the moment; he thrusts out a statement, snatches it back, and then advances it more circumspectly. 'I have *loved* more than anyone,' he writes in 1872, 'a presumptuous phrase that means "like anyone else", and perhaps more than a man chosen at random.'

There was still in Flaubert a strain of bombast, uneasily allied with a harsh self-criticism. He indulged both by recapitulating his past, dissecting it and yet romancing about its intensity. The more he repeated to himself and others the events of his youth, the more outstanding and stylized they became; Eulalie Foucaud assumed in the sixties a passionate significance she had not possessed in 1840, while Elisa was identified with a universal feminine ideal. But in society there was a distortion of Flaubert's attitude: he developed, under pressure, a mask which improved on the spurious personality he had sometimes affected in his adolescence, a mask of bluff joviality, genial and terrible by turns. It was all the more convincing because it was true, and yet only a fragment of the truth. It enabled him to parade some of his feelings, while keeping the others under lock and key. Essential generosity and absolute loyalty combined in him with a whimsical humour; he created an imaginary world that interpenetrated with reality; Bouilhet became 'Monsieur l'Archevêque', Flaubert was his vicar-general, and there was a series of secondary characters, from Onuphre, the valet, to Zéphyrin, a pimply seminarist, the Archbishop's nephew. But this façade could not deceive acute observers. In their portrait of Flaubert in *Charles Demailly* (1860) the Goncourts describe him as 'a man who has had something killed under him in his youth, an illusion, a dream perhaps. Deep in his nature there is a rumbling of anger and a yawning of ennui at the unavailing ascension to some Paradise.'

While he was still struggling with the plan of *Le Château des cœurs*, Flaubert was brooding precisely on this element in himself: aspiration and its decay, the blue Romantic flower blown in a morning. It was his own history and the history of a generation. Fulfilment had always cheapened desire, and desire wavered and flagged. He had longed to go to the Pyrenees and then been bored by the waterfalls. Italy, his dream, had wearied him with its art galleries. In Paris he had found, not pleasure, but the discomforts of poverty. Despite his yearning for the East he had been sated with Egyptian temples and sat moodily by the Nile, thinking nostalgically of the Seine and Croisset. Above all, love, which had seemed the culmination of sweetness and delight, was realized in a surreptitious escapade with his mother's servant, a tumultuous liaison with an inferior blue-stocking, and casual transactions first with prostitutes and then with courtesans. Life, like the personality, had lost its savour, or rather life never had any savour. Flaubert's experience led to the conclusion that the sharpness of pleasure was only tasted in anticipation; reality was flat and dull; all his wisdom was reduced to the crackling of thorns under a pot, and he resolved to embody it in a picture of his generation with the sardonic title, *L'Education sentimentale*.

It was a novel far removed in conception from *Bovary*. Like *Salammbô* it involved a redoubtable documentation, but although it was far narrower in scope than the conjuring-up of Carthage, its implications were deeper. In contained, in fact, the pith of Flaubert's thought, his verdict on life; and it grew round a concentrate of his emotional experience. As he wrote it, he traced back the origin and development of his relations with Elisa Schlésinger and wove them into the broad pattern of contemporary life. He was not attempting an autobiography, for that was a wish he had long since outgrown; but he was taking the richest episodes in his private experience, linking them with the lives of his friends, which he had watched at close quarters, and following out these personal histories as they looped and twisted in the complex fabric of society. This subtle and intricate scheme demanded exertions comparable to any that Flaubert had yet undertaken. 'Happily', he wrote in April 1864, 'I am now working hard on the plan of my big novel about Paris. I am beginning to understand it, but I have never asked so much of my poor brains.' And the plan was only the beginning of his labour, for once its outlines were clear he had to accumulate the minutiae that were to form the substance of the book. For his picture of Carthage he had fallen back on professional historians and specialists, but in a novel about modern Paris from 1840–51, dealing with the decline and fall of Louis Philippe and of the establishment first of the Second Republic and then of Louis Napoleon's régime, there was no work of scholarship available, and he had to nourish his memory and imagination on whatever documents could be obtained and on the recollections of his friends. He started, in fact, a considerable piece of historical research that required abnormal clarity, sense of perspective, and judgement if it was to be adequately terminated; and his first reading was in Socialist theory—Fourier and Saint-Simon —combined with the Liberal Catholicism of Lamennais and Lacordaire.

Paris became more than ever necessary to his work, for it was the only place where much of his material could be found. He spent the winter there, usually from late November to the middle of May, and, since the hunt for documents had no season, he also made occasional trips in the summer. Socially his fame had brought him elevation, and from 1864 onwards he was seldom in Paris without visiting the Princess Mathilde. She was a niece of Napoleon I and therefore a cousin of Napoleon III, to whom she had, for a short time, been virtually affianced. But in 1840 she married Anatole Demidoff, a Prince of San Donato, obtaining a separation ten years later; and for two decades she kept up an unexpectedly durable liaison with the sculptor, Nieuwerkerke. Under the Second Empire her position was equivocal; for though the enemies of the régime treated her as a Bonaparte and a target for abuse, her salon was known to be intellectually advanced and anticlerical, and the Goverment regarded her with some disfavour as a patroness of unorthodoxy. She was a jealous, violent, impetuous woman, less intelligent than she imagined, but possessed of enough personal charm to keep the friends whom her behaviour would otherwise have alienated. Since the Dîners Magny were almost an extension of her salon, Flaubert encountered several of his acquaintances when he first visited her at Saint-Gratien, and it was a place to which he returned with pleasure. Scold him and upbraid him as she did, the Princess Mathilde was a loyal and reliable friend, and it is alleged that in the rather awestruck deference with which Flaubert treated her, there was the first flush of a sentiment stronger than mere liking.

Flaubert, however, remained a bourgeois at heart, and nowhere more than in his private life; snobbery found no place in his values. In 1863 his niece Caroline, then seventeen, had met a Rouen wood-merchant called Commanville and the preliminaries of marriage had been arranged. Commanville was an excellent name with a faint tinge of nobility, and the man who bore it conducted an extensive import business with evident success. Caroline was set on the match: did not 'Caroline de Commanville', with its intrusive 'de', gild and transmute the flatness of 'Caroline Hamard'? What was more, although her tiny dowry had gone to slake the thirst of her father, Emile Hamard, who was leading a life of aimless intoxication in Paris, Commanville had raised no difficulties; he could afford to dispense with the money. But a sudden discovery threw the whole marriage in peril and Flaubert was summoned home to Croisset. Both Commanville's parents were dead, and when his own birth-certificate was examined, he appeared on it simply as 'Ernest-Octave'. This he explained as mere carelessness, but his father's marriage-certificate referred similarly to 'Louis-Germer-Augustin, called Commanville'. His grandfather was designated as 'Jacques-Philippe, ship-master', and Commanville seized on the chance that Philippe might conceivably be a surname, went to the courts and obtained civic status as 'Ernest-Octave Philippe'. It was a fortunate stratagem, for Commanville's grandfather was in fact the illegitimate child of a certain Madeleine Ballue, and Caroline, if she wished to marry

Commanville, should by rights have become 'Caroline Ballue'. As it was, she had no title to 'Commanville', with or without its 'de'.

Flaubert's attitude in all this deception was clear. At first he had been doubtful about Commanville's suitability—doubtful with an instinctive prescience—but once his approval was given, he connived with vigour. 'My poor niece married to a pauper', he told Caroline, 'is such an atrocious idea that I cannot entertain it for a moment. Yes, dear, I should emphatically prefer you to marry a grocer who was a millionaire, rather than a great man who was poverty-stricken.' Commanville had the money, Caroline was determined to marry him, and Flaubert pronounced a blessing on their union.

There was, in fact, a sharp discord between the opinions Flaubert expressed at the Dîners Magny and his actual manner of life; he denounced humanity in general and befriended it in particular. But anyone who saw him only on public occasions could easily be deceived, and it needed the benevolent perspicuity of a George Sand to uncover his diffident tenderness. They had met in 1859, but their friendship dated from 1863, and three years later she visited Croisset for the first time. She was seventeen years older than he, still warm in her affections and generous in her enthusiasms; but although advancing years had not clarified her mental processes, her hot indignation at injustice had simmered down to a universal goodwill. She had a natural perception of the redeeming qualities in any man or woman; indeed she sometimes noticed these qualities to the exclusion of any others, and her exaggerated benignity irritated, when it did not move, Flaubert. But she understood him and helped him to explain him to himself. 'You are', she told him, 'one of the *very few* who have remained receptive, sincere, in love with art, uncorrupted by ambition, unintoxicated by success. In short, you will always be twenty-five because of all kinds of ideas which, according to our senile young folk of today, are outmoded.' And again: 'You flatter yourself when you hope to be angry with *everything and everybody*. You couldn't. Like all tender-hearted people, you are weak in the face of suffering.'

George Sand expended a matronly solicitude on Flaubert; she

advised him about his health, mental and physical, his relations with women, his solitude; she argued with him about literature, life, and sex. There was indeed a pleasant irony in the way she defended strict monogamy, at least in certain cases, while Flaubert attacked it. And in her more playful moods she wrote him illiterate letters as Goulard, while he adopted the severer role of Reverend Father Cruchard of the Barnabites, Spiritual Director of the Ladies of Disillusion.

It was the happiest period of Flaubert's life. He was conscious and proud of his talent, liked and respected by his most eminent contemporaries. His mind had attained its full maturity, and though persistently inflamed by the foolishness of the bourgeoisie and the pattern of existence itself, it was soothed, as much as was ever possible, by the consolations of fame and a realized vocation.

The apogee of his career fell during the flamboyant period of wealth and luxury that marked the final years of the Second Empire. High prices increased the gap between poverty and riches; despite the improvement in working conditions a large section of the proletariat lived on the verge of starvation, and improvidence invaded all classes of society. Industrial workers squandered their wages on drink, bourgeois lost and made fortunes in an orgy of speculation, and the nobility led futile lives of self-indulgence. In the provinces, especially in the country, a measure of stability was preserved, but Paris, evolving swiftly as it was under the guidance of Haussmann, became the cynosure of social climbers, profiteers, rips, and courtesans. It is no doubt easy to exaggerate, easy to confuse the glittering surface with the grey reality that lies beneath; and it would take more than a few years of lush prosperity to subvert the perennial solidity of French bourgeois life. But Paris was almost a new city; between 1851 and 1866 its population sprang from nearly a million to close on two; and the fresh arrivals were provincials drawn to the capital by stories of easy money and quick fortunes. In this atmosphere stock-jobbery became a disease and honest labour a make-shift. There was scarcely an intelligent observer who, whatever the degree of his personal involvement, did not feel alarm at the headlong rush to acquire wealth and dissipate it.[2] Paris was the city of men and women without roots.

The Court was frivolous and Napoleon III's entourage unimpressive. 'We are hastening to our decline', wrote that hostile but acute observer, Horace de Viel Castel, in 1864. 'That which was young about the Emperor has now grown old, and that which, but four years ago, was not quite corrupt, is now entirely so.' And again: 'We are ruled by gamesters and political intriguers. It is a sad spectacle.'

It was the upholstered period of the expansive crinoline; in Paris postilions and broughams were *de rigueur*, while Morny, the Emperor's half-brother, boasted a phaeton. Pedestrians stared at the procession of coaches and gossiped about their occupants, who, for their part, supplied ample matter for scandal. Concerts, plays, masked balls were the nightly distractions of the Court, and lavish receptions took place at the Tuileries. At first the Emperor had feared public opinion and, since musicians might describe what they had seen, dancing at Fontainebleau had been to a barrel-organ. But he soon overcame his inhibitions and in 1856 he inaugurated the receptions at Compiègne. Each lasted a week: the morning was free; in the afternoon one either went hunting, for which the Emperor donned his yellow and gold uniform and the meet rode off in three-cornered eighteenth-century hats, or one visited the castle at Pierrefonds, which had been restored, even to its crenels and dungeons, by Viollet-le-Duc; and in the evening there was dinner, accompanied by military music, and then dancing.

Because of his work on political economy and the biography he was preparing of Julius Caesar, Napoleon III prided himself on being a writer, and in spite of the hostility he had created in the literary world by his policy of censorship and repression, he was anxious to attract men of letters to his circle. Prosper Mérimée had a friendship of long-standing with the Empress, and it was partly due to him that invitations were sent to such men as Dumas *fils* and Octave Feuillet. Lists were drawn up of authors who could suitably be invited to official functions, and in 1860 Flaubert's name creeps on after nonentities like A. de Beauplan, Nadaud, Latour-Saint-Ybars, and M. Uchard.[3]

Just as he had been as a student, Flaubert always remained a provincial in Paris, too bluff and forthright to fit into the suave atmosphere of salons and house-parties.[4] He distrusted honeyed words and disliked amorous intrigues, and his brusque and noisy sense of humour did not suit the fashion of shy allusion and topical repartee. At a dinner in 1860 he innocently asked who Markowski was—Markowski, the most famous dancing-master of the epoch; and shortly before his death one of his friends remarked: 'The more that fellow Flaubert visits Paris, the more of a provincial he becomes.'

But provincial as he was, he was not proof against the flattery of being invited to Imperial functions, and in 1864 he visited Compiègne for the first time. One would like to know more about Flaubert in this environment of parlour games, tuft-hunting, blandishment, and banqueting. Du Camp describes him undertaking a spirited defence of Victor Hugo and being tactfully dissuaded from reciting passages of *Les Châtiments* when his opinion was challenged; but that is all. He was at one time planning a novel about the Second Empire, but it was never more than a vague project, and the only material that remains of his observation of Napoleon's Court is in Zola's work, *Son Excellence Eugène Rougon*, for which Flaubert supplied many of the details.[5]

He was also invited to the Tuileries, he stayed with the Princess Mathilde at Saint-Gratien, and he attended at least one ball given by Prince Napoleon. In short, though not aspiring to the iridescent pleasures of the *bohème dorée*, he lived at a pace he had never dreamed of hitherto, and what with his friendship with Jeanne de Tourbey and Charles-Edmond, editor of *La Presse* and secretary to Prince Napoleon, he incurred debts far in excess of his modest income of 7,000 francs a year. His mother asked him to earn money by writing for the papers, but he refused, out of respect for art; and in perplexity she consulted her notary. 'You cannot believe', she wrote, 'how happy I should be to see [Gustave] behave reasonably.' Flaubert denied that he was extravagant or indulged in a life of dissipation: his expenses were the result of moderate hospitality, mainly at Croisset. But when he estimated his liabilities at over 5,000 francs, Mme Flaubert was first shocked at the high figure and then suspicious that it was a device to obtain ready cash. She preserved the sense of thrift inbred in a member of the professional classes, and though she was fond of him, she probably regarded Gustave's life as frivolous and self-seeking compared to the labours of Achille at the Hôtel-Dieu. However, the situation had to be met, and after much heart-burning she decided to sell her farm near Nogent. It fetched between 60,000 and 70,000 francs.

The official favours of which Flaubert was a recipient culminated in his nomination as a Chevalier of the Legion of Honour, a trivial enough decoration in itself, but belated amends at least for the prosecution of *Bovary*. By this time, however, he was deep in *L'Education sentimentale*, deep in the web of illusion that had destroyed the savour of living. It was at once a book about the past and the present, about the inexperience of the past interpreted by the knowledge of the present. But as he wrote he assimilated new material. 'I relate to this work (as my habit is)', he said, 'everything I see and feel.' And fortune assisted him; for by far the most moving episode in the book is chapter VII of Part III. Frédéric is weary of his insipid, passionless life.

'Late in March 1867, at dusk, as he was alone in his study, a woman entered.

"Madame Arnoux!"

"Frédéric!"

She took him by the hands, drew him gently towards the window, and gazed at him, repeating "It is he! It is he!"

In the dim evening light he saw only her eyes beneath the veil of black lace that hid her features.'

The chapter is a masterpiece of Flaubert's art, so delicate in its interweaving of the strands of emotion and irony that it defies translation. Before she leaves, Mme Arnoux removes her hat, and the lamplight falls on her white hair. She cuts off a lock, gives it to Frédéric, and slips away. The episode summarizes with almost unbearable poignancy the theme of the book and is an aesthetic fulfilment of all that goes before. But thanks to Gérard-Gailly we know that it cannot have formed part of the original plan; for he has proved that late in 1864 or 1865 Mme Schlésinger did in fact

visit Croisset. She was staying with a friend at Vernon, and
Gérard-Gailly has discovered a certain Georges Mercier, then a
boy of about fourteen, whom she asked, with some delicacy, to
accompany her. No doubt Flaubert modified and reshaped the
interview for the purpose of his book; in particular, it is clear that
he could not suspect Mme Schlésinger, as Frédéric suspects Mme
Arnoux, of 'coming to offer herself', and it is unlikely that Mme
Schlésinger ever uttered words so eloquently final as: 'Farewell,
my friend, my dear friend! I shall never see you again! This has
been my last womanly act. My soul will be with you always. May
heaven shower its blessings on you.' But whatever she may have
said, Flaubert felt that such phrases were implicit in her departure
and he made the tacit emotions of their interview articulate.[6]

But Flaubert was concerned with the characteristic psychology
of his generation, not with his private development. 'Delving into
the personality of others,' he says of Frédéric, 'he forgot his own
—perhaps the only way not to suffer from it.' And similarly he
delved into the minds of his contemporaries. He grafted their
experience onto the stock of his own emotion, creating a new
unit. Mme Schlésinger was put alongside Mme Delessert, who had
been Du Camp's mistress,[7] and Du Camp, Mérimée, and Schlésinger were introduced under suitable masks to rub shoulders with
Flaubert's friend, Mme Sabatier, and his enemy, the Rouen deputy,
Pouyer-Quertier. Incorporating episodes from his own life that
were full of a private significance, he had to organize and remould
them so that they acquired a comparable significance for the
reader; and though he depicted, in Frédéric Moreau, some of his
own feelings and ideas, he consciously diminished Frédéric's personality in order to express the hazy mind to which real emotion
became ever more elusive and evanescent. In some ways, Frédéric
Moreau is even a satire on Flaubert. Just as Flaubert, on his way
to Brittany with Du Camp, had seen the great canopy-bed of
Diane de Poitiers at Chenonceaux and longed to sleep in it, so
Frédéric, wandering through Fontainebleau with Rosanette, shows
her a portrait of the royal mistress:

'He asked her if she would not have liked to be that woman.

"Which woman?"'

"Diane de Poitiers!"

He repeated: "Diane de Poitiers, the mistress of Henry II!"

She uttered a little "Ah". That was all.

Her silence clearly proved that she knew nothing, she did not understand.'[8]

Flaubert is half-mocking himself; the feeble enthusiasms of Frédéric are distorted echoes of his own desires.

But Frédéric's uncertain hold on reality needed a foil in exacting descriptions of social life, and Flaubert worked with a will. He read exhaustively in the newspapers of 1847 and 1848 and he ransacked the memories of his friends. From Sainte-Beuve he obtained an account of the Neo-Catholic movement in the forties, and from George Sand a description of the Revolution of 1848. She procured for him a first-hand report by Barbès of the ill-treatment he had received in 1841, and Maurice Schlésinger supplied recollections of Le Club des Maris et des Femmes. Feydeau, with his commercial experience, summarized the fluctuations of the Paris Bourse in the summer of 1847, and another friend described working-class life in Lyons and found out the coach-times from Paris to Fontainebleau in 1848. Flaubert himself drove in a coach along the banks of the Seine to remind himself of the itinerary of the old river-steamers. He visited porcelain factories, travelled to Fontainebleau and made a plan of the forest, sketched the Champ de Mars as it was when horse-racing still took place there, inquired about the fashions of 1847, and attended an operation for laryngeal diphtheria at the Hôpital Sainte-Eugénie.[9] In short, he took every possible precaution to avoid error. There is even evidence of his zeal among the Notices to Correspondents in *Notes and Queries* of 27th February 1869:

'G. F. will find eight articles on the Calves' Head Club in "N. & Q." 1st S. vols. iii, viii, ix and xi.'

But the labour was wearisome and Flaubert was soon uttering his usual complaints. 'I am overwhelmed by the difficulties inherent in my book. . . . In seven weeks I have written fifteen pages, and even then they are not worth much. . . . I am working like thirty niggers, but I have got involved in a subject that is unmanageable because of its simplicity and abundance. The more I write, the less facility I have. Yesterday I spent ten hours at a stretch on three lines, and they are still unfinished! . . . Left-wingers won't forgive me this book any more than diehards!'

There was no work in which Flaubert revealed himself more than in *L'Education sentimentale*: he incorporated so many of the events and situations of his life that were significant in relation to the subject. But from the casual way he referred to Mme Arnoux —'a mediocre personage', he described her to one of his friends— it is clear that he did not completely identify any character with a counterpart in reality; and although the distortion that overtook his models is consciously aesthetic, the reader must have a lurking suspicion that with Mme Arnoux, at any rate, Flaubert allows his ideal of woman to blur the features of Mme Schlésinger. On her first appearance aboard the river-steamer she assumes an exotic beauty: 'He supposed her of Andalusian origin, Creole perhaps; had she brought that negress back with her from the West Indies?' Now although Mme Schlésinger was never a pallid, ethereal creature like the typical Romantic heroine, there is no suggestion that her rather lush attractions were anything but French; Devéria's portrait of 1846 shows her as buxom but fair-skinned, and Flaubert, when he first describes her in *Les Mémoires d'un fou*, speaks merely of a 'brown neck flecked with crimson' and 'an energetic, masculine expression that would eclipse blond beauties'. But while she has no Creole element, something very like it is apparent in Flaubert's feminine ideal. There is already a hint in his affection for the Princess Mathilde, who seemed, even to the taste of her time, hard and heavy in feature. But there is stronger evidence than that. Speaking of Flaubert's encounter with Eulalie Foucaud de Lenglade, the Goncourts referred in their *Journal* to 'women from Lima', of which she was one, and for some years Mme Foucaud was thought to be a Peruvian. When it became clear that she was a Marseillaise, the Goncourts were discredited: they were supposed to have embroidered on the truth. But it is surely more likely that the embroiderer was Flaubert, who improved on his stories every time he told them, and the likelihood becomes almost a certainty when, later in the *Journal*, the Goncourts describe Flaubert at the Dîner Magny sketching his conception of the perfect woman—'so Turkish and so *dirty* an ideal that everyone chaffs him'. Mme Arnoux is therefore not just a portrait: although Flaubert's desire originally crystallized round Mme Schlésinger, her figure has attracted to itself other qualities he associates with beauty. After more than thirty years love preserves some of the overtones of *Les Mémoires d'un fou*, and the ideal is still 'some brown-skinned woman with burning eyes [who] would fold me in her arms and whisper the language of the houris'. It is a crowning irony that *L'Education sentimentale*, dealing as it does with the gulf between desire and its fulfilment, should demonstrate, in the portrayal of the most significant female character, just such a divergence in the mind of the author. Mme Arnoux, who is the quintessence of Frédéric's Romantic longing, exists in the novel both as a real figure and an idealized allurement; but there is a parallel discrepancy between the real figure she presents in the novel and the Mme Schlésinger of Flaubert's life.

On 16th May 1869 *L'Education sentimentale* was finished. Flaubert placed it in a filing-case in his study, and to contain its bulkiness he ordered a special box of white wood from his local carpenter so that he could carry it to Paris and wait, without embarrassment, on the Princess Mathilde.

The book was brought out on 16th November, at an inauspicious moment. Hostility to the Second Empire was becoming more vocal with *Le Réveil*, *La Marseillaise*, and *Le Rappel*, and in September the International had met at Basel and condemned private property. In October soldiers fired on miners who were on strike at Aubin; there were disturbances in Paris; and Republican deputies demanded the convocation of the Corps Législatif. Napoleon, thus challenged, hesitated and conferred with Ollivier. The country was apprehensive; and in the tense and precarious atmosphere the sale of books, as always, slumped to virtually nothing.

The critics were as hostile to the new book as they had been to *Salammbô*, and the public did not buy it. Neglect and incomprehension were the reward for what Flaubert felt to be his masterpiece, and he was abused once more for immorality. The title, as he felt later, was misleading: it should have been *Les Fruits secs*. The moral he intended his reader to draw was that the fruit, which seemed so succulent and appetizing on the tree, tasted dry and bitter when it was picked. Better, then, to leave it untouched, where it could still give pleasure. Better, like Frédéric and Deslauriers, to run away from a brothel than to sample professional love-making. Better, in short, to preserve your innocent illusions than to see them shattered. Such a moral would no doubt be unpalatable, but at least it had meaning. Most critics, however, interpreted the ending of the book, which is precisely the brothel visit, as a recommendation to debauchery, and, if they deigned to give the book a review, did so with reluctance and distaste. Of a hundred and fifty copies that Flaubert sent out to his acquaintances, only thirty were acknowledged.

There was no book by which he set greater store, and no criticism wounded him more than that directed against *L'Education sentimentale*. Where there was misunderstanding, he imagined hostility, and where there was hostility, he imagined an organized plot. He had diagnosed the ills of society and his diagnosis had been either rejected or ignored. 'Ah!' he said to Du Camp two years later, as they stood on the terrace by the water-front and surveyed the fire-blackened shell of the Tuileries, the Cour des Comptes, and the Palais de la Légion d'honneur, 'if people had understood *L'Education sentimentale*, none of all that would have happened.'

Notes to Chapter Eleven

1. Berlioz was also considered as composer and both Catulle Mendès and Barbier were approached at different times as librettists. Eventually the libretto was completed, more or less under Flaubert's supervision, by Camille Du Locle and set by Reyer. It was first performed in Brussels in 1890 and last revived in Paris in 1938.

2. For instance, Champfleury was already denouncing Paris in 1843 (J. Troubat, *Saint-Beuve et Champfleury* (1908), p.28); the

Goncourts deplored the change repeatedly in their *Journal* (e.g. i, 167, 345); George Sand called Paris 'un gouffre de luxe et de vie factice' (*Correspondance*, iv (1883), 158). The percentage of illegitimate children was probably rising (compare E. Levasseur, *Histoire des classes ouvrières* (1903–4), ii, 771, with Larousse, *Grand dictionnaire universel* (1865–90), xii, 1424).

3. See *Les Papiers secrets du second Empire* (1870), No.3, pp. 72–4. Flaubert's name comes last and is somewhat preceded by Bouilhet's.

4. His picture of Mme Dambreuse's salon in *L'Education sentimentale* is a little unconvincing.

5. A few fragments have also recently been published by Marie-Jeanne Durry in *Flaubert et ses projets inédits* (1950), pp. 253 ff., 376 ff.

6. Almost every line of the chapter could serve as a basis for commentary, so closely are fact and fiction intermingled. But there is a most interesting slip which has been pointed out by Ernest Bovet. Mme Arnoux describes how she first realized Frédéric's affection. 'It was one evening when you kissed my wrist between the glove and the sleeve. I thought: "But he loves me . . . he loves me!"' Frédéric certainly did behave thus earlier in the book; but it was Rosanette he kissed, not Mme Arnoux. The action clearly had a particular significance for Flaubert, and, being associated with love, was detached from Rosanette and transferred to Mme Arnoux.

7. Maurice Parturier identified Mme Dambreuse of *L'Education sentimentale* with Mme Delessert, but Auriant has recently adduced damaging arguments against the identification (*Koutchouk-Hanem* (1942), pp. 119–123). It is, however, still possible, and even probable, that Flaubert borrowed some traits from Mme Delessert.

8. *L'Education sentimentale*, Part III, ch. i.

9. However, he could not stand the sight of the child choking on the operating table, and when Dr. Chaume made the first incision, he fled. Not having witnessed the operation from beginning to end, he was not prepared to describe it; in *L'Education sentimentale*, therefore, Mme Arnoux's child is not operated on, but cured by the rare accident of coughing up the false membrane.

Chapter Twelve

THE RECKONING

'Les gens comme nous doivent avoir la religion du désespoir.
Il faut qu'on soit à la hauteur du destin, c'est-à-dire impassible
comme lui.' Letter to Feydeau, October or November 1859.

L'*Education sentimentale* heralded the break-up of Flaubert's
world, and a shadow already overhung its publication:
Bouilhet was dead.

For some years he had been fighting against ill-health, and
despite the success of his play, *La Conjuration d'Amboise*, in 1866,
he worried about the future. He lived quietly at Mantes with
Léonie Leparfait and her son, Philippe. She was a farmer's
daughter, who had been brought as a girl to Rouen by a wealthy
nobleman and then abandoned, and her liaison with Bouilhet was
fifteen years old. Apart from occasional escapades with Flaubert in
Paris, Bouilhet lived a bourgeois life, but because of his irregular
position he was not accepted in bourgeois society. His precarious
and lonely situation involved him in long moods of depression,
but when, in 1867, he was appointed Librarian of the Municipal
Library in Rouen, the post, which afforded him both financial
security and proximity to Croisset, seemed to solve his personal
problems. His health, however, failed to improve. In spite of himself, he became sensitive and irritable, and yet without specific
symptoms of disease. Visiting Paris in the summer of 1869 to discuss textual changes in his latest play, he could scarcely drag himself from the station to the Odéon and back again. The doctors
whom he belatedly consulted advised him to take the waters at
Vichy, but here he was considered incurable, and he was sent
home to Rouen. He had been afraid of learning the truth, but at

last he called on Achille Flaubert and was told that he stood no chance. He wanted to marry Léonie, but she refused. When his two pious sisters arrived from Cany to harass him into repentance, he turned them out of the house; a copy of La Mettrie stood by his bedside. On 18th July, rather suddenly, he died.

Flaubert was in Paris, and on receipt of the telegram bearing the news, he hurried to the station and waited two hours in the scorching heat before the next train left. He and d'Osmoy headed the handful of mourners,[1] but the funeral was too poignantly grotesque even for his taste, and when the speeches began, he had to be led away. 'I have just buried part of myself,' he told the Princess Mathilde, 'an old friend whose loss is irreparable.' And in another letter: 'I say to myself: What is the good of writing now since he is no longer there?' But his grief was not so selfish as these quotations might imply. All the love of which Flaubert's nature was capable had been spent on Bouilhet and he had magnified the importance of the man and the significance of his work. But now Bouilhet was dead, Flaubert realized how great a place he had occupied as critic and friend. Six months later he could say: 'In losing my poor Bouilhet I have lost my *accoucheur*, the man who saw more clearly into my thought than I did myself. His death has left a gap of which I grow daily more aware.' Bouilhet was 'my literary conscience, my judgement, my compass', and the task of orientation, of self-knowledge, was made immeasurably harder. Not that Bouilhet often supplied ideas or gave Flaubert a new direction; but the acuity of his mind hastened Flaubert's realization that in certain cases the thought was obscure, the tone ambiguous, the characterization false or insufficient. Left on his own, Flaubert was unlikely to blunder or grope, but he felt less confidence in his judgement if it was unfortified—less certainty that he was right in the face of all his critics.

Of his local acquaintances, the man that stood closest to him was Jules Duplan, whose companionship dated back to the days of Le Poittevin. He had a keen, accurate mind and a fund of hard sense, and he willingly unearthed facts for *L'Education sentimentale*; but he was a personal friend rather than a literary adviser, and although he knew *Les Mémoires d'un fou* and *Novembre*, he was not really an initiate of the arcana.

Perhaps Flaubert's melancholy was deepened by harking back once again to his youth; for as soon as *L'Education sentimentale* was finished, he had disinterred the manuscript of *La Tentation de saint Antoine* and decided to rewrite it completely. The new text was to incorporate scenes and ideas that inevitably echoed his conversations not only with Bouilhet but with Le Poittevin; *La Tentation* had been the occasion of the greatest disappointment in his life, a disappointment that might have been calamitous, and in returning to the old subject he was in part trying to efface that failure and to record a final, definitive success. But a success with a difference. For his trend of thought had greatly altered since 1856, and his abstract conception of the book ran sharply counter to the ideas he had fondled at Croisset in 1849, before his journey to the Middle East. While he was still meditating his approach, he began his inevitable documentation and was once again a familiar figure in the great libraries of Paris.

But Bouilhet's loss was only the first, although the bitterest, of a series of misfortunes. In October 1869 Sainte-Beuve succumbed to a long illness, and before 1870 had half run its course, both Duplan and Jules de Goncourt were dead. Flaubert's spirits sagged beneath the accumulation of calamity, as though each bereavement not only afflicted him in itself, but intensified the mourning in which he was already plunged. Sainte-Beuve had not always been a friend; indeed Flaubert had at one time regarded him as an enemy, an apostate, *ce lymphatique coco*; and although Sainte-Beuve's moderate praise for *Bovary* had created a feeling of mutual sympathy strong enough to survive their disagreement over *Salammbô*, Flaubert preserved a certain suspicion of the man, not only because he wrote for the papers when he had apparently no need, but because, like Taine, he stressed the historical context of a work of art at the expense of its inherent beauty. Moreover Sainte-Beuve, who was himself a notorious amateur of Paphos, spread rumours that Flaubert was appallingly vicious. Still, he was irreplaceable, and Flaubert, who seems to have borne him no malice, lamented his disappearance for personal reasons and for the gap it left in the thinning ranks of the Romantic generation. Duplan's death, on the other hand, was an intimate bereavement. But that of Jules de Goncourt, again, had wider implications, and it brought home to Flaubert the transient happiness he had known in Paris. 'Of the seven of us who attended the first Dîners Magny', he told George Sand, 'there are only three left.' Gavarni, who had died in 1866, Bouilhet, Sainte-Beuve, and Jules de Goncourt— they had taken with them the warm expansiveness of the early meetings.[2] Jules de Goncourt, in particular, was associated with many of Flaubert's social activities. Despite their differing notions of style and the novel, each had found the other a congenial companion, and Flaubert had not only frequently visited the Goncourts in their exquisitely furnished, exquisitely lit, and exquisitely over-decorated rooms in the rue Saint-Georges, but had met them in the salons of Jeanne de Tourbey and Mme Sabatier and drunk with them at the Café Riche.

As the century drew near its eighth decade and Flaubert moved into his late forties, it seemed already that the period of easy enjoyment was over. In a few months the network of friendship that had maintained his spirits had been torn to shreds, and the distressing sense of loss gnawed into his personality. While the society in which he had flourished began to disintegrate, he felt that a parallel disintegration was impending in his own mind. Each new blow racked him. His life had been built up on his friendships, and as they were eliminated one by one, the superstructure tottered. No woman had played so influential a part in his life as Alfred Le Poittevin or Louis Bouilhet; even Elisa Schlésinger's role was essentially that of a vision, an ideal, rather than a living figure. The feminine mind could not take in or accept his high conception of art and preferred to bask in diffuse emotion; and Flaubert therefore reserved his intensest thought for men. But where he thought most intensely, he felt most deeply, because of his natural predisposition and deliberate policy; and his male friends were the focal points of his most personal and characteristic feeling. Idealist and Romantic that he was, he made no allowance for their shortcomings: he was absolute and uncompromising in his demands, and the inevitable disappointments startled him each time into indignant resentment. He found it impossibly hard to conceive that a friend of his should have other duties and affections, which might challenge his own position, or that unadulterated Flaubert was too drastic a treatment for the most resilient constitution.

His solitude became more acute and morose. His mother was growing old, and her anxious disposition was exacerbated by deafness and chronic depression. Moreover, 'my niece, whom I love as a daughter, is not living with me'. Caroline Commanville, in fact, was full of social aspirations: she and her husband had at one time begun to negotiate for the Château of Miromesnil (for the possession of a château would confer an undeniable *cachet*), and they had bought a town-house in Paris and a country-house near Dieppe. She attended balls, gave receptions, cultivated distinguished friends. Flaubert, who still signed himself, rather pathetically, 'ta vieille Nounou', wondered uneasily whether in this whirl of gaiety she still found time to read and think. Occasionally she came to stay at Croisset or entertained him at Dieppe, and he looked forward to their meetings for months in advance. In all manner of ways—upbringing, education, and ideas—she was his child, and he followed her life with the imaginative participation of a father, worrying about her health, inquiring about her friends, behaving with an almost apprehensive respect towards her husband.

But Flaubert was not the man to ignore a debt to a friend, and there was some consolation for his loneliness in the publication of Bouilhet's work. Du Camp exaggerates with typical malice when he says that Flaubert regarded Bouilhet as the greatest poet of the nineteenth century; Flaubert would certainly have awarded the palm to Hugo. But he held Bouilhet in high esteem, far higher than Bouilhet stands in the critical judgement of our own generation, and he considered it his duty to disseminate his work.[3] In particular, he found the manuscript of *Mademoiselle Aïssé*, a play that was completed a month before Bouilhet's death, and he determined to have it produced. It had already been accepted by the manager of the Odéon, and Flaubert insisted on its being proceeded with; but although the first performance had been planned for January 1870, complicated delays and prevarications held up

the rehearsals till July. Meanwhile he collected as much of Bouilhet's verse as had not appeared in volume-form, entitled it *Dernières Chansons*, and wrote a preface in which he vigorously expounded Bouilhet's ideas of art and used them as a weapon with
which to belabour his opponents. Bouilhet 'hated', says Flaubert,
'this new maxim that "one should write as one speaks"'; and
Bouilhet's preferences are exalted into universal artistic ideals. Flaubert also planned to erect a monument to Bouilhet's memory, and
when he discovered another play in manuscript, *Le Sexe faible*,
which was only a fragment, he called in d'Osmoy and they tried to
complete it.

He was still short of money, and at George Sand's suggestion,
his publisher Michel Lévy visited him at Croisset and offered him
an interest-free loan. But it was on condition that his next book
should be sold for the same sum as *L'Education sentimentale*, and
Lévy was so pressing with his generosity that even Flaubert's
suspicions were aroused.

In any case, expensive pleasures were no longer possible. On
19th July 1870, France declared war on Prussia and the Second
Empire survived for a bare six weeks. Flaubert's first reaction was
one of cynical detachment. 'The good Frenchman', he told
George Sand, 'is going to fight: (i) because he thinks he has been
provoked by Prussia; (ii) because savagery is the natural state of
man; (iii) because war contains a mystical element that entrances
the mob.' He was accustomed to stand aloof from social and
national conflicts and to proclaim his indifference, whichever side
won. 'As for the idea of a native country,' he had written over
twenty years earlier, 'i.e. a certain portion of territory drawn on
the map and separated from the others by a red or blue line, no!
My native country is the land I love and therefore the land I dream
of, the land where I am at home. I am as much a Chinaman as a
Frenchman, and I derive not the slightest pleasure for our victories over the Arabs, because I am grieved at their defeats.' Flaubert was consistently loyal to this point of view. He had too keen
an awareness of the universal baseness of human nature to deceive
himself about the virtues of any race or people, or to imagine that
France was the depository of a truth denied to Germans, Turks,

Chinese, or Eskimos. In politics he was equally critical of all classes or parties: 'The great moral of this reign will be to show that universal suffrage is as stupid as the divine right of kings, though slightly less odious.' And somewhat later: 'The whole dream of democracy is to raise the proletarian to the level of stupidity attained by the bourgeois.' But he did not deny the existence of a superior truth: he maintained that it was international, the possession of a handful of eminent minds, and the only form of government that obtained his sanction was government by mandarins, because mandarins were most likely to possess the knowledge and preserve the scientific attitude necessary in good rulers.

When, therefore, the Prussian armies began to close on Paris and Napoleon III was deposed, Flaubert still laboured to keep his detachment: he had, at least, no tears to shed over the collapse of the Second Empire. But the constant expectation of news put him in a fever of anxiety and he stifled in the atmosphere of Croisset. One of his neighbours had hallucinations; another, speechless with fear, fled to Belgium; a third barricaded his iron gate with planks. The Nogent cousins had arrived in force, and Flaubert was awakened either by the monotonous sound of one of them spitting or by his mother quarrelling with her maid. The only tolerable companion was Dr. Fortin, who had a house further along the bank and called several times a day, seeking consolation for his wife's infuriating calm.

Like D. H. Lawrence in the 1914–18 War, Flaubert followed the news with so intense an imagination that he shared the physical suffering of his countrymen: he actually became one with the soldier dying on the battle-field, or with the peasant, tied to a tree, gazing on the smouldering ruins of his farm. Several times he threatened to go to Paris and take part in the siege that seemed inevitable; but the practical limit of his initiative was to register as a male nurse at the Hôtel-Dieu and to get himself elected Lieutenant in the National Guard. A letter of 27th September runs: 'Today I begin my night patrols. I have just given a fatherly talk to my men and told them I shall pass my sword through the belly of the first who falls back, while they must shoot me if they see me running away.' He conducted military excursions in the wood of Canteleu and went to Rouen for lessons in the art of war. Nevertheless the Prussians continued their advance, and late in October Flaubert and his brother officers, unable to cope with a militia that took no cognizance of orders, resigned *en bloc*. He was in no mood to read or write and could do nothing but collect and distribute rumours. Caroline was in England and he passed on to her naïve assurances that the war was not yet over. But even when the war did end, there was nothing to look forward to. 'What is terrible in this war is that it makes you *evil*. My heart is now as hard as a stone, and whatever happens, we shall remain stupid.' And a few days later: 'The Latins are done for! Now it's the turn of the Saxons, who will be eaten up by the Slavs. And so it goes on.'

The days and weeks brought no sign of the Prussians, though the road was open. Flaubert tried to find some ground for hope. He exaggerated the valour of the French troops straggling through Rouen, and repeated every rumour suggesting the position might improve: the army of the Loire was planning an attack, Bourbaki was on his way from Lille, Bazaine would escape and relieve Paris, Trochu would make a devastating sortie. One morning he called on his friend Lapierre, the editor of *Le Nouvelliste*, and informed him confidentially that an army corps had broken out of Paris and reached Vernon on its way to liberate Rouen. 'But what is your authority for this news?' asked Lapierre. 'Why, the milkman.'

At last, however, the Prussians renewed their push down the Seine till they came to the sea. The house at Croisset was occupied by seven privates, three officers, and six horses, and Flaubert and his mother, leaving only a servant behind, took rooms in Rouen. Postal communications had broken down and there were no papers. Mme Flaubert was so weak that she could walk about the house only by leaning against the walls and furniture. Flaubert, who spent his days obtaining hay and straw for the invaders, likewise felt the crushing impact of defeat and surged with disgust and rebellion. 'I should like', he cried, 'to live in a place where one doesn't have to hear the drum, to vote, and to fight—far away from all these horrors, which are even more stupid than they are abominable.' But there was no escape; Prussian helmets lay on the bed at Croisset, and Prussian sabres clanked on the pavements of Rouen. Flaubert's brother, Achille, tried to jump off the bridge. Flaubert himself, through the nights, had the death-rattle of a dying man and was indeed convinced he would die. 'My mind is not my own', he had already written in September. 'I feel as though cataracts, rivers, oceans of grief are pouring over me. At times, I am afraid of going mad.' When he knew he must leave Croisset, he was seized with a wild fear that all his possessions would be taken and destroyed, and in a febrile distraction he grasped random armfuls of papers, letters, notes, and books and threw them into the fire. What was burnt he did not know himself. In Rouen he was sick almost daily and thought he had cancer of the stomach. Worst of all, his nervous attacks, which had been quiescent for years, returned to harrow him. His constitution, in fact, despite its apparent robustness, was incapable of withstanding the combined assault of personal bereavement and public calamity, and as his mental distress intensified, his physical condition deteriorated.

Several times in his life he had been present at scenes of violence and even disaster, but it was as an observer: now he was embroiled. With the rational part of his mind he still clung to the idea of superior detachment and longed for the Olympian impartiality of a man like Goethe. But his temperamental instability swamped his intellectual defences as though they were mere sandcastles, and he became an involuntary participant in the hatred of Prussia. Even then, however, he could not swallow the popular cant that France would be purified by defeat. 'No! Misfortune makes men selfish and wicked and stupid.'

When the Prussians left Croisset late in January, he was anxious to return and find what damage had been done. In fact, all his literary possessions had been respected and he had lost nothing but a dressing-case, a few pipes, a portfolio, and a paper-knife. But after three months of occupation the house smelt of greased boots, and the walls had to be repapered and the rooms repainted. By April he was back in his study, exhausted after the longest period of intense suffering in his life but resolved to pick up *La Tentation* where he had left off. And two months later he had so far recovered that Edmond de Goncourt, dining with him, could note with startling inaccuracy: 'He has remained the same—a literary man first and foremost. The cataclysm seems to have passed over him without distracting him in the faintest degree from the impassive construction of his book.'

Although, as before, he sat at his table at Croisset, with his customary notes and pipes and quill-pens around him, he could not, by this continuity, impose continuity onto his environment. After the Second Empire had come the Third Republic; after war, the Commune. The Princess Mathilde was in Brussels, where indeed Flaubert had visited her in March, and his surviving friends were scattered and stricken. Some had acquitted themselves with signal bravery: d'Osmoy, for instance, had been a captain in the *francs-tireurs* and then fought against the Communards; and Alfred Maury had kept the tricolor flying about the Archives all through the Commune, while pursuing his researches about the Etruscans. Renan was one of the few who kept a level head: most, in Flaubert's eyes, were candidates for Bedlam.

In personal relations the war had been nowhere so baneful as to the Schlésingers. Of the children, the first, Maria, was illegitimate, while the second, Adolphe, was born in wedlock. When, in 1856, Maria married Christian von Leins, the Mayor of Stuttgart, her birth-certificate had to be produced, and she apparently guessed the truth. At any rate, she created a violent scene with her mother and identified herself with the nation of her father and husband, becoming a rabid Francophobe. Adolphe, on the other hand, was a Frenchman, and while Maria gloated over the German victories, he was fighting in the French army. Family tension was increased by the death of Maurice Schlésinger in February 1871. In his will he had been obliged to leave his property to his two children; for if it had been left to his wife, only Adolphe would have inherited from her. All three met at Trouville and quarrelled so fiercely that strangers intervened. Adolphe ceded to his sister his share in the Hôtel Bellevue at Trouville, with the result that when Mme Schlésinger wished to stay there, she had to appeal to

Maria's grudging hospitality. Maria, for her part, detested her brother and mother and did not hide her detestation.

When Flaubert heard of Maurice Schlésinger's death, his letter to Elisa went astray. He wrote again, tenderly. For the first time in his life he could express his affection without fearing that his letter would fall into the wrong hands and be misinterpreted. 'My old friend, always dear, yes, always!' he began, but even for her he would not set foot in Germany, and since his mother's incapacity also prevented him from travelling so far as Trouville, he hoped that she would visit Croisset. 'You must forewarn me so that I do not miss your visit. Do you remember the last?'

Elisa came to Croisset, for one night.[4] She was a frail, white-haired woman of over sixty and Flaubert himself was middle-aged. It was thirty-six years since their first meeting at Trouville, and the fact that there was no longer a barrier between them gently emphasized the knowledge that no barrier was necessary. A further chapter of ironic pathos was thereby added to Flaubert's private and unwritten *Education sentimentale*, for although Elisa remained his ideal—*chère et vieille amie, éternelle tendresse*, as he apostrophized her—she preserved only a wisp of her one-time beauty and power. It seemed almost unbelievable that she was still alive; she symbolized and recalled days that appeared, in retrospect, braver and happier, and Flaubert, with a kind of nervous piety, reverenced her as tenderly as he had ever done. They met again several times, in Paris and at Croisset, and in 1872 he attended her son's marriage and cried like a child.

His last letter to her is dated October the same year and strikes the old chord—*ma vieille amie, ma vieille tendresse*. We do not know if he wrote to her again or even if he learnt the fate of her declining years. It is perhaps too much to hope that he remained ignorant; for there is one more glimpse of Mme Schlésinger.

In September 1881 Du Camp had spent a long day hunting near Baden. The weather was hot and the partridges elusive. Feeling tired, he crossed a railway embankment, climbed a hill into a spruce-wood, and lay down in the shade. Nearby the iron gates of Illenau lunatic asylum were open, and he saw a group of women emerging on their daily exercise. They walked in twos, accompanied by their attendants. The nearest drew his attention by her air of misery: she glided along listlessly with downcast eyes, tufts of white hair escaping from a battered straw hat. She had no teeth and her slippers were in pieces. As she passed by, their eyes met and he recognized her: Mme Schlésinger had succumbed to the final misfortune.[5]

Notes to Chapter Twelve

1. Bouilhet's biographer, the Abbé Letellier, points out that Flaubert is quite incorrect when he says in his letter to Du Camp: 'Il y a eu un enterrement très nombreux, deux mille personnes au moins!' In fact one is always a little sceptical when Flaubert has motives for deceit in personal matters of this kind.

2. The other three members were Gautier, Edmond de Goncourt, and Flaubert. Flaubert stopped going to the Dîners Magny in 1868.

3. Bouilhet wished that after his death his unpublished work should be dealt with by a committee consisting of Flaubert, d'Osmoy, Du Camp, and Caudron. It is not certain whether a committee was ever constituted or whether the latter three gave Flaubert any assistance, apart from d'Osmoy's co-operation in *Le Sexe faible*.

4. For a long time Mme Schlésinger was referred to as 'Maria' by Flaubertistes, largely because she was 'Maria' in *Les Mémoires d'un fou*. But when Flaubert refers to her visit to Croisset in 1872, he speaks of 'Mme Marie Schlésinger'. It is hard to believe that 'Marie' is a slip of the pen. Was it a name used by Flaubert alone? Schlésinger, at any rate, always called her 'Elisa'.

5. She died in 1888.

Chapter Thirteen

TEMPTATION AND
THE STAGE

'Ce qu'il y a de sûr, c'est qu'il y a (en moi) du moine. J'ai toujours beaucoup admiré ces bons gaillards qui vivaient solitairement, soit dans l'ivrognerie ou dans le mysticisme.' Letter to Louise Colet, 14th December 1853.

Mme Flaubert was weak and querulous; having worried all her life about either her husband, her children or her granddaughter, she worried now about herself. Hypochondria aggravated her depression and deafness cut her off from her friends. Health, or rather ill-health, had become her only topic of conversation, and she fretted continuously because, whether she stayed at Croisset or at the Commanvilles' villa near Dieppe, she was away from either Gustave or Caroline.

The gradual decay of his mother's mental and physical powers distressed Flaubert, but not acutely; the fact that she was increasingly hard to live with bred in him sufficient irritation to mask his grief. But when she died in April 1872, he reeled at the blow: it was the culmination of this period of bereavement and privation, and he could scarcely find in himself the strength to withstand the shock. She had been part of the accepted routine of his life, and to remain at Croisset without her was to inhabit a world that had suddenly lost its support. 'In the last fortnight I have realized', he said, 'that my poor dear mother is the person I have loved the most. It is as though part of my bowels had been torn out!'

Flaubert, as always, valued highest what he no longer possessed;

he was a virtuoso in the nuances of *desiderium*, and his acutest feelings derived from the past—or rather from that part of the present which echoed the past. He had never wavered in his affection for his mother, but now that she was dead, his fondness grew, because it was no longer impeded by temperamental quirks and vagaries. His picture of her was refined of its roughnesses and approximated to an ideal, so that she became a hazy figure highly charged with emotional associations. Hers was yet another ghost that lingered at Croisset.

He was now only a tenant of the place, for Mme Flaubert had left it to Caroline with the provision that Flaubert should have the usufruct until his death. And although he inherited both property and money, it seems that certain conditions were attached which prevented him, except in abnormal circumstances, from touching anything but the interest and rents. No doubt Mme Flaubert was suspicious of his extravagance and wished to preserve the family wealth for Caroline; but her qualms were needless, for Flaubert was too old and sad to hanker after the gaiety of Paris. He detested anything to do with money—legal forms, questions of administration, problems of investment—and was glad to entrust some of his capital to Commanville.

A recurrent occupation of these years was a monument to Bouilhet's memory. Before war broke out, Flaubert had obtained the approval of the Mayor of Rouen for the erection of a fountain with a bust on top, but the advent of the Prussians had swept the scheme aside, and when it was mooted again in 1872, there was apathy and phlegmatic opposition. Flaubert chafed: he was the only active member of the committee formed for the purpose and he was determined to force the project through. He lobbied local politicians, roused journalists, and pestered his friends. But the citizens of Rouen were more hesitant than he about Bouilhet's merit, and although literature was normally a topic they ignored, pompous discussion began about Bouilhet's standing as a poet and a dramatist. When the Municipal Council eventually refused to put up a fountain even though funds were provided, Flaubert was furious. He speedily accumulated his facts, demanding, for instance, from one of his friends a list of statues recently erected to mediocre contemporaries, and he drafted an open letter to the Municipal Council. Lapierre originally promised to bring it out in *Le Nouvelliste de Rouen*, but on reading it he hastily changed his mind; and so Flaubert sent it to *Le Temps* of Paris, which was as much read in Rouen as *Le Nouvelliste* and had a wider circulation elsewhere.

The letter appeared on 26th January 1872, and it was a bombshell. Instead of reconciling his opponents he insulted them. He took the arguments against erecting the fountain and demolished them one by one, and when he felt that the last whinny of protest had died down, he lashed his victims in an apostrophe that was to become famous: 'Conservatives who conserve nothing . . . The French nobility compassed their own destruction by having, for two centuries, ideas worthy of menials. The end of the middle class is in sight because they have ideas worthy of the rabble. I do not observe them reading other papers, enjoying different music or indulging in loftier pleasures. Both classes display the same love of money, the same respect for the accomplished fact, the same need for idols in order to destroy them, the same hatred of all that is superior, the same spirit of disparagement, the same crass ignorance! . . . If you wish to be respected by what is below you, respect what is above you! . . . Enlightened classes, be enlightened!'

The effect, naturally, was to confirm his opponents in their obstinacy.

He wrote the letter while he was in Paris, with Bouilhet much on his mind: the rehearsals of *Mademoiselle Aïssé*, interrupted by the war, had been recommenced, and Flaubert, having no confidence either in Chilly, the Director of the Odéon, who was ill, or in Duquesnel, the Co-Director, who was incompetent, organized the play himself, planning the production, rehearsing the actors, and spending days in the Cabinet des Estampes to design suitable costumes. On the first night, 6th January, he actually shifted the properties for act I, and two days later he was still leading the figurants onto the stage. All that could be done for his friend's memory he did, but he was unable to win over the critics: most of them found the play wearisome; the audiences, though appreciative, were thin; and after about twenty performances *Mademoi-selle Aïssé* was taken off.

Dernières Chansons had just come on the market, and Flaubert, with his debt to Bouilhet acquitted, at least for a time, could turn back to *La Tentation*, which was two-thirds finished. Even his mother's death did not deflect him for long from the task; work was an analgesic. 'Meals by myself, at this empty table, are cruel', he wrote early in May. 'But this evening, for the first time, I reached the dessert without tears. Perhaps I shall get used to this solitary, unsociable life.' Paris, which he visited for Adolphe Schlésinger's marriage, gave him a chance of seeing George Sand for the first time since 1870 and of staying a night with the Princess Mathilde at Saint-Gratien; but he was liable to violent attacks of misanthropy, and in one of these moods he returned to Croisset. There, in July, *La Tentation* was finished.

He hesitated to publish it, feeling uncertain both of the work and of its probable reception; but in December 1873 he was prevailed on to part with it, and it was on sale early in the next year. According to Du Camp, Flaubert always regretted his decision and wished he had kept *La Tentation* among his papers, undisclosed. At any rate it was adversely criticized, partly, as Flaubert thought, because he was a friend of the Princess Mathilde, and had been a guest at Compiègne, but principally, as Thibaudet points out, because it still breathed the heady atmosphere of 1848.[1]

Not that Flaubert's conception of the book had not altered as he grew older; but even the dedication—'To the memory of my friend, Alfred Le Poittevin'—revealed how the subject was bound up with his formative years. First with Le Poittevin and then alone, after his illness, he had peered into the dark recesses of his mind; and thus he had passed on to Saint Anthony the effects of his nervous probing of the imaginative power, subjecting the hermit to visions and temptations that explored the gamut of desire. He showed up, in fact, the appalling fragility of the human intellect, and he did it with a malice and pleasure that were anything but objective. But his aim was more philosophic than in 1849: then he had been content to describe the temptation, to convey all its detail and colour, but now he was trying to generalize its significance and to make of Saint Anthony the representative, not merely of Gustave Flaubert, but of humanity.

Flaubert was no metaphysician, but he kept abreast of the general philosophic trend of his day. His thought, as it developed, ran roughly parallel to the ideas current in educated society: he had read Creuzer and *Faust* in the thirties, Victor Cousin in the forties, Taine and Renan twenty years later. But although he learnt to express his attitude differently, it showed little variation: it merely hardened and acquired a wider application than to himself. On the whole, when he read philosophy, he sought reasons for the point of view he had already adopted. The reasons may have been bad, but in this way he was practising the instinctive epistemology that determined his methods as a writer: knowledge, to be genuine, had to be experienced emotionally, and it followed that once an idea had been seized on intuitively and assimilated, he could then look for a rational justification.

Among nineteenth-century novelists Flaubert had no rival in his capacity for perceiving inconsistency and presumption, particularly in other people; and he was as honest as any man can be in his analysis of himself. But in so far as he underwent influences, they all accorded with the natural bent of his personality; he selected ideas because he needed them, or already agreed with them. One never feels with Flaubert that he is being pushed into an uncongenial position by the force of unanswerable logic. The logic is there, but as a servant; the position is uncomfortable, but not uncongenial. In fact, Flaubert's final outlook is the same as his outlook as a child, but revised, annotated, and enlarged: life is still the nauseous smell of cooking escaping from a vent.

In the last version of *La Tentation* some of Spinoza's ideas persisted, and in fact he continued to read Spinoza up to his death, rhapsodizing over the religious sense of 'that so-called atheist'. He echoed, for instance, Spinoza's rejection of anthropocentricity and dwelt on the contradictions between the sects and the cults. But he no longer contrasted science and religion; for in the years since he had last confronted Anthony with the Devil he had studied Haeckel and Herbert Spencer, and the latter, in particular, fired his enthusiasm. 'Germany', he informed a friend, 'has no one to touch that thinker.'

Tracing the influences of philosophers on Flaubert is a hazardous task because, even though he read them, there is no proof that he understood what they were saying. The only control is in chapter VIII of *Bouvard et Pécuchet*, in which sporadic distortions are deliberate. But there can be little doubt that what appealed to Flaubert in Spencer was the evolutionary reconciliation between science and religion, and the emphasis on the unknown mystery that escapes all the gropings of dogma. In Flaubert's eyes the truly religious man was he who perceived the ultimate inscrutability of the universe, the man whose mind was so free from passion and prejudice that he was resigned to the inconceivable complexity around him. The true saint would be like Spencer's man of science: 'He learns at once the greatness and the littleness of the human intellect—its power in dealing with all that comes within the range of experience, its impotence in dealing with all that transcends experience. He, more than any other, truly *knows* that in its ultimate nature nothing can be known.'[2]

But Saint Anthony was not a man of science and did precisely claim an insight which, in Flaubert's view, was impossible. Saint Anthony therefore was not a truly religious man, and in the third *Tentation* Flaubert tempts him—not, as before, with desires, but with truth. Some of the old sins naturally recur—gluttony, lust, avarice—but the essential opposition to the saint is conducted by Hilarion, a former disciple who had apparently taken lessons from Haeckel. Anthony is thus not a simple anchorite but a scholar, argumentative and learned, and discussions replace wrestlings with desire. Anthony, in fact, is not tormented, only harassed.

Flaubert, with his persistent capacity for visualizing, remained an epicure of temptation and still, even at this stage, envied the saint's opportunity for contemplating excess. But just as he transferred the emphasis from emotion to idea, so, in the last version of *La Tentation*, his attitude to history swung from the picturesque conception of Michelet to the lucid accuracy of Taine and Renan. Both men he knew well, and he consulted Renan frequently over points of detail, borrowing his books, appealing to his expert knowledge. Alexandrianism therefore became no longer a gaudy panorama but a subject for special study, from which the essential ideas of religion could be teased out. And there was a similar tightening on the construction of the book, so that Anthony's visions could be rationalized as hallucinations, taking root in his solitude and boredom, growing in power as the darkness thickened, culminating in the terrible apparition of Damis and Apollonius at midnight, and fading away at dawn.

The methodical study of the Orient had grown fashionable; Burnouf and his successors had delved into Buddhism and presented it to their contemporaries. Western intellectuals who had lost their Christian faith and hoped to find another, turned to Eastern religion and its denial of the world. For some the extinction of the individual in Nirvana offered solace for the mechanized cruelty of their own epoch and civilization; others embraced an unrelieved pessimism, and Schopenhauer's *World as Will and Idea*, fifty years after its publication, began to reach a wide public.

Flaubert read Schopenhauer and it was perhaps under Schopenhauer's influence that in *La Tentation* of 1874 he abandoned the old Romantic antithesis between love and death and treated death as an illusion. At any rate the pessimism of Schopenhauer and Spencer gradually overclouds the philosophy of Spinoza. Not that Flaubert ever lost his admiration for the *Ethics*, but he remained unconvinced. In fact, art was the subject on which he would dogmatize; there was no other range of ideas he took so seriously that he could not admit the truth of their opposites, and his incorrigible, fluctuating scepticism is the despair of his commentators. Even in religion he stood aloof, expressing opinions that were valid for only twenty-four hours. He had been brought up in a Voltairian household, and his conditioned response to the Church and the priesthood was mockery. Much as he liked the Dominican Father Didon, for instance, he could not accept him as a friend: the cassock was an absolute disqualification.

Although Flaubert differed from most of his literary contemporaries in having a natural solidity of character and outlook, his roots, firm as they were, were bourgeois only. His stability was social, preserving fragments of a class ethos; it inherited what constructive ideas it still maintained, from the Catholic conception of the family. While accepting the advantages of this background, Flaubert enriched it with the humanism implicit in a wide culture, but humanism underwent a curious metamorphosis as it passed through his mind and temperament. Just as Baudelaire, though broadly accepting the standards of orthodox Christianity, had turned them upside down and become a conscious Satanist within the framework of a Catholic world-picture, so Flaubert, appropriating humanistic canons of judgement, inverted them to justify an inhuman misanthropy. The parallel is not exact because Flaubert neither sought to practise inhumanity nor used his own standards to condemn himself. But there is a sharp discrepancy between the source of his values and the actual use to which he puts them.

Religion interested him psychologically, but its power over him went deeper. Indeed Henri Guillemin has maintained that Flaubert's adoration of beauty was in reality adoration of the Godhead, that he was 'a predestined Christian, a Christian unaware of himself, whether voluntarily or not'. The argument is attractive, but subjects the word 'Christian' to an intolerable strain. There is at least no doubt of Flaubert's mysticism. He writes, for instance: 'Above life, above happiness, there is, as it were, a blue incandescence, a tenuous, unmoving expanse of heaven, whose brightness, as it reaches us, has the power to set worlds in motion. The glory of genius is only the pale reflection of this hidden Word.' Added to this glimpse of a dazzling unearthly beauty, there is a feeling of personal selection which approximates to the doctrine of grace, and a self-dedication which resembles the priestly calling. Moreover, Flaubert rejected out of hand the facile belief in human perfectibility and spoke of 'the curse of Adam, in which, fundamentally, I believe'. But he was too sceptical even to be an avowed theist, and although in moments of great emotion he wished to pray and to call on God, his considered opinion reduced the Deity to a remote abstraction who had no particular concern with human beings. As for Christianity, Flaubert combined a tender respect for the person of Jesus with a caustic denial of Christian mercy. Justice, for him, came first, and he was continually inveighing against the way in which, in politics and society, justice was ignored. Not that he himself in private life exacted an eye for an eye, but he was at pains to disguise his tender heart and would have been insulted if his charity and solicitude had been called Christian. He seems, indeed, to have regarded Christianity as a spent force, and there is a passage written for the third *Tentation*, but subsequently omitted, in which Jesus dies again in the streets of nineteenth-century Paris. The only two elements in Catholicism to which Flaubert responded were subordinate to the main tradition and divergent from it: the hatred of life, the negation of life's goodness, which he thought he discovered in Catholic philosophy, and, concomitant with it, the rigorous self-abasement of asceticism. But his own religious feeling, if such it can be called, was diffuse—a kind of creatureliness before the mystery of creation. 'What draws me above all things', he wrote in 1857, 'is religion. I mean all religions, not one rather than another. Each dogma on its own repels me, but I consider the feeling that created them as the most natural and poetical in humanity. I don't like philosophers who find there only fraud and foolishness.'

Despite his belief in Original Sin, Flaubert did not feel involved in humanity to a culpable extent; his conception of stupid futility flowed from a savage awareness of his own shortcomings, but this awareness did not amount to guilt. He strove for moral detachment, which is a sort of objectivity; and though by temperament and situation he could not attain it even if it were attainable, he was still not a whole-hearted participant. By the limited extent of his participation and by the realization of the sorry process in which he was caught up, he therefore felt that he escaped the full burden of human sinfulness. Moreover, his concept of sinfulness was intellectual and aesthetic: it was sinful to deceive oneself, to indulge in humbug, to deny beauty. There is no trace in Flaubert's mature work of evil as it existed for Baudelaire; his perception of what was wrong was intuitive but analysable, and if challenged, he would probably have traced it back to the humanistic ideal.

La Tentation is thus not valid from a Christian standpoint; or rather it is inadequate. But whatever qualifications may be made of Flaubert's conception of good and evil, there is no doubt of

his integrity. In his correspondence one often catches him resort-
ing to minor hypocrisies, stumbling into contradictions, wriggling out of requests. But the impression he left on those who knew
him well was of complete frankness and even naïvety: 'Among the
literary people I have mixed with in my life', writes Edmond de
Goncourt, 'I know only one man who is quite *pure*, in the
highest sense of the word, and that is Flaubert—who, as everyone
knows, has a habit of writing so-called immoral books.'

This, too, was Flaubert's character in friendship, a genuine
openness of heart. 'My main remembrance', says Henry James, 'is
of a conception of courtesy in him, an accessibility to the human
relation, that only wanted to be sure of the way taken or to take.'
And because he gave more generously, his sense of loss was more
acute as his friends disappeared one by one. In October 1872 it was
the turn of Gautier, a pillar of the Romantic generation, whose
influence on Flaubert dated back to the years at Rouen *collège*.
Flaubert had united with Gautier in trenchant denunciations of the
bourgeoisie, and Gautier gone meant one true artist the less, suffo-
cated no doubt by the noxious atmosphere of the Third Republic.
'I respected him as a master', said Flaubert, 'and I loved him as a
brother. I don't pity him. I envy him.' Within a year Feydeau too
had died—'the one I shall miss least of all the friends I have lost
in the last four years. Still, he *was* my friend.' Feydeau's *Daniel* had
been accepted as worthy successor to *Bovary*; it enjoyed great success, and Feydeau, who catered for the public taste rather like a
restaurant-keeper, gave himself airs. Although Flaubert despised
such weakness, he found Feydeau a congenial, if unstable, character, and when the man was first ruined financially and then stricken
with paralysis, he was not only anxious and distressed, but took
steps to ensure that the pension granted under the Second Empire
should be renewed by the Third Republic.

It was at this period that Flaubert became intimate with Edmond Laporte, a Parisian who managed a lace factory at Grand-
Couronne, six miles down the Seine from Rouen, and had built a
house on the bend of the river, almost opposite Flaubert's. They
met in 1865, through Duplan, and after Duplan's death they were
increasingly drawn together. Laporte was a keen hunter and an

excellent shot, no writer himself, but possessed of those qualities of loyalty and devotion that Flaubert missed among the literati of Paris. He was a willing source of information, undertaking minor researches, and visiting Rouen Library on Flaubert's behalf. Flaubert, if he were in a hurry for information, packed a letter in a parcel and sent it to Laporte by the river-boat that called both at Croisset and Couronne; Laporte usually replied by return.

But the best friend of Flaubert's last years was Turgeniev, who had left Russia in 1855 and lived in either Baden or Paris with the Viardot-Garcias. He was a slender, moon-faced, squeaky-voiced person, chronically uncertain of himself. Like Flaubert he had enthusiastically adopted the Romantic world-picture, but found it inadequate and sought a corrective in the disciplined observation of reality; and although he derived his only conception of value from the beauty inherent in human activity and his outlook was therefore more sentimental than realistic, Flaubert liked and admired him—liked him, perhaps, because of his faults. For Flaubert, despite his malignant, corrosive misanthropy, was sentimental in his personal relations, and sought as his friends those who were not hard and practical but were still capable of generous effusions and extravagant self-abandonment for the sake of an idea. Moreover Turgeniev was an artist: he handled French almost as easily as Russian and had a fine sense of discrimination between what was genuine and original and what was shoddy and false. But Flaubert soon found that he was an exasperating friend, lavish with promises but hesitant in their accomplishment. Not that he was in any way disloyal or insincere. But he was repeatedly undertaking to come to Croisset and at the crucial moment being crippled by an attack of gout and postponing the visit. The gout was an eternal evasion; once in 1868 it did fail to keep Turgeniev away, but all through the summer and autumn of 1872 he was threatening to descend on Flaubert and hastily cancelling the project. Such typical procrastinations, recurring every year, irked and infuriated Flaubert, who grumbled about Turgeniev's 'flabbiness' and called him a 'soft pear'. But their relations were better expressed in a letter of March 1873, in which Flaubert said: 'Now you are the *only human being* for whom I have any consideration, the only man of letters in the world, the only friend remaining to me.'

The exaggeration is pardonable but misleading. In particular Flaubert still had, in George Sand, a friend whose affection and solicitude were equal to any demands. Each criticized the other: Flaubert, for instance, blamed her benevolence. 'In spite of your big sphinx-like eyes, you have seen the world in a golden haze.' She, on the other hand, was concerned with his health, for the shock of war and of bereavement had dealt him blows from which he had not recovered. He was irritable, emotional, irascible, now bursting into tears and now exploding with anger. The possibility of madness or suicide obsessed him; he slept badly, was exhausted by trifles, and felt at moments that his head was dry and empty; the disgust caused by his contemporaries sometimes mounted, he himself realized, to a mania. He even feared that, as Du Camp had forecast with characteristic tact, his brain had begun to soften.[3]

George Sand felt instinctively that Flaubert's life, especially since the death of his mother, lacked any proper emotional outlet. He was active—as much as ever in his career; but his huge labours at Croisset and febrile exertions in Paris were not counterbalanced by any settled tenderness. Caroline bestowed occasional weeks upon him but they were not always happy ones, and George Sand, with an affection that was at once vague and penetrating, wished he could find himself a wife or mistress or even a long-forgotten child. Bouilhet's death she attributed in part to the desiccating use of mind, and she feared that the same destiny might overtake Flaubert. So far as she could, she tried to incorporate him in her own family. As the midnight chimes at Nohant rang in Christmas Day 1871, she and her son and daughter-in-law thrice cried out Flaubert's name, and when she told him, he was moved to tears. Periodically he visited her at Nohant, they met in Paris, or she came to Croisset. One of the latter occasions was made memorable by their attendance at the Père Legrain's puppet-show—she a venerable figure with white hair and an old-fashioned cap, while he was recognizable by his long drooping moustache and pince-nez. *La Tentation de saint Antoine* was still being played to packed benches, and Legrain, apprised of the presence of distinguished visitors, appeared in front of his booth and announced: 'Ladies and gentlemen, the author is in the audience and is honouring us by attending a performance of his work.' Flaubert was delighted.

But such episodes were all too rare, and George Sand realized that it needed a strong personality to attenuate Flaubert's unhappiness. 'How you are tormented and distressed by life!' she wrote. 'For all you complain about is life. It has not been better for anyone, at any period. . . . There is one person who could change you and save you and that is Hugo; for by one side of his character he is a great philosopher, and yet he remains the great artist which you need and which I am not. You must see him often. I think he will calm you down; I, for my part, am no longer turbulent enough for you to understand me.'

Hugo had been back in Paris since the collapse of the Second Empire and had achieved the dignity of an institution. He was the rallying point for left-wing thought as well as the doyen of contemporary French letters. But although Flaubert frequented him and savoured the easy charm of his personality—charming, at least, when no politicians were in the offing—even Hugo could not by himself cure or even perceptibly lighten the melancholy into which Flaubert had settled. It was not an enervated, pathetic gloom, but a ferocious penetration of humbug and self-deception; and because it derived from abnormal awareness and sensitivity it could not be treated by comforting platitudes. Flaubert saw further into the motives and nature of human activity than any but a handful of his contemporaries; he had deliberately cast off the protective carapace of insouciance and self-satisfaction and had bared himself to the full impact of a tormenting and wearisome life. Moreover he intensified the impact by his peculiar emotionalization of knowledge: the world not only appalled him, but racked him. If there was a cure, it must be a metaphysical one—the glimpse of some ultimate reconciliation that would transform the pattern of futility and suffering into one of significant beauty. Flaubert was denied any such intimation; and being left with only beauty to illuminate his darkness, he achieved the best justification of which he was capable.

His attitude to the public was wary, like his attitude to his publisher. But although he was careless of his own profits, he demanded for his friends what he would not demand for himself. The cost of printing Bouilhet's *Dernières Chansons* had been borne nominally by Philippe Le Parfait, but in fact by Flaubert; Michel Lévy's task was simply that of distribution. When, early in 1872, Flaubert became convinced that Lévy, having netted a comfortable profit, was making not the slightest attempt to advertise or sell the book, he burst into his office, denounced him passionately, and swept out again without waiting for an answer. 'Lévy', he declared, 'is a monster of rapacity and bad faith.' Attempts at reconciliation were made, but by the end of the year, the break was complete.[4]

Flaubert was determined that if he could not find a suitable publisher, his books would not go into print. But he discovered a congenial acquaintance in Georges Charpentier, who in 1871, at the age of twenty-five, had succeeded his father as head of the house bearing his name. In these hands Flaubert felt that his interests were safe, and before the publication of *La Tentation* he politely refused to be godfather to Charpentier's boy, whom the parents wished to christen Antoine.

In 1869 Flaubert had taken a flat on the fourth floor of a house in the rue Murillo, so as to save money and be nearer Caroline's *hôtel*. The accommodation was tiny but newly built, and there was a pleasant outlook onto the Parc Monceau. The furniture was simple and the walls, though hung with a flowery cretonne, were bare. Apart from an Arab saddle he had brought back from Africa and a gilded Buddha he had purchased in Rouen, there were no ornaments. He had a jar full of quill-pens and another full of clay pipes, about the size of thimbles, which he offered to his friends. Visitors he expected on Sundays, and as soon as the bell rang, he threw a piece of red silk over the table to hide his work. Turgeniev, Daudet, Edmond de Goncourt, and later Zola and Maupassant were his familiars, and he received them with his customary bonhomie, dressed in a flowing gandurah, with goffered frills, and a tarboosh on his head. But in spite of his hospitality there was a curious dearth of visitors—a dearth which struck Edmond de

Goncourt forcibly. Flaubert, he noted, 'is famous and talented and a very good fellow'. Why should he be so little sought after? As a host he was genial and entertaining, even if he had an unhealthy bias for open windows. Perhaps the reason for his obscurity lay in the fame he had achieved; he was known primarily as the author of *Bovary*, a book he had come to dislike and even revile, and his subsequent work, when it obtained a hearing, had been interpreted in the *Bovary* spirit. Once burdened with a reputation for immorality, Flaubert was unable to clear his name; and because he was also pictured as a kind of hermit, who only left his lair in Normandy to hibernate in Paris libraries and who never, under any circumstances, dabbled in journalism, the portrait of a rather carnal-minded misanthrope was complete.

At Croisset he was even more deserted. Laporte gave him a wolf-hound which he christened Julio and rarely took for walks. But although his friends, especially George Sand, urged on him the need for exercise, he resisted. Sometimes he would stroll down to the *pavillon* by the river or along the avenue of lindens that he called his *gueuloir* or up the other avenue of yews leading to the statue of Mercury. In warm weather he went swimming, for swimming was the only sport that appealed to him. But most of his time at Croisset he spent in his study, with Pradier's bust of Caroline to remind him of his youth, and two mummied feet, stolen from the Caverns of Ma'abda, unfortunately blackened by his servant and adapted for use as paper-weights, to recall the greatest adventure of his manhood. He collected bric-à-brac of all kinds—amulets, primitive musical instruments, arrows, copper plates, glass necklaces, Greek and Egyptian arms, plaster masks, and mouldings of bas-reliefs. He even kept an old hat of his mother's to fondle from time to time, and he grew attached to his possessions and hated change. In 1873, however, he spent 1,000 francs on alterations, cleaning some of his pictures, repairing the more dilapidated furniture, and installing in the stairway two Chinese monsters Laporte had given him.

At forty he was already hopelessly nostalgic, and by the time he was fifty, his musings were all about the past. He preserved his old ambitions in a modified form: some were merely pointers to what might have been, but some still lured him on. Above all, he longed for fame as a playwright. He did not consider the rejection of *Le Château des cœurs* as definitive, and when he discovered the fragment of *Le Sexe faible* among Bouilhet's papers, he was fired to complete it. Carvalho, who managed the Vaudeville, was encouraging and promised to perform the play in winter 1873–4; and Flaubert, working feverishly, finished it in April 1873. Meanwhile he had conceived a play of his own, *Le Candidat*, a fierce satire on the political nullity of the time, and, at Carvalho's suggestion, he wrote it in the summer and autumn. At this, Carvalho, who was a skilled negotiator, asked to put it on before *Le Sexe faible*, in which lengthy revisions had suddenly become necessary, and Flaubert, pressed by d'Osmoy and Turgeniev, gave way. Rehearsals began in January 1874 and the première took place on 11th March.

It was an unmitigated failure. The public, which came expecting to be amused, was treated to a play in which Flaubert attacked all shades of political opinion with impartial ferocity. Disappointment turned to hostility: Flaubert's pathos was mocked at and his humour derided. No doubt the *chef de claque* was incompetent and the audience included some dandies and Stock-Exchange speculators who hardly appreciated the vigour of Flaubert's disapproval. But the loyalty of his friends and the support of his actors could not disguise the fact that *Le Candidat* stood no chance; Flaubert felt that the subject was suitable but that he had spoilt it. Seeing Delaunoy, his best actor, coming off the stage with tears in his eyes decided him: on the fourth night he withdrew the play.

As for *Le Sexe faible*, it could not, after the failure of *Le Candidat*, be produced at the Vaudeville, and after having it rejected at the Théâtre Français and the Odéon, Flaubert presented it, to the consternation of his friends, at such third-rate theatres as Cluny and the Gymnase. But even there it was condemned, and the manuscript returned to Croisset for good.

Zola says that during the rehearsals of *Le Candidat* Flaubert discussed five or six other subjects which, if the public reception was encouraging, he hoped to treat dramatically. After 11th March 1874 he did not mention them again.

Notes to Chapter Thirteen

1. It is curious that Alfred Nion, a schoolfellow of Flaubert's, should have discovered in the book a flavour of Quinet's *Ahasuérus*. The influence of *Ahasuérus* is fairly strong on Flaubert's immature work, but little of it persists after 1849.

2. Herbert Spencer, *First Principles* (Final edition), ch. iii, §21.

3. At least he writes on 1st September 1872: 'Maintenant j'ai peur de la rage. Cette sotte idée est un des symptômes de mon ramollissement.' And this passage should surely be linked with his letter of 27th–28th February 1853: 'Je crois que le ramollissement de cervelle diagnostiqué par Du Camp n'arrive pas encore.' Du Camp should perhaps bear some responsibility for Flaubert's hypochondria. The phrase recurs like an obsession in a letter to Raoul-Duval of 30th January 1880: 'Il y a ramollissement de la cervelle publique.'

Dr. Russell-Davis points out that Flaubert displays at this period many of the symptoms of involutional melancholia. And there is another suggestion which should be mentioned. In 1849 Flaubert informed Chevalier that he was syphilitic, adding that the infection dated back many years and blaming it for his nervous symptoms (M.-J. Durry, *Flaubert et ses projets inédits* (1950), Appendice, pp. 403–4). But the Wassermann reaction was not available till 1907, and in its absence diagnosis would be extremely difficult once the primary stage of the disease was past (i.e. within a few months). It is, in fact, unlikely that the disease was diagnosed early, and although Flaubert's glossitis of 1854 may have been due to habitual overdosing with mercury (the traditional treatment), there can be no certainty that he had syphilis. But even if he did, it can hardly have affected his 'epilepsy'; for the only possible form of syphilis that fits his symptoms is G.P.I., the normal course of which is so different from that of Flaubert's nervous illness that it can be discounted. In any case, the first attack of 'epilepsy' occurred much sooner after the putative infection than could be explained in this way.

4. Flaubert received 800 francs for *Madame Bovary*, 10,000 for *Salammbô*, 16,000 for *L'Education sentimentale*. Lévy also made him an *ex gratia* payment of 500 francs for *Bovary* in view of the book's success.

Chapter Fourteen

RUIN AND RENOWN

'*Je crois que le cœur ne vieillit pas; il y a même des gens chez qui il augmente avec l'âge.*' Letter to George Sand, 23rd–24th January 1867.

Ever since he had been able to formulate, document, and justify his scorn for the human race, Flaubert had threatened to fix it permanently and in detail. He had already traced out in *Bovary* the deceptive lure of the Romantic ideal and in *L'Education sentimentale* the unpurposeful ambitions of his generation; but he had not attempted to judge mankind in general, and although the idea had several times beset him, there had been on each occasion some more pressing task to be disposed of. But after the completion of *La Tentation* the moment was ripe. He was in his fifties and felt old and forsaken; the society in which he had found at least a precarious footing had collapsed, and a new order was growing up, in France and Europe, which seemed at once democratic and totalitarian. Whereas the values for which he stood had been tolerated in the old scheme of things, in the new they were menaced by external hostility and internal vacillation. Moreover although each of his books had been written as part of a personal hygiene, he was, at this age, little concerned with the future: so far as it existed for him, it was black. He had long considered happiness mere vanity, at least for himself, and life was such a burden of toil and suffering that he was sometimes surprised at his own persistence in undergoing it. He lived in a constant state of indignation—indignation at bourgeois ineptitude, political humbug, artistic shoddiness, and moral degradation—and, since he had long ago taken the measure of himself, his gaze was fixed on the detailed operations of society. Politics, economics, law, journalism, philosophy, literature, all galled and infuriated him. He was, in fact, an altruistic misanthrope.

When, therefore, in the summer of 1872, he began to turn over the plan of *Bouvard et Pécuchet*, he was doing more than express a disgust created by particular circumstances in a particular temperament. Because of his lucidity and penetration he had a sharp consciousness of the vast tracts of ignorance and imbecility in his own mind—tracts which most of us prefer to ignore—and he had a pitiless perception of the same inadequacies in other people. He hated human frailty; he resented its operation; and he dealt with it in the mass, so that his vision was of universal folly. From *Bovary* to *La Tentation* there had been a gradual hardening in his outlook, a tensing of his style, a desiccation of his imaginative faculty. But he made up for the loss with an increasing command of intellectual abstractions, and in *Bouvard et Pécuchet* his thought culminated in the analysis of two minds groping for the certainty of knowledge and failing miserably and abjectly to attain it. As the structure and content of his books became more characteristic of Flaubert's personality, their scope widened in compensation, and they acquired added point and ferocity. So *Bouvard et Pécuchet* is more devastating in conception than any of its predecessors. While *La Tentation*, even in its latest version, had been based on the instability of emotion and the fluctuations of faith, *Bouvard et Pécuchet* attacked the basic presupposition of the modern world— that knowledge is easily available and easily assimilated. The book suggested an incompatibility between mind and truth.

Flaubert's conception involved a prodigious labour—a labour far outreaching the maximum of his efforts hitherto; he was to show his two characters tackling a fresh department of knowledge in each chapter, summarizing the best authorities, stumbling on contradictions, falling into confusion and landing in either mental perplexity or physical embarrassment. Because they were to sample a cross-section of modern knowledge of all kinds, he himself had to undertake a preliminary survey of each field; he must discover what was correct before he could discover error; and when he had a summary notion of current orthodoxy in each particular subject he was obliged to explore popular textbooks and garner mistakes. If his satire was to have point, it must reach beyond Bouvard and Pécuchet to the sources they used; as Flaubert's stalking-horses, the two men were naïve and well-meaning, ready to believe what they were told, and he was a t huge pains to demonstrate that they were merely the focus for contradictions and blunders that derived from established authorities. He was therefore obliged to undertake a documentation at which the brain of the hardiest researcher might reel—a documentation covering, in minute particulars, agriculture, chemistry, anatomy, physiology, medicine, geology, archeology, history, literature, politics, gymnastics, spiritualism, philosophy, religion, education, and much more. 'You have to be mad,' he wrote, 'and absolutely frantic, to start a book like this.'

If the subject had not forced itself upon him, Flaubert could never have attempted it. He was ill, tired, and dejected; Bouilhet's plays and the Rouen monument made heavy demands on his time and energy; he was busy with *Le Candidat* as well as *Le Sexe faible*, and was still trying to place *Le Château des cœurs*; moreover he was continually and characteristically at the disposal and service of his friends.

His book, however, did possess one tonic virtue: it forced him to travel—in 1873 to Rambouillet and Mantes in search of the right background; in 1874 to Alençon and Caen. The same summer, obeying his doctor who told him he was a hysterical old woman, he spent a month in Switzerland, mostly at Rigi-Kaltbad. It was a gloomy episode, for Flaubert picked a hotel that was full of supercilious English and monumental Germans. He scarcely spoke to a soul, and was so lonely that in an expansive moment he nearly kissed three calves he found in a field. Fortunately Laporte arrived to bring him home, and Laporte was excellent company. It was with him that Flaubert had made his trip though Normandy earlier the same year, and with Laporte's connivance he was addressed by inn-servants as 'Monsieur le Ministre' or 'Monsieur l'Ingénieur'. If a maid entered his room, he usually contrived to be dictating a letter to Laporte—a letter that described a blood-curdling crime. When Laporte arrived at

Rigi-Kaltbad, Flaubert thoughtfully offered him a shower; had one himself; drenched their clothes by carelessly manipulating the apparatus; failed to turn off the tap; and, naked and shivering, had to call the hotel staff, who arrived in gaping droves. Returning through the Customs, Laporte, who knew his friend's taste, announced his identity as 'Laporte, President of the Chamber of Commerce at Grand-Couronne'. Flaubert, next through the turnstile, was met by a brusque: 'And you?'—'Flaubert, Secretary to the President.'

He found a ready accomplice for this kind of farce in Laure de Maupassant's son, Guy. After being expelled from Yvetot seminary for some sentimental verse, Guy had been sent to Rouen *lycée*, and his mother had given him an introduction to Bouilhet, a friend of many years' standing. Bouilhet had taken a paternal interest in his versifying and afforded him mild encouragement. After Bouilhet's death Mme de Maupassant recommended Guy to Flaubert, who promised to supervise his work and create openings. They knew one another well from about 1872, when Guy was twenty-two. He was a thick-set, swarthy, blunt-mannered countryman, who relieved the tedium of his clerkship at the Admiralty by week-ends of boating on the river. Flaubert's interest in him was at first a kind of tribute paid to Mme de Maupassant and, beyond her, to Alfred Le Poittevin; for Guy bore a startling likeness to his uncle. 'I am sometimes even afraid,' Flaubert told Guy's mother, 'especially when, in reciting verse, he lowers his head.' But he added: 'I think our young man is rather an idler, not particularly keen on work. I'd like to see him start a substantial book, even if it were detestable.'

Flaubert was highly susceptible to the charm of Maupassant's personality and soon spoke of him with enthusiasm. He was less fervent about Maupassant's poetry, but discovered talent in his work and subjected him to a long apprenticeship, gradually turning him away from verse to prose. More or less weekly, Maupassant submitted passages which Flaubert scrutinized and discussed; and he absorbed, at least temporarily, Flaubert's doctrine of objectivity. Flaubert treated him as a disciple, although an independent one, and became an approving confidant for the lubri-

cious escapades which dominated Maupassant's life even as they
were later to dominate his imagination. Periodically, indeed, Flaubert recalled him to literature and dogmatized severely about the
natural antagonism between women and work; but when, in 1875,
Maupassant composed an obscene playlet, *A la Feuille de Rose,
Maison turque*, and had it performed to a select audience in the
studio of the painter, Maurice Leloir, Flaubert was a delighted
spectator and was most anxious that it should be put on again for
Turgeniev's special benefit.[1]

Flaubert, in fact, was not a consistent mentor because he had
no respect for authority. The years had scarcely modified his attitude: he regarded the assumption of office as an experiment in the
grotesque, and all officials as humbugs. He remained the boy he
had been at Rouen *collège*—a rebel, by turns sulky and boisterous.
He still read forbidden literature in the dormitory and cocked a
snook at his masters; but the dormitory was now at Croisset and
his masters were the blatant publicists of Paris. The conventions
of society were only the stupid rules and regulations of the *collège*;
the drum-beat had only been muffled. 'If ever I take an active part
in the world', he had told Chevalier, 'it will be as a thinker and
demoralizer.' And that he had become—a demoralizer who not
only undermined society, but shook the whole basis of reasonable
emotion and logical thought. 'Ah!' he cried in 1871, 'how tired
I am of the ignoble workman, the inept bourgeois, the stupid
peasant and the odious priest.' These people shared responsibility
for the social structure, combining, even in their dissidences, to
set hypocritical deceivers in places of power; and Flaubert thrilled
with exquisite pleasure if some Rouen or Paris celebrity lost his
mask of moral eminence. He had been delighted when the vice-
principal of Rouen *collège* was discovered in a brothel. He was
equally pleased in December 1876, when two men were detected
in a compromising situation near the Champs-Elysées. One was
Chouard, a stupid and dirty jeweller's boy; the other, who
threatened to horsewhip the policeman who arrested him, was
Eugène Lebègue, Comte de Germiny, the able and intelligent son
of a former Governor of the Bank of France, himself Municipal
Councillor of Paris, Secretary to the General Council of the Seine,

churchwarden in the parish of Saint Thomas d'Aquin, Vice-President of the Institution of Clubs for Catholic Working Men and editor of the *Revue Catholique*. 'You cannot imagine how I've suffered', Flaubert wrote to Maupassant, 'having no one to talk to about this good Germiny! Can you picture the disturbance this business must have caused in the Hôtel des Farces and the *Garçon's* speech for the defence?'

Flaubert preserved the outlook that had created *Le Garçon*; he was so anxious to prick each bubble of fame and reputation that they evidently contained, even at this stage of his life, some lingering attractiveness and plausibility. Mature years had not slowed down his spontaneous response, whether to horror, folly or untruth. Thus he believed implicitly that his contemporaries had a rooted 'hatred for literature'; and when a journalist, in a short article, spoke of the bare walls of Flaubert's Paris flat as hung with pictures worth a fortune, he was convinced that the misstatement was either part of a campaign of vilification organized by Rouen municipality or a manifestation of the personal animosity he had aroused in Villemessant, king of all journalists. Similarly, when he read the trial of Mme Gras, an ageing courtesan who arranged for her rich young lover to be blinded with vitriol so that she could marry him in greater security, Flaubert was horrified to the point of being ill. He was, in fact, only pleased with evil and corruption when they fitted into the ironic pattern of the grotesque; his sense of the grotesque was a barrier against suffering, a means of laughing at it, and when that barrier could not be used, Flaubert received the full impact, and writhed. His endless vituperation of the bourgeois was similarly a defence, precisely because it was a counterattack; he had acquired a habit of obloquy that protected, as it relieved, him. His friends, like Lapierre who edited *Le Nouvelliste de Rouen*, did not take his ferocity too seriously. Indeed Lapierre maliciously provoked it, and in one of his letters he describes how, one evening, 'friend Flau trampled on social prejudices with his customary vigour, piling the old parties onto the new ones so as to make a gigantic Russian salad. At ten o'clock we cleared away the wounded and the dead and our friend returned to Croisset, scornfully puffing his cigar-smoke through the coach window at 100,000 Rouennais, his mortal enemies.'

He was still a bourgeois in his loyalties, even if he had overcome the bourgeois attachment to comfort and wealth. The proof came in April 1875, when Commanville, who had been in financial difficulty since the war, revealed that he could not meet his creditors. Since Caroline had been married under the dotal system that was common in Normandy, she was able to transfer only part of her property to Commanville; and unless he received immediate and substantial backing, a crash was inevitable. Flaubert was appalled, but did not hesitate. At the thought of his family being tainted with bankruptcy he put his fortune at their disposal. He gave up his flat in the rue Murillo and took rooms on the same landing as the Commanvilles in the rue du Faubourg Saint-Honoré; he drastically reduced his expenditure; he sold his entire property at Deauville; in all, he abandoned to his niece and her husband 1,200,000 francs, in return for which they promised him a small allowance. At one time it even appeared that he would have to get rid of the house at Croisset, and he faced the prospect with horror but courage. George Sand immediately asked what the price would be; if she could afford it, she would buy the house and let Flaubert live there for the rest of his life. But her generosity was not called upon. Flaubert's friends came to his aid, and both Laporte and Raoul-Duval, the lawyer and deputy, guaranteed 25,000 francs—more out of respect for Flaubert than liking for Commanville. Although Flaubert himself was left without a penny, Commanville's name was saved; but that was small consolation to the firms involved. For Flaubert's money and his friends' loans and guarantees did not cover a quarter of the sum required, and the Rouen bank of Pécuchet, Lainé et Cie failed. A new company—Faucon, Pécuchet et Cie—was formed on 1st July 1875, with the specific purpose of liquidating Commanville's affairs, and it was with this bank that Flaubert conducted all subsequent negotiations.[2]

Even Commanville's failure did not open Flaubert's eyes. It made him slightly more sceptical, but did not reveal to him that both his niece and her husband were far more concerned about their own standing and fortune than about his own affection; he was an expedient and little else; after his death he would be a source of income. Unlike the merchants of Rouen, he readily shared Commanville's optimism that the business could be set on foot again, and he expected his friends to agree. In personal relations he was afflicted with a becoming blindness; he exaggerated Louise Colet's talent, Bouilhet's eminence, Caroline's sensibility, and Commanville's commercial acumen; he was so anxious to believe the best that he convinced himself of it; he was the most doting of uncles, the most wilfully credulous of patrons.

But just as Caroline's success gladdened him, her peril cast him down; and apart from his own privations the anxious months of 1875 bore heavily upon his courage and strength. 'I feel he is stricken,' Turgeniev wrote to George Sand, 'and more deeply than he perhaps thinks himself. He has tenacity without energy, as he has pride without vanity. Misfortune enters his soul as though it were butter.' It may have been because of his anxiety that Turgeniev wished to visit Croisset; at any rate, now that the trip was impossible, his gout no longer troubled him, and all through the summer and autumn he exasperated Flaubert by demanding to come for a night. The two men did not meet till November, when, with Commanville's bankruptcy staved off, Flaubert went to Paris for the winter and found Turgeniev 'nicer than ever'.

Before this, Flaubert had spent six weeks at Concarneau with his friend Georges Pouchet, the natural historian.[3] His nerves hindered him from writing letters, but he bathed almost daily and took long walks. The sight of Pouchet placidly absorbed in dissection roused his envy: scientists were spared emotional disturbance. After the stresses and alarms he had passed through, he felt unequal to the task of *Bouvard et Pécuchet*, and he set the work temporarily aside and turned to a subject that calmed and satisfied him: the medieval legend of Saint Julian Hospitator. Saint Julian's life was told in a window of Rouen Cathedral which had been presented late in the thirteenth century by the Corporation of fishermen and fishmongers; and because of the little statue of Saint Julian he had seen at Caudebec when in 1846, after his illness, he was exploring the district with Du Camp and Bouilhet, the theme may have been associated with tranquillity in Flaubert's mind. Certainly, in these darkening years, he broke away from the crabbed desperation of *Bouvard et Pécuchet* and achieved an un-affected supernaturalism in which the powers of light were, for once, triumphant; and despite the difficulties of technique, obscu-rities of detail, and problems of tone, he enjoyed the writing. 'It puts me in a cleaner environment than the modern world and does me good.'

With *Saint Julien* finished, he needed two more *contes* to make up a volume, and immediately, in February 1876, he embarked on another subject that recalled his youth. It was the tale of an old servant he had met as a boy at Trouville, and he linked her life with the visits he and his sister had paid to Pont-l'Evêque.[4] In *Un Cœur simple* he dispensed with irony; mocking laughter gave way to a sad pity. 'I want to move tender hearts to compassion and tears', he said, 'for I am tender-hearted myself.' He wrote espe-cially to please George Sand and to show that his reputation for hardness was undeserved. But it would not have been Flaubert if, in describing Félicité's parrot, he had not obtained a stuffed bird from Rouen Museum and kept it on his work-table; and for her death he relied heavily on Grisolle's *Traité de la pneumonie*.

Like *Saint Julien*, *Un Cœur simple* has the luminous simplicity that comes of a life surveyed and interrelated; events are no longer pressing forward into a dark and menacing future, but cohere in a unified pattern. It is as though Flaubert, after his personal trials, had transcended the harsh conception of *Bouvard et Pécuchet* and granted that a humble life of sacrifice and duty, however innocent of critical intelligence, possessed an intrinsic beauty and therefore an intrinsic meaning. To describe the accident that befell Félicité on the Honfleur road, Flaubert harked back, as Gérard-Gailly has shown, to the first incidence of his illness outside Bourg-Achard. The procedure is important, for it involves a parallel between Flaubert and Félicité, if not some degree of identification, and implies that if he could discover a pathetic but significant beauty in the life of the old servant, he also accepted the significance of his own suffering. It is a hint rather than an indication—a hint that Flaubert was not confining value to art but extending it to life, which for so long had seemed a 'foolish joke'. The accident outside Bourg-Achard and the years of tormented sensitivity from which there was no escape might after all have an unsuspected worth; and Flaubert was hovering on the brink of that exacting and courageous belief.

While writing *Un Cœur simple*, he was reminded of another thread in his life by the death of Louise Colet in March 1876. It cost him a morning's brooding, and he wrote to Troubat, who had been Sainte-Beuve's secretary, asking him to come and talk about her. For Louise Colet had receded into virtual oblivion: after the publication of *Salammbô* she tried to renew relations, and when he brought out his preface to Bouilhet's *Dernières Chansons*, she wrote him an anonymous and abusive letter in verse; but they did not meet, and if Flaubert ever referred to her, it was with the weary memory of an ancient irritation. She, however, was still obsessed with the man who had been for seven years her lover, and although she tried to cast him out in *Une histoire de soldat* and *Lui*, he remained to haunt her with the realization of failure. Her health was bad and grew worse; but she was continuously and vehemently active on behalf of various controversial causes, particularly herself. In 1869 she managed to be invited to the opening of the Suez Canal, and she travelled up the Nile. Her purpose, as she realized, was to find 'as a living mummy one of those seductive *almehs* whom [Flaubert] employed to wound my feelings and revolt me in the accounts of his travels'. But Kuchiuk was no longer at Esneh, and Louise returned home, to die six years later, poverty-stricken and neglected.

Louise Colet's death meant only a temporary interruption in the writing of *Un Cœur simple*—an episode that aroused Flaubert to the absoluteness of the past, the remote petrifaction of his early manhood, but did not stir him to grief. In June, however, George Sand died, without having read a line of *Un Cœur simple*. Flaubert attended the funeral at Nohant and broke down at the sight of the coffin. 'It was as though I were burying my mother for a second time.' His genuine distress at the loss was enhanced and intensified by his incurable nostalgia for what was absent and intangible; his greatest friendships culminated when his friends were dead, and the monotonous importance of bereavement in his life derived from the bitter paradox that his closest approaches to happiness were retrospective, vitiated with unreality. Happiness meant more to him as the occasion for it receded. It was a flavour lingering on the palate, and Flaubert fastened on it greedily, trying to create a spurious memory of satiety. So he was delighted to see Gertrude Collier (Mrs. Charles Tennant) when she visited France in October; she brought back Trouville and the days which Flaubert liked to think of as carefree and entirely devoted to Romantic aspiration. 'My old friend, my youth', he called her; and he gave the too sweeping assurance: 'During the long years I lived without knowing even your whereabouts, there was perhaps not a single day when I did not think of you.'

More than ever he was a victim of doubt and hesitation. Bouilhet and George Sand had both helped him to overcome his perplexities and narrow the gap between ambition and achievement; and without them he lacked encouragement and stimulus. As he wrote his third *conte*, *Hérodias*,[5] dealing with Salome's dance and John the Baptist's death and portraying the racial conflict between Jews and Romans, he was uncertain of his work and had no one to consult. For the facts he resorted as usual to the authorities: Baudry, Renan, Clermont-Ganneau. But when it came to the conception, there was only Turgeniev whose judgement he relied on; and although *Hérodias*, in spite of its intricacy, was successfully completed, *Bouvard et Pécuchet* was another matter. It had been temporarily laid aside, but Flaubert continued to meditate on it. Others had misgivings. Zola had said at the start: 'It is a pity none of his friends dares dissuade him from the book he is beginning.' And Turgeniev wrote to Flaubert in 1874: 'The more I consider it, the more I think it is a subject to treat *presto*, like Swift or Voltaire. . . . Suppose you spin it out and are too learned . . .?' Flaubert replied that he could only give the book weight and power by handling it seriously and that he very well realized the danger of monotony; but Turgeniev was not convinced, and in 1876 he received a letter from Taine, to whom Flaubert had just shown the first chapter and the plan of the whole. '[Flaubert] requested my opinion', said Taine; 'I was evasive and asked for time to reflect; and now I consult you.' Taine's main criticisms were that because of the dullness of Bouvard and Pécuchet their misfortunes would be without interest; that, however brilliant in execution, the book would fail to be amusing; and that only specialists could understand the errors made by the two clerks. 'I have always been frank with [Flaubert]', Taine concluded; 'I love and respect him greatly; he is a man of feeling, loyal and honest. I should like to behave towards him as a good friend of long-standing, and I do not know what to do. He would bear no resentment for my outspokenness. But I am afraid of discouraging him to no purpose.' Having spoken to Turgeniev, Taine apparently felt that he could do no more, and apart from briefly summarizing his objections in a letter to Flaubert, he let the matter drop; while Turgeniev, with his rather flaccid benevolence, was unable to prevail against Flaubert's patient determination.

Since 1874 Flaubert had occasionally met the elusive Turgeniev at Le Dîner des Cinq (or Le Dîner des Auteurs sifflés), which was held at the Café Riche. It was a more select successor to the Dîner Magny, and since membership was confined to playwrights whose work had been hissed off the stage, there were only three other regular diners; Daudet, Edmond de Goncourt, and Zola. Flaubert hated walking back to his flat alone, no doubt afraid of having an attack in the street, and Zola accompanied him. On other occasions, if he dined out, Maupassant usually took him home.

Despite his avoidance of publicity his fame grew yearly. Although the general public misunderstood him, his literary contemporaries perceived his worth. There could no longer be any question of comparing him with Duranty, Feydeau, and Champfleury, and if a comparison had to be made at all, it would be in the spirit of Turgeniev, who sent Flaubert a copy of *War and Peace* and added: 'I consider [Tolstoy] the foremost living writer. You know who, in my opinion, could contest his place.' Apart from Hugo, whose genius was unchallenged but who, as a novelist, stood outside the main tradition, there was in France no imaginative writer of corresponding stature. Flaubert stood head and shoulders above Daudet and Edmond de Goncourt, and Zola, though already notorious, had yet to justify his rather transient glory-

P   225

Flaubert's detachment and integrity, his struggle for perfection, and the years of self-dedication that went into each book, all contributed a more resistant and durable basis for greatness than the accepted methods of intrigue and publicity; in the end, he dwarfed Du Camp. As for the Academy, the goal of so much legitimate and illegitimate endeavour, he despised it and seized any convenient opportunity to pay it his disrespects; he treated it as a pretentious body of impostors of the same stamp as the vice-principal of Rouen *collège* and the Comte de Germiny—impostors who used the art of literature as a means for self-advancement and celebrity. So despite his position as a master of the modern novel he escaped the taint of respectability, and innovators and iconoclasts could still look up to him as the incorruptible defender of new ideas. No one, indeed, could be more friendly than Flaubert to young writers. Outspoken he might be, but never brutally harsh; he welcomed the faintest streak of originality and stressed its significance. However busy he was with his own work and Bouilhet's affairs, he made time to read the novels he was sent and to give copious comments. Edouard Gachot, Daniel Darc, Paul Alexis, François Coppée, Jean Aicard, Léon Hennique were some of those who profited. And his generosity did not stop there; for he used his influence to find journalistic and literary posts for his protégés, and Maupassant was only the most outstanding of a long list of his beneficiaries. His activities were not even confined to literature: several times he requested the Croix d'honneur for deserving soldiers; he had a certain Carle appointed bailiff at Envermeu; and when Laporte was himself ruined in 1877, Flaubert took energetic steps to install him in a suitable official post.

1877 was the crucial year for Bouilhet's monument. Controversy raged in Rouen Municipal Council, and Flaubert, irritated by the obtuse attitude of his fellow-citizens, was ceaselessly dinning into his eminent friends the necessity for downright and aggressive action. The negotiations had suffered many ups and downs. One of the most embarrassing setbacks occurred when Caudron, the Treasurer of the Committee for the erection of a monument, lost his reason: delicate approaches had to be made to recover the large amount of money subscribed. But the obstacles were overcome, and in September Flaubert learned with gratification that the Council had at last granted a spot for Bouilhet's bust in a cant on the new Municipal Library.

Before this, *Trois Contes* had been published, first as newspaper serials and then in volume form. Apart from Brunetière, who had just joined the staff of the *Revue des Deux Mondes* and apparently felt the need to adopt Buloz's dislikes, the reception was universally warm and admiring. Flaubert's friends were delighted and even the reviewers in the popular Press felt that their requirements were satisfied. Théodore de Banville summarized opinion by speaking of 'three complete and perfect masterpieces', and Saint-Valry, in *La Patrie*, added with a tinge of unconscious prophecy that Flaubert's 'ideas, talent, and artistic devices . . . are somehow condensed and epitomized in a final synthesis'.

As *Un Cœur simple* was coming out in *Le Moniteur*, a dinner was given in Flaubert's honour at the Restaurant Trapp, near the Gare Saint-Lazare. It was organized by the so-called 'Médan group' who met in summer at Zola's property at Médan. They comprised Hennique, Paul Alexis, Maupassant, Huysmans, and Céard, to whom was added Mirbeau, and they invited Zola and Goncourt to the occasion. The menu was specially selected:

> Potage purée Bovary
> Truite saumonée à la fille Elisa
> Poularde truffée à la Saint-Antoine
> Artichaut au cœur simple
> Parfait 'naturaliste'
> Vins de Coupeau, liqueurs de l'Assommoir.[6]

The papers announced the birth of the Naturalist school. But if the columnists had crept within earshot, says Céard, they would have heard Flaubert praising Boileau, denouncing all literary systems, and thundering against *isms* of every description— particularly the Naturalist absurdity.

Notes to Chapter Fourteen

1. It was in fact performed once more in Becker's studio on 19th May 1877, but Turgeniev does not seem to have been present. It dealt with a young married couple who entered a brothel under the impression that it was a hotel. Flaubert was so keen that he attended the rehearsals as well. He is described, in the hot summer of 1875, as clambering up to Leloir's studio on the fifth floor, discarding his overcoat on the first, his frock-coat on the second, his waistcoat on the third, and arriving at the top in his underwear, with a pile of clothes on his arm and a top-hat still on his head. The description is rather suspect.

2. Both Pécuchet and Lainé were ruined. Having entitled his new book *Bouvard et Pécuchet*, Flaubert was distressed at the co-incidence of Pécuchet's name, especially as he respected the banker as an honest upright man. Pécuchet solved the problem by dying shortly afterwards.

Flaubert's finances are complicated and obscure and likely to remain so. He was highly secretive about his position, but it seems that at Christmas 1871 he already had to raise money on Commanville's behalf (v. *Lettres inédites à Raoul-Duval*, commentées par Georges Normandy (1950), pp. 147–51).

3. He was the son of Félix-Archimède Pouchet (1800–72), who had taught Flaubert at Rouen *collège*.

4. Félicité of *Un Cœur simple* is also partly modelled on Julie, the maid who had helped to bring up Flaubert. In spite of failing eyesight she still got about—in fact she survived Flaubert—and he liked her to come over after dinner and talk about his mother, father, and sister.

5. Like the other two stories, *Hérodias* was associated with Flaubert's home and youth. The subject was portrayed on a familiar tympanum of Rouen Cathedral—over the side door, north of the main front.

6. Apart from Flaubert's works, the menu alludes to Edmond de Goncourt's *La Fille Elisa* (1877) and Zola's *L'Assommoir* (1877), in which one of the principal characters is a zinc-worker called Coupeau. *Vin de copeaux* (*sic*) is new wine clarified with chips.

Chapter Fifteen

CROISSET'S DOOM

'"J'aimerais mieux ne pas mourir," comme disait Marat. Ah! non! assez, assez de fatigues.' Letter to George Sand, December 1875.

In September 1877 Flaubert took Laporte on a short trip through Normandy. The immediate occasion was to discover a suitable setting for the third chapter of *Bouvard et Pécuchet*. He wore a soft hat and an expansive red kerchief, and armed himself with two cudgels and two carpenter's pencils. The latter were weapons against Marshal Mac-Mahon, on whose political escapades Flaubert blamed the declining sales of *Trois Contes*; and his irritation against the Marshal was increased by the abuse of genitives on election posters. 'Monsieur . . . , candidat du gouvernement du Maréchal de Mac-Mahon, duc de Magenta' was the normal formula, and it evoked the exasperated question: 'Come, Laporte, how can anyone vote for such barbarians?' Flaubert had christened Mac-Mahon 'our modern Bayard', and he inscribed his opinion on any convenient surface, including walls and station seats. Once, according to Laporte, they were sitting together in a station bus when a fellow-traveller, who had been staring long at Flaubert, leant across and asked: 'Don't you come from Montauban and travel in fats?' 'No,' said Flaubert, 'vinegar.'

By this time he was very bald and rather fat; he had lost almost all his teeth and only his round eyes still hinted at the Apollonian beauty of his youth. He was profoundly conscious of his physical decline, and the relentless disintegration of the small section of society in which he had found a niche added to his burden of ill-health and apprehension. He was frightened at the possibility of a lingering disease and alarmed by the tempting velleity of suicide; neither maturity nor middle age had callused over his raw sensibility or brought him nearer to an Olympian detachment, and in his fatigue and discouragement there was a frequent and implacable desire for death.[1]

Bouvard et Pécuchet thus combined intellectual maturity with emotional awareness; Flaubert surveyed life in a broader sweep than hitherto, but reacted with all his old immediacy. That *Bouvard et Pécuchet* was not his last word on every aspect of existence was already shown in *Trois Contes*; but it was a considered judgement and the two clerks not only explored vast tracts of human intellectual endeavour but summarized, in their own activities, much of its folly and self-deception. In this folly and self-deception Flaubert had his own part; Bouvard and Pécuchet, though reaching out to the universality of Don Quixote and Sancho Panza, bore also a significant likeness to Flaubert and Bouilhet and even to Flaubert and Du Camp. Flaubert did not except himself from the general stupidity; he no longer believed, like René, in a private and exclusive fate; he was caught up in the predestined and inescapable *bêtise*, but at least he perceived it, and he derived some superiority from the virtue of self-consciousness. But although he was partly generalizing the conflict in his own soul, he was also enjoying his loudest hoot at authority; for the great failing of Bouvard and Pécuchet is their uncritical acceptance of what they are told, and by accumulating contradictions and inanities Flaubert was exposing the Germinys of the intellectual world and amusing himself immensely in the process.

Bouilhet said of him: 'There is no more moral man than you, and no one who likes immorality more: a piece of stupidity delights you.' The remark fits Flaubert at every stage of his career: he laughed at the lady who visited the Hôtel-Dieu when he was a child, he laughed at Chamas in Cairo, and he was still laughing at Germiny and Pinard. He derived an unholy joy from any manifestation of obtuseness and studied it with an excited curiosity. The trivialities of conversation, in which otherwise intelligent people behaved like automata, gave him especial pleasure, and he compiled *Le Dictionnaire des idées reçues*, a breviary of current cliché dating back to the forties, in which the stock remarks of Rouen and Paris bourgeois were put into permanent cold storage. *Le Dictionnaire* supplied the normal repertoire of the *Garçon*, and Flaubert itched to publish it, with a preface in which he would solemnly justify the book as an attempt to consolidate tradition. As it was, he used it for all his works about contemporary life— *Madame Bovary, L'Education sentimentale, Le Candidat, Un Cœur simple* and *Bouvard et Pécuchet*. It formed the skeleton of Homais's personality, and turning its pages, one meets a scarifying analysis of the commonplace. There are such entries as:

Angels—Suitable word in love and literature.

Beard—Sign of strength.

　　　Too much beard makes the hair fall out.

　　　Useful to protect ties.

Budget—Never balances.

Crowd—Always has good instincts.

Cypress—Only grows in cemeteries.

Doubt—Worse than denial.

English—All rich.

English women—Be surprised that they have pretty children.

Erudition—Scorn it as the sign of a narrow mind.

Genius—Pointless to admire it: it is a neurosis.

Inspiration (poetic)—Caused by sight of the sea, love, woman, etc.

Rhyming dictionary—Shameful to use one.

Yawn—Say: 'Excuse me, it isn't boredom but indigestion.'

Flaubert's sense of humour was dual. On the one hand he loved uproarious farces, dervish dances, and enormous hoaxes; on the other he found a savage, complex pleasure in the discomfiture of self-satisfied and ponderous nitwits. But because the second pleasure was a mechanism of defence against the society with which he was in conflict, it extended over the whole nexus of law and punishment, of respectability and moral eminence. Unless one is prepared to justify the tension that permanently existed between Flaubert and society, his amusement is disproportionate. The laugh is bitter and personal, springing from an acceptance of folly and corruption as incurable. It is a laugh of revenge, not a reformer's satire. How mild is the occasion and how sharp the response, comes out even in Flaubert's youth. In 1845 he writes: 'The most trivial saying sometimes strikes me with rare wonder. There are gestures and intonations I cannot get over, and imbecilities that almost give me vertigo.' And two years later: 'A gendarme is essentially ludicrous; I cannot look at one without laughing. It is grotesque and inexplicable—the effect this pillar of society has on me, like public prosecutors, justices of any kind and professors of literature.' But the comic effect of a gendarme and even a literary professor is not usually overwhelming, and the intensity of Flaubert's reaction is proof enough that his amusement masks other, less respectable emotions. That these emotions were suppressed or at least canalized was an achievement; but a greater achievement was their depersonalization, so that in *Bouvard et Pécuchet* they lost the stamp of idiosyncrasy and acquired a wide and indeed universal validity. Even so, Flaubert was grumbling all his life that his friends had no sense of humour, and few of them followed him in the more distant ramifications of his feelings for the grotesque. In his last years he obtained a volume of verse written by doctors and inflicted it on his visitors. When they failed to respond, he was puzzled and disappointed, and confided one day: 'It's strange: nowadays I laugh at things no one laughs at any more.'

Flaubert planned the second volume of *Bouvard et Pécuchet* as a monument of inanity.[2] In so far as the book was a comic novel, it attained the peak of its comedy in the dicta and opinions collected by the two clerks when they abandoned all hope of becoming knowledgeable and reverted to their former occupations as copyists. They were apparently to buy old papers by weight from a nearby factory and to write down and classify any passage that struck them as significant. In this occupation they preserved their integrity; for after slight hesitation they transcribed a letter from a local doctor who spoke of them as harmless fools; and they also acquired a critical sense that made them wince at folly. Flaubert, for the purpose of his book, was obliged to bestow on them something of his own feeling for the ludicrous and the stupid, and one can gather an idea of how he would have built up his second volume by glancing at the material he had collected. It is of redoubtable proportions: the documentation for *Bouvard et Pécuchet* comprises over 11,000 pages of plans and drafts, and sixty dossiers of notes; and although only a small part of this was intended for the collection of the two copyists, it must be augmented with the papers that were found among Laporte's effects after his death. Flaubert amassed evidence of folly all his life; it was the counterpart for his documentation of grotesque suffering and crime. Céard describes how, when *Bouvard et Pécuchet* was under way, Flaubert would enliven the Sundays in his Paris flat by producing files of blue paper and booming out his favourite enormities. He was particularly pleased when he discovered, in a textbook of rhetoric, that *vaillance* was a good word in verse; it must have recalled the extravagances of *Jenner*.

Nonsense of all kind was his pabulum: quirks of style, naïveties of thought, ignorant blunders, and pompous absurdities. And because no one who writes can escape floundering sooner or later and, in fact, the folly of *Bouvard et Pécuchet* is therefore a permanent characteristic of the human race, Flaubert had gleanings from his most revered masters as well as from his pet abominations, and was even involved himself. Famous names jostled with nonentities:

'Water is made to hold up those huge edifices that we call ships. Fénelon.

'In Egypt women prostituted themselves publicly to crocodiles. Proudhon, *De la célébration du dimanche* (1850).

'The melon was divided by Nature into slices so as to be eaten by the family; the pumpkin, being larger, can be eaten with neighbours. Bernardin de Saint-Pierre.

'I have often heard men deplore the blindness of Francis I's Council, which turned down Christopher Columbus's offer of India. Montesquieu, *Esprit des lois*. [Note by Flaubert: Francis I ascended the throne in 1515; Christopher Columbus died in 1506.]

'Bacon, a man ignorant of all the sciences and whose basic ideas were all false. De Maistre, *Examen de la philosophie de Bacon*.

'[Napoleon] was certainly a great winner of battles; but apart from that almost any general is his superior. Chateaubriand, *De Buonaparte et des Bourbons*.

'It is a pity Molière does not know how to write. Fénelon.

'Molière is a squalid mountebank. Bossuet.

'Shakespeare himself, however uncouth, was not entirely unread or ignorant. La Harpe, *Introduction au Cours de la Littérature*.

'The grocery trade is respectable. It is a branch of commerce. The army is even more respectable because it is an institution whose purpose is order. Jules Noriac, *Les Nouvelles*, 26th October 1865.

'As soon as a Frenchman crosses the frontier, he enters foreign territory. L. Havin, *Courrier du dimanche*.

'The breasts of woman may be regarded as objects of pleasure and utility. Murat et Patissier, *Dictionnaire des Sciences médicales*.

'The wealth of a country depends on its general prosperity. Louis Napoleon, quoted in *La Rive gauche*, 12th March 1865.'

Flaubert did not foresee great difficulties in the organization and arrangement of his second volume, but the first cost him the most exacting labour of his life. Apart from the inherent and depressing monotony of the subject and the sheer physical exertion of accumulating facts, he was faced with artistic problems that were almost insuperable; and although sustained by the conviction that his plan was '*superb*', he flagged beneath his own demands. Moreover *Bouvard et Pécuchet* was composed at a time of continuous distraction and worry, and Bouilhet's plays, Bouilhet's fountain, Maupassant's affairs, and Commanville's bankruptcy all drained the vigour that might have gone to writing the book. At the height of his anxieties Flaubert set it aside and produced *Trois Contes*, but from May 1877 again all his effort was directed to its completion. His correspondence for almost eight years echoes the familiar complaints, doubts, self-questionings, and scruples, with occasional sighs of satisfaction and flashes of pleasure. 'I am now reading up chemistry (of which I understand nothing) and Raspail's medicine, not to mention Gressent's *Potager moderne* and Gasparin's *Agriculture*. . . . I flounder and scratch out in despair what I have written. Yesterday evening it

gave me violent stomachache. But I'll do it: I *must*. . . . My pro-
logue will be complete tomorrow; to finish it, all I need is to walk
through the kitchen garden with a candle in the dark. . . . The
difficulty with such a subject is to vary the cast of the sentences. If
I succeed, it will be, quite seriously, an *artistic triumph*. . . . At
certain moments this book dazzles me with its immense scope.
What will become of it? . . . Here I am in the toughest part (it can
be the noblest) of my infernal book, i.e. metaphysics! Making
people laugh at innate ideas! . . . Do you know how many volumes
I have had to absorb for my two fellows? More than 1,500! My
dossier of notes is eight inches high. But this superabundance of
documents has enabled me to avoid pedantry—I am sure of that. . . .
The mere notion of finishing the book bears me up, but there are
days when I weep with fatigue.'

Throughout this period Laporte showed himself the best of
friends. He bought reviews in which Flaubert's work was discussed; collected material for *Bouvard et Pécuchet*; spent week-ends
at Croisset; slept there specially on New Year's Eve 1876 so as to be
first with good wishes; brought baskets of rennet apples from
Grand-Couronne; and in January 1877, when he was ruined,
remarked simply to Flaubert that it was a further link between
them. Flaubert showed his gratitude by sending Laporte the
morocco-bound manuscript of *Trois Contes* and by striving to
find him a new post. But it was a debt of gratitude that could never
be settled because it was continually renewed, and Flaubert, who
christened Laporte his sister of mercy, felt his obligation with
particular keenness when, in January 1879, he slipped on the ice at
Croisset and cracked a fibula. Laporte hurried over in appalling
weather, slept at the house and acted as amanuensis. Flaubert
was forced to remain in bed for a fortnight and then to creep about
on crutches. But that was the least of his trials, for *Le Figaro* had
published an account of his mishap ('Je suis HHHindigné!'), and
he was overwhelmed with sympathetic letters of inquiry, which
all had to be replied to, at a considerable expense in stamps.

But the accident was a mere inconvenience, and Flaubert was
far more seriously concerned about his financial position. He was
entirely dependent on Commanville, and even if he was content

with such precarious support, his friends were anxious. They had apparently discussed the best course before approaching Flaubert; at any rate, on 3rd February, a week after the accident, Turgeniev visited Croisset, and, waiting till the Commanvilles had left, he delicately broached his proposition. Flaubert had already heard of it from Taine and had rejected it indignantly. Silvestre de Sacy, the Librarian of the Mazarine, was dying, and his post, which carried a salary variously estimated at between 3,000 and 8,000 francs, involving one day's attendance a week, would shortly be vacant; the money would be enough to keep Flaubert solvent and relieve him of anxiety, and Turgeniev, using all his powers of persuasion, gave Flaubert a sleepless night and carried away permission to go ahead. Flaubert acquiesced with painful reluctance; he regarded the post as a kind of pension. 'Those who have ruined me', he told Du Camp, 'are in duty bound to keep me fed—and not the Government.' But Turgeniev, having broken down Flaubert's defences, cherished high hopes of success and postponed his visit to Russia in order to press home the advantage. The only other candidate was Frédéric Baudry, the Librarian of the Arsenal, and Flaubert's supporters included Victor Hugo, Paul Bert, the Senator Cordier, Du Camp, the Princess Mathilde, the Charpentiers, Edmond de Goncourt, Zola, and Mme Adam; moreover the Minister of Public Instruction, on whom the appointment depended, was Agénor Bardoux, one of the friends of Flaubert's youth.

But the plans went awry. Dufaure's Ministry fell on 4th February and was succeeded by Waddington's; on 12th February or 13th Turgeniev called on Gambetta and was ill received; Le Figaro got wind of the interview and published a dramatized account, which wrung from Flaubert bitter tears of humiliation. Agénor Bardoux left the Ministry of Public Instruction, and Sénard, the defender of Bovary, who had played a prominent role in the formation of the new Government, solicited the Mazarine post on behalf of Baudry, who had the advantage of being his son-in-law. On 14th February Sacy died, and three days later Baudry's appointment was announced.

But in spite of his repulse and his burning resentment at the publicity lavished on his private affairs, Flaubert did not abandon all hope. Turgeniev, who had convinced him that some kind of additional income was essential, continued his negotiations, and in March Flaubert admitted rather nervously to Caroline: 'I have every reason to believe that I am going to be *offered* a pension, and I shall accept it, although I am profoundly *humiliated* (and I require absolute secrecy).' The Commanvilles did not wish Flaubert to take the post and bore a particular grudge against Laporte and Turgeniev, both of whom had overcome his unwillingness. But Commanville's lame attempts to recommence his business were not taken seriously in Rouen, and when he sold his saw-mill in March, even Flaubert admitted that it had fetched a paltry sum. Under these circumstances pride was a luxury; Flaubert was even afraid that he might have to keep himself by giving private lessons; he made a mysterious trip to Paris in May, and by June he knew that his post was certain. In due course he received a letter from Jules Ferry, who had succeeded Bardoux, informing him that from 1st July he had been appointed Supernumerary Librarian at the Mazarine, with an annual salary of 3,000 francs and no residential obligations. 'It is charity', said Flaubert with some acerbity; and he threatened to treat the money as a loan which would be repaid after his death. In fact, no trace of Flaubert's name has ever been found in the archives of the Mazarine, and it seems highly probable that mention of the Library was only a device to obtain his consent and that he was actually receiving a State pension.

Meanwhile Commanville was harassed by his creditors. In 1877 a further loan had been arranged, and, as usual, it was Flaubert's friends who supplied the bulk of the money, with Raoul-Duval and Laporte to the fore. Laporte renewed his guarantee, but he had lost his fortune, and if Faucon, the banker, brought pressure on Commanville, Laporte would have to mortgage his house in Paris. The situation recurred in 1878, and out of respect for Flaubert Laporte still complied, though with reluctance. He had no illusions about Commanville, who had plunged further into hazardous speculations and showed no inclination to cut down his rate of expenditure; but these suspicions were not properly shared by

Flaubert, who was blinded by affection, lacked any business sense, and asked only to be rid of all financial preoccupations. When a crisis arose, Caroline continually worked on him, bewildering him with facts and figures and persuading him to appeal to his friends; and although he was puzzled, he trusted her advice. 'I persist', he wrote to her in March 1879, 'in not understanding what guarantee I can offer Faucon, since I have nothing left. He asks for my promise; I give it him; but I cannot keep it. So I am a rogue.' And he echoed a sentence of hers with some perplexity: 'Our heads are as well worth saving as anyone else's.'

'Vieille Nounou' was out of his depth; he hardly realized that the Commanvilles had nicknamed him 'the consumer' and resented even the wood that he burned. So when, in September, they pressed him to write to Laporte for a further guarantee, he acquiesced, producing a tortuous and stilted letter, but concluding: 'Whatever you decide, nothing will be changed between us.' Unfortunately Laporte was no longer at hand; in June, thanks largely to Flaubert's efforts, he had been appointed Inspector of Labour at Nevers, and he moved immediately. He was almost fifty and thinking of marriage. Now that he knew Flaubert to have a modest independent income, he was the less ready to help Commanville, especially as he had no confidence in the use to which his money was put. And so he declined.

To Flaubert his action must at first sight have appeared normal and reasonable, if disappointing, but neither Caroline nor her husband were capable of Flaubert's magnanimity. Four years earlier, at the time of Commanville's deepest anxiety, Caroline had written to Laporte: 'Do not fail to come to Croisset even when my uncle has gone. I very much wish to shake your hand and am happy to count you *among our true friends*.' But since then Laporte had encouraged Flaubert to apply for the Mazarine post, and when he refused to renew his guarantee, his last qualification as a friend had evidently vanished. Commanville put it bluntly: 'Laporte ran the risks of my fortune: I go down, he goes down with me. If he helped me with his signature, it was out of pure vanity, in order to become a closer intimate of Flaubert.' And husband and wife, forcing their resentment onto Flaubert, profited by his innocence in all business matters to convince him that Laporte was guilty of a betrayal. In October the break was complete and Flaubert was cruelly hurt; but doubts lingered in his mind and in December he was still writing to Caroline: 'I continue to think very often of my ex-friend Laporte. That's an affair I found it hard to stomach.'

The winter that ushered in 1880 was correspondingly unkind. It snowed fiercely in December and a murky fog cut all communications between Croisset and Rouen. Flaubert remained grimly in his study, despondent and lonely, but determined not to leave for Paris till his last chapter was under way. There were occasional visits from his friends, but apart from a few gifts, like caviare from Turgeniev, Christmas was marked only by passing beggars ringing the bell. In January *Le Château des cœurs* began to appear in *La Vie moderne*, edited by Bergerat and published by Charpentier; but Flaubert's pleasure was immediately spoilt because the illustrations not unnaturally failed to reproduce his own conception of each scene, and because the tableaux, for purposes of serialization, were foolishly divided in the middle. He was furious with Charpentier on this account; and Charpentier, despite his urbane culture and easy personality, increased his irritation by lacking the essential virtue of a publisher—that of prompt payment.

Although Flaubert was alone at Croisset, he could not devote himself entirely to his book; there were three or four letters to write every day, and he received a weekly batch of two or three novels, sent by his juniors for criticism. To these obligations of eminence he responded generously but not always willingly: they made heavy inroads on his time. But when, in February, he heard that Maupassant was in trouble, he hastened to his rescue. The occasion was the publication of two pieces of verse, 'Au bord de l'eau' and 'Le Mur', which had originally appeared in *La République des lettres* in 1876. In November 1879 *La Revue moderne et naturaliste* reprinted them, somewhat refurbished, with 'Au bord de l'eau' rechristened 'Une Fille'. This immediately gave a handle to the local opponents of Harry Alis, who edited the *Revue*, and Allien, who printed it; if these two men could be convicted, they would lose their political rights. Intrigues led to action, and about 10th

February proceedings were decided upon.³ Maupassant, in alarm, appealed to Flaubert, who speedily exploited his influence. But even Raoul-Duval, Bardoux, and Mme Adam could not halt the ponderous process of the law, and as a last resort Flaubert wrote an open letter to Maupassant, published in *Le Gaulois* of 19th February, in which he tartly recalled the prosecution of *Bovary*. It had its effect and Maupassant went unmolested.

Flaubert was also worried about his brother Achille, who had been in failing health for some years; and although Achille had always been remote from him in interests and temperament, Flaubert heard, perhaps for the first time, the call of the blood. He was, in fact, beginning to perceive the result of his withdrawal, for his faculty of emotion, though still rich and eager, had little to expend itself on. He was prodigal of affection and could find few takers. His niece, of whom he was so blindly and paternally fond, was usually out of range, and Maupassant, whom he regarded half-jokingly as his disciple, was unable to visit him often. His only companion was the dog. There are indeed many stories of Flaubert in these years sentimentalizing over children; and they are certainly true. 'That's what I lack', he had told George Sand: 'a granddaughter like yours.' For a child represented the continuance of life at which he had rebelled; and although a child could only grant him emotional relief if he accepted the inherent value and significance of each individual human destiny, he was on the brink of that acceptance. It did not enter into his conscious philosophy or the calculations of his art, but it had begun to effect a surreptitious change in his sense of values. Under the compulsion of a solitude that he had once deliberately chosen and now felt to be inadequate, Flaubert slowly turned away from the denials of his youth—the spirit that had prompted him to tell Louise Colet: 'May my flesh perish utterly; may I pass on to no one the boredom and degradation of life.'

He was still glad to see old Julie, and her respect for him was enhanced: she had heard at the grocer's that he was a 'great writer'. No doubt she felt that his fame excused some of his peculiarities, for he was certainly individual. At home he usually wore a magnificent dressing-gown which Turgeniev had sent him from

Russia. 'This royal garment plunges me into dreams of absolutism and lust', Flaubert said when he received it. 'I should like to be stark naked inside it and shelter Circassian women.' It was really a kind of medieval *houppelande*, cascading in dark brown folds to the floor, and in summer he replaced it with a gay robe of lighter texture but similar design. Dressed in ample and formless trousers held up by a girdle, he looked vaguely ecclesiastical, and once when the Archbishop of Rouen, on a visit to Croisset, gave alms to a short-sighted beggar-woman who had importuned him, the old creature hobbled away croaking 'Thank you, Monsieur Gustave'. Flaubert indeed had his eccentricities: if he dined in Paris, he preferred a private room so that he could take off his jacket and boots. And so far as he was known at Croisset, it was as a bizarre figure, perhaps even a maniac. According to legend, passers-by peered at him through the iron gates, and Lapierre recognized a Rouen confectioner who brought his wife and two children to Croisset every Sunday morning and sat on the parapet, gazing at the study. Local inhabitants who had seen Flaubert pacing to and fro and heard him thundering out his prose spoke of him quite seriously as 'the barrister'. And it is certain that when the riverboats went down to La Bouille on Sundays, passengers pointed out Flaubert as he came into sight through the trees, while he, not to be outdone, stared back with sardonic curiosity and even bought a pair of opera-glasses to observe the expressions of the bourgeois massed on deck. 'He is an eccentric', one local inhabitant is reported to have said. 'Today he is quietly living at home; tomorrow he packs his bags and is off to Carthage. We don't think much of that in Rouen.'

For some years Lapierre had organized a celebration on 27th April, the day proper to Saint Polycarp. The saint was credited by Saint Irenaeus with the habit of suddenly blocking up his ears and crying out: 'O good God, for what times hast Thou kept me that I should endure such things!' And Flaubert, who claimed to be a reincarnation of the saint, was invited as guest of honour to a dinner at which his plaints and prejudices were vigorously echoed and parodied. The festivities in 1880 were a triumph for Lapierre and his wife: Flaubert received thirty letters and three telegrams, including the homages of the Archbishop of Rouen, the Italian cardinals, and the Corporation of floor-polishers; flowers were expected from Nice, and among other, more practical gifts, Flaubert was presented with an old tooth as a relic of the saint. He was celebrated in verse and acclaimed with music. But although the ceremony warmed his heart, he was unable to enter completely into its spirit; and when a girl ran up to him and put on his head a garland so big that it fell round his neck, he muttered, 'I feel like a grave-stone'.

Two other events gladdened him, each the consummation of year-long labour and affection. In February he had received the proofs of *Les Soirées de Médan*,[1] a collection of stories by Zola and his associates; and one glance at the volume showed Flaubert that 'Boule de suif', Maupassant's contribution, eclipsed the rest. He was not to know that it was probably the peak of Maupassant's achievement. '"Boule de suif", the story by my disciple,' he wrote, ' . . . is a masterpiece; I stick to the word, a masterpiece of composition, humour, and observation.' And then in March arrangements were concluded for Sauvageot, a Rouen architect, to proceed with Bouilhet's monument; it was to be ready in October.

Flaubert had in fact reached the harvest of his endeavours, and even with *Bouvard et Pécuchet* he was well into the final chapter and on the verge of the last scene but one. In May he was leaving Croisset for two months in Paris, and although he was returning in summer, he hoped to finish his second volume in September and to go to the capital for at least a year. He had enough of the solitude of Croisset and needed the distraction of cheerful company. On Easter Sunday he entertained Zola, Daudet, Charpentier, and Goncourt for a night; Maupassant met them at the station and Flaubert received them in a broad Calabrian hat, promised to make them drunk, encouraged them with salacious humour, and bade them farewell with tears in his eyes. But such entertainment was too much of an evasion to mollify his discontent for long, and because the pleasure involved a partial limitation of feeling and a drugging of the sensibility, the subsequent reaction was all the more acute. It was impossible for him to cheat himself.

He planned to leave for Paris on Saturday, 8th May. On Friday

he invited his neighbour, Dr. Fortin, to dinner and read him some
Corneille with verve and conviction. When he got up on Saturday,
he took his usual bath, examined his correspondence, and smoked
several pipes. About 10.30 he felt unwell and called for help. The
maid hurried to fetch Fortin, but he had just left by boat, and when
she returned, Flaubert was still standing in his study, slightly
dazed, rubbing his temples with eau-de-Cologne. He lay down on
his divan and asked with difficulty for Hélot, a Rouen doctor. But
the cook had already gone for Dr. Tourneux, Fortin's deputy.
When Tourneux arrived, he found Flaubert lying back unconscious. His heart fluttered weakly and stopped. Death was apparently due to apoplexy.[5]

Lapierre was immediately informed and sent out telegrams. The
Commanvilles came in the evening, and were followed by Maupassant, who washed the body and watched over it for three
nights. Edmond de Goncourt and Claudius Popelin, the poet and
painter, arrived on Monday, stunned by the news. Laporte, who
had learnt of Flaubert's death in his morning paper, sped to
Croisset and was turned out of the house: the Commanvilles did
not forgive easily. On Tuesday, the day of the funeral, the Paris
train brought Zola, Daudet, Coppée, Banville, Céard, and many
more. The only journalist was Chincholle of *Le Figaro*.

Starting from Flaubert's house at Croisset, the procession
followed the road by the river till it reached the dusty track leading up to Canteleu. A short service was held in the church, during
which the five rustic chanters bungled their responses with equani-
mity. The procession then wound its way into Rouen and up again
to the Monumental Cemetery. The mourners numbered between
two and three hundred, of whom perhaps ten were Rouennais;
and although little knots of passers-by collected to stare at the
Parisian celebrities, many did not know who was dead and at the
name of Flaubert thought of Achille and Achille's father. A picket
of soldiers was waiting at the cemetery—the inevitable and banal
tribute to a Chevalier of the Légion d'honneur, but otherwise the
municipality was indifferent and unrepresented. Lapierre said a
few words by the graveside, and the coffin was lowered into the
tomb. By a distant iteration of the Flaubertian grotesque the

coffin stuck: it could be neither raised nor lowered and the grave-diggers grappled with it in vain. After an embarrassed pause the mourners departed, leaving Flaubert rammed obliquely into the ground.

Although Goncourt, Zola, and Daudet returned to Paris together, some mourners stayed in Rouen for a meal in Flaubert's honour; but when they sat down to table, it became plain that there were thirteen of them. Banville, who was wildly superstitious, insisted on some other diner being found, and Bergerat, after several rebuffs, came back with a private on leave, who had never heard of Flaubert but was longing to meet Coppée. The day ended with a riotous banquet in which Flaubert was entirely forgotten.

As soon as the proceedings were decently over and Flaubert's affairs had been wound up, the Commanvilles were anxious to sell the house at Croisset. A profit of 60,000 francs, which they had recently made on some ground on the Quai des Canadiens, had been swallowed by Commanville's creditors; Croisset, on the other hand, belonged entirely to Caroline and would fetch a considerable sum. Accordingly, in May 1881 it was sold for 180,000 francs; in June it changed hands again at the same figure; and two months later demolitions began.

Flaubert, who in his lifetime had been a financial failure, became an excellent proposition now that he was dead; and while Du Camp hastily hitched his own memory onto Flaubert's fame, Caroline published *Bouvard et Pécuchet* and prepared a mutilated edition of the correspondence. Even Croisset became a profit-making concern, and by 1885 a large and promising distillery was in full operation where the house had formerly stood. Only the little *pavillon* by the towpath survived the destruction, as it still survives today; and if Flaubert could revisit the scene of his labours, it would give him a delicious sense of the grotesque to know that the distillery was not allowed to last and that on the precise spot where he once wrote *Bovary*, there is now a huge and prosperous paper-factory.

Notes to Chapter Fifteen

1. A characteristic expression, which it may be as well to give in French, is that of 8th May 1879: 'La tristesse me submerge! mon bouquin m'accable! J'ai quelquefois des maux de tête, comme hier soir, où il me semble que je vais crever—et des crises de larmes!—enfin, c'est complet.'

2. It is, however, fairly clear that the second volume would begin with chapter IX. Precisely what was to comprise the second volume is a vexed question that has been discussed in detail by Descharmes, Demorest, and Dumesnil, but not answered for certain. It appears that Bouvard and Pécuchet were to plunder Flaubert's *Album* (or *Sottisier*) and probably to make use of his *Catalogue des opinions chic*. It is hard to distinguish between the latter and the *Dictionnaire* and doubt has long existed whether the *Dictionnaire* was involved at all. The question has, however, been settled in the affirmative by M. J. Durry (*Flaubert et ses projets inédits* (1950), pp. 228–30).

The second volume would really be a kind of international 'This England', without left-wing bias.

3. Defentry Wright, properly called Minturn, the author of a *nouvelle* entitled *Adnia*, was also summoned to appear before the *iuge d'instruction*.

4. He may have received the proofs of *Boule de suif* only and not seen the complete volume till it appeared in April.

5. This abbreviated description is based on the accounts of Tourneux and Maupassant, who are more reliable than Zola or Du Camp. (Du Camp did not even attend the funeral.) But there is a strong tradition in Rouen that Flaubert committed suicide, and although Gérard-Gailly dismisses it scornfully, M. Edmond Ledoux adduces facts that are certainly hard to explain away. Some of M. Ledoux's arguments have recently been published by Georges Normandy (*Lettres inédites à Raoul-Duval* (1950), pp. 266–8), but until more evidence comes to light, the conventional account must stand.

M. Ledoux maintains that Flaubert hanged himself in his bath. He certainly had secret causes for distress: it appears that rumours were circulating about the probable sale of Croisset, and it is possible that Flaubert heard from Pouchet, if not from Fortin, the true nature of Maupassant's disease. It seems, however, more likely that the task of finishing *Bouvard et Pécuchet* would have strengthened him against the temptation of taking his own life. If Flaubert committed suicide, it was an impulsive act in a moment of depression.

Chapter Sixteen

THE HEART OF
FLAUBERT

*'Je pense souvent avec attendrissement aux êtres inconnus,
à naître, étrangers, etc., qui s'émeuvent ou s'émouvront des mêmes
choses que moi. Un livre, cela vous crée une famille éternelle dans
l'humanité.'* Letter to Louise Colet, 25th–26th March 1854.

Conflict was the condition of Flaubert's life, a condition established as soon as our knowledge of him begins. It was a conflict that he instinctively deepened and perpetuated. Beginning as the search by a lonely spoilt child for his particular superiority, it developed into a mockery of the bourgeois, a dislike of his schoolmasters, and an ultimate rejection of all the authorities in the social structure. Its roots lay in his feeling of individual worth, in his conviction of a truth ignored or denied by orthodox judgements. But although the conflict set him at odds with his environment, it was matched, and perhaps created, by the conflict within himself. For there is in Flaubert's mind, even as a child, an ambiguous attitude to life in which two opposite judgements are interlinked. On the one hand he was disgusted and nauseated by the whole business of living long before he had any chance of trying it for himself; and though premature disillusion is a commonplace of Romantic literature, there is no reason why Flaubert, with his prosaic, matter-of-fact background, should have adopted it unless it satisfied some inner compulsion of his nature. On the other hand his disgust was intensified and even contradicted by his persistent aspirations towards a world of high meanings, sudden revelations, delicious enjoyments, and endless pleasure, in which his desires, long pent up in the grey tyranny of Rouen, would have free rein—a world which, as it took him years to discover, did not and could not exist.

This conflict is not in itself unusual; but it is immediately enhanced and elevated to another order of significance by Flaubert's perception of beauty and his overwhelming response to it. For with beauty he became aware of ugliness; and there developed a further, parallel conflict between beauty and ugliness, which found its summary and culmination when they paradoxically co-operated to produce the grotesque. The grotesque was in fact a unification of the vision which, on other planes, Flaubert was continually striving to complete; and his career as an artist was a sustained effort to balance and present these diverse elements as they shifted and intersected at different junctures of his life.

This is the context of his nervous malady; for though it darkened his labour and wore down his resolution, it was only part of the anguished sensibility that made pain so near and happiness so remote. By his illness Flaubert's predicament was intensified. He was characteristically the man of the nineteenth century, but endowed with an intellectual and moral awareness of his situation. Apart from his own special problems, the political and metaphysical complications of his epoch bore down upon him, especially as he grew older; and the same complications beset him as an artist. The art to which he was wedded involved such aloofness, such anarchism, that it needed an abstract justification which he was quite unable to supply. He felt its compulsion, but although he dedicated his life to its pursuit, he was cut off by his scepticism from any explanation of its transcendent power over him and was obliged, when he spoke of its source, to use the terms of a mystical agnostic or to refer bluntly to an escape from life. On his own showing he had no right, whether economic or moral, to withdraw from society, exist on the labour of others, and dedicate himself to a pursuit that was justified solely because it appealed to him; and though it takes a dogmatic and utilitarian view of art to say that Flaubert was wrong, he was only right, if he *was* right, by virtue of values and realities that he was uncertain of and even denied.

Flaubert's individual predicament as a man was his gain as an artist, and in so far as it was capable of being reshaped and generalized, he exploited it in his work. But apart from the use to which he put it artistically, his life was significant in itself. That he was sometimes childish and always neurotic is of no importance in the last analysis; it is clear, too, that his affair with Louise Colet was trivial; and it seems, as the man stands in his final nakedness, that even his love for Elisa Schlésinger manifested rather than decided his outlook. Scanning his labyrinthine personality, one may look in vain for an easily comprehensible pattern, and even his unflinching devotion to his artistic ideal is complicated by drifting desires and uncertain beliefs. Loyal in friendship, ruthless in enmity; naïve in personal relations, piercing in his analysis of strangers; doubtful of himself, positive of his goal; modest but obdurate; tender-hearted but misanthropic; exasperating but lovable—Flaubert is so rich and formidable a personality that he must baffle summary and simplification.

He stands, firm and downright, in the main path of literature, offering a permanent challenge. His honesty, versatility, and bracing independence of thought and feeling raise him above all but a handful of his contemporaries and ensure that his significance as a man is not confined to the historical context of nineteenth-century France but persists into later ages. Although and because he is unique, he is the representative of the literary artist, and the external circumstances in which he reached that status have now disappeared and are unlikely to recur.

Not that he has escaped heavy criticism: he is accused of ignoring the turmoil within himself, of failing to transcend his period, of concentrating on his personal preferences to the neglect of wider and more important questions. Such statements are easy to make and hard to refute, for they depend on inexplicit standards of judgement; but in so far as they can be related to agreed and ascertainable facts, they are unlikely to survive unmodified a systematic examination of his life.

Flaubert's life, however, cannot vindicate his position as a novelist, which stands or falls by the intrinsic merit of his work; but ultimately, in a profound sense, his general significance as a man is reduced to his particular significance for himself. And again one strikes on a contradiction. For although he hated life he persisted daily in a suffering that is barely imaginable. Indeed his persistence amounts to choice; for not only did he make up his mind as a child that the process of living was futile and savourless, but he tortured himself with the study of his emotions, coldly dismembering and intellectualizing them and, in turn, conjuring up further emotions to deepen his intellectual perception. If Flaubert's life was a catalogue of suffering, it was because he instinctively fastened on suffering as the element that could integrate his personality. But had his suffering any meaning? The question is presumptuous but asks itself; and if we turn it back on Flaubert, he gives two answers. On the one hand, he dismisses life as a sorry joke with no discoverable significance; on the other, he finds in it, from *Madame Bovary* to *Un Cœur simple*, a possibility of beauty which is not primarily human, and he pursues his own existence with no likelihood of alleviating his burden, but with an evident conviction that the toil is worth while. Flaubert was not the man to shrink from suicide, but suicide, when it occurred to him, was a temptation and not a way out. Life, in fact, had coherence and purpose even in denying itself; although detestable it was significant, and it possessed meaning in a pattern that was meaningless. Moreover art was not outside that pattern but part of it, and Flaubert had a lurking, continuous sense of mystery, according to which all things were possible, whether believed in or denied by the frail human intellect. He was himself the plaything of obscure, transcendent compulsions whose validity was unknown and unknowable; and, generalizing from his doubt and his incapacity to resolve it, he maintained that all conclusions about the world were futile because they were reached by the unreliable instrument of the mind and based on assumptions that were laughably inadequate. But as he grew older, he was less inclined to contradistinguish the value of art from the value of life and readier to perceive in human destiny a beauty and significance which did not derive entirely from the factitious invention of the artist but were independent and intrinsic. He was groping his way towards an acceptance and died without achieving it; his final

attitude was still of uncomprehending resignation—the attitude of
Saint Anthony hunching his shoulders in prayer, or Bouvard and
Pécuchet returning to their old occupation as copyists; but there
was a hint that the long darkness was beginning to lift, that the
night of temptation and distress was coming to an end, and that
some answer might at last be vouchsafed to his schoolboy
entreaty:

> *Messieurs les démons,*
> *Laissez-moi donc!*
> *Messieurs les démons,*
> *Laissez-moi donc!*

SELECT BIBLIOGRAPHY

✫

Note. An extensive list of books can be found in the bibliographies of H. P. Thieme (1933), H. Talvert and J. Place (1928–"oo"), and S. Dreher and M. Rolli (1948).

1. FLAUBERT'S WORKS

(*a*) Chronological table of Flaubert's major works, as they first appeared in volume form.

> *Madame Bovary. Mœurs de province.* 1857.
> *Salammbô.* 1863.
> *L'Education sentimentale. Histoire d'un jeune homme.* 1870.
> *La Tentation de saint Antoine.* 1874.
> *Le Candidat, comédie en quatre actes.* 1874.
> *Trois Contes.* 1877.
> *Bouvard et Pécuchet. Œuvre posthume.* 1881.
> *Correspondance.* 1884 and subsequent editions.

(*b*) Editions

The standard edition of Flaubert's works is that published by Conard (1910–36), but the text is not uniformly reliable. An edition with full apparatus criticus is being brought out by La Société Les Belles Lettres (Les Textes Français). The Conard edition of the Correspondence in nine volumes includes most of the important letters known to exist, as well as one pastiche, but the dating is not always accurate and there have been omissions and alterations in transcribing the text. A comprehensive edition of the Correspondence is being prepared by René Dumesnil, Jean Pommier, and Claude Digeon.

The following are the more important publications supplementing the Conard edition:

SELECT BIBLIOGRAPHY

Paysages de Grèce. Extraits inédits des 'Notes de voyage' de Gustave Flaubert (Hiver 1850–51). Annales romantiques, t. 8, 1911, pp. 358–71.

René Dumesnil: *Essai de nomenclature et de classement des lettres inédites de G. Flaubert à E. Laporte.* Bulletin du bibliophile, 1936, pp. 213–23, 253–9, 315–19, 389–98, 470–4, 518–21, 568–9.

Lettres à Maupassant commentées par Georges Normandy. Paris. 1942.

Lettres inédites à Tourgueneff. Présentation et notes par Gérard-Gailly. Monaco. 1946.

Lettres inédites à Maxime Du Camp, Mᵉ Frédéric Fovard, Mme Adèle Husson et 'l'excellent Monsieur Baudry' publiées par Auriant. Sceaux. 1948.

Lettres de Grèce. Notes et commentaires de Jacques Heuzey. Paris. 1948.

Jean Pommier: *Quelques lettres de Flaubert et de Bouilhet* (1846–56). Bulletin du bibliophile, 1949, pp. 161–86, 225–37.

Madame Bovary. Nouvelle version, précédée des scénarios inédits. Textes établis par Jean Pommier et Gabrielle Leleu. Paris. 1949.

Lettres inédites à Raoul-Duval commentées par Georges Normandy. Préface de Edgar Raoul-Duval. Paris. 1950.

2. FLAUBERT'S LIFE, ETC.

(*a*) Books

Adam, Juliette: *Mes sentiments et nos idées avant* 1870. Paris. 1905.

Albalat, Antoine: *Souvenirs de la vie littéraire.* Nouvelle édition. Paris. 1924. *Gustave Flaubert et ses amis.* Paris. 1927.

Auriant: *Koutchouk-Hanem, l'Almée de Flaubert.* 3e édition. Paris. 1943.

Bergerat, Emile: *Souvenirs d'un enfant de Paris.* 4 vols. Paris. 1912.

Bertrand, Louis: *Gustave Flaubert, avec des fragments inédits.* Paris. 1912.

Blossom, F. A.: *La Composition de 'Salammbô'.* Baltimore and Paris. 1914.

Canu, Jean: *Flaubert auteur dramatique.* Paris. 1946.

Coleman, A.: *Flaubert's literary development*. Baltimore and Paris. 1914. See also Fay, F. B.

Colet, Louise: *Une histoire de soldat*. Paris. 1856. *Lui*. Roman contemporain. Paris. 1860.

Colling, Alfred: *Gustave Flaubert*. Paris. 1941.

Commanville, Caroline: *Souvenirs intimes*. Prefaced to editions of Flaubert's Correspondence.

(Curtis, G. W.): *Nile Notes by a Traveller*. London. 1851.

Degoumois, Léon: *Flaubert à l'école de Goethe*. Geneva. 1925.

Demorest, D.-L.: *L'Expression figurée et symbolique dans l'œuvre de Gustave Flaubert*. Paris. 1931. *A travers les plans, manuscrits et dossiers de 'Bouvard et Pécuchet'*. Paris. 1931. See also Dumesnil, René.

Descharmes, René: *Flaubert avant* 1857. Paris. 1909. *Un ami de Flaubert. Alfred Le Poittevin. Œuvres inédites*. Paris. 1909. *Autour de 'Bouvard et Pécuchet'*. Paris. 1921. And Dumesnil, René, *Autour de Flaubert*. 2 vols. Paris. 1912.

Digeon, Claude: *Le dernier visage de Flaubert*. Paris. 1946.

Dubosc, Georges: *Trois Normands*. Rouen. 1917.

Du Camp, Maxime: *Egypte, Nubie, Palestine et Syrie*. Paris. 1852. *Le Nil. Egypte et Nubie*. Paris. 1855. *Orient et Italie*. Paris. 1868. *Souvenirs de l'année* 1848. Paris. 1876. *Souvenirs littéraires*. 2 vols. Paris. 1882–3.

Dumesnil, René: *Flaubert*. Son hérédité, son milieu, sa méthode. Paris. 1905. *En marge de Flaubert*. Paris. 1928. *Gustave Flaubert, l'homme et l'œuvre*. Paris. 1932. *Flaubert et 'l'Education sentimentale'*. Paris. 1943. *Le grand amour de Flaubert*. Paris. 1945. *Flaubert et 'Madame Bovary'*. Paris. 1945. *'Madame Bovary' de Gustave Flaubert*. Paris. 1946. And Demorest, D.-L. *Bibliographie de Gustave Flaubert*. Paris. 1937. See also Descharmes, René.

Durry, M. -J.: *Flaubert et ses projets inédits*. Paris. 1950.

Fay, F. B. and Coleman, A.: *Sources and Structure of Flaubert's 'Salammbô'*. Baltimore and Paris. 1914.

Fischer, E. W.: *Etudes sur Flaubert inédit*. Leipzig. 1908.

Gérard-Gailly: *Flaubert et les fantômes de Trouville*. Paris. 1930. *L'unique passion de Flaubert*. Paris. 1932. *Les Véhémences de Louise Colet*. Paris. 1934.

Goncourt, Edmond and Jules de: *Charles Demailly* (1860). Nouvelle édition. Paris. 1893. *Journal.* 3 séries. 9 vols. Paris. 1888–96.

Guillemin, Henri: *Flaubert devant la vie et devant Dieu.* Paris. 1939.

Jackson, J. F.: *Louise Colet et ses amis littéraires.* New Haven. 1937.

James, Henry: *Notes on Novelists, with some other Notes.* London. 1914.

Lapierre, Charles: *Esquisse sur Flaubert intime.* Evreux. 1898.

La Varende, Jean de: *Grands Normands.* Etudes sentimentales. Rouen. 1939.

Letellier, L.: *Louis Bouilhet,* 1821–1869. Rouen. 1919.

Maupassant, Guy de: *Des Vers* (Lettres de Mme Laure de Maupassant à Gustave Flaubert). Paris. 1908. *Œuvres posthumes II* (Etude sur Gustave Flaubert). Paris. 1908. *Pierre et Jean.* Paris. 1909.

Mauriac, François: *Trois grands hommes devant Dieu.* Paris. 1931.

Maynial, Edouard: *La vie et l'œuvre de Guy de Maupassant.* Paris. 1906. *La Jeunesse de Flaubert.* Paris. 1913. *A la gloire de Flaubert.* Paris. 1943.

Moore, T. Sturge: *Art and Life.* London. 1910.

Riddell, A. R.: *Flaubert and Maupassant: a literary relationship.* Chicago. 1920.

Roy, H.: *Le Docteur Charles Cuny.* Paris. 1930.

Sand, George: *Correspondance avec Gustave Flaubert.* Paris. 1904.

Seillière, Ernest: *Le romantisme des réalistes: Gustave Flaubert.* Paris. 1914.

Shanks, L. P.: *Flaubert's Youth,* 1821–45. Baltimore. 1927.

Tarver, J. C.: *Gustave Flaubert as seen in his works and correspondence.* London. 1895.

Thibaudet, Albert: *Gustave Flaubert.* Paris. 1922.

Zola, Emile: *Les Romanciers naturalistes.* Paris. 1881.

(*b*) Articles

Ambrière, Francis: *Les ennuis d'argent de Gustave Flaubert.* Mercure de France, 1st November 1934, pp. 519–34. *La fabrication de 'l'Education sentimentale'.* Mercure de France, 15th February 1938, pp. 184–90. *La fabrication de 'Salammbô'.* Mercure de France, 15th September 1938, pp. 717–22.

SELECT BIBLIOGRAPHY

Auriant: *Mme Bovary, née Colet.* Mercure de France, 1st June 1936, pp. 247–81.

Bart, B. F.: *Flaubert's itinerary in Greece.* Publications of the Modern Language Association of America, June 1950, pp. 371–87.

Bertrand, G.-E.: *Un pastiche de Flaubert pris pour un original.* Mercure de France, 15th January 1932, pp. 436–40.

Bouilhet, Louis: *Lettres à Louise Colet.* Revue de Paris, 1st and 15th November 1908, pp. 5–24, 280–302.

Bovet, Ernest: *Le Réalisme de Flaubert.* Revue d'histoire littéraire de la France, 1911, pp. 1–36.

Descharmes, René: *Lettres inédites d'Alfred Le Poittevin à Gustave Flaubert.* Annales romantiques, t. 7, 1910, pp. 65–71, 132–42, 183–98. *Par les champs et par les grèves.* Annales romantiques, t. 8, 1911, pp. 195–203.

Dumesnil, René: *Quatre épisodes de la vie sentimentale de Flaubert.* Mercure de France, 15th September 1932, pp. 5–37. *Notes sur 'l'Education sentimentale'.* Mercure de France, 1st February 1936, pp. 449–62. *Le Sottisier de Bouvard et Pécuchet.* Mercure de France, 15th December 1936, pp. 493–503.

Le Poittevin, Alfred: See Descharmes, René.

Martino, P.: *Notes sur le voyage de Flaubert dans la régence de Tunis et en Alger.* Mélanges Vianey. Paris. 1934. Pp. 447–57.

Parturier, Maurice: *Autour de Mérimée.* '*Les Forces perdues*' *et* '*l'Education sentimentale*'. Bulletin du bibliophile, 1931, pp. 487–92, 533–9.

Spencer, Philip: *Censorship of Literature under the Second Empire.* Cambridge Journal, vol. 3, 1949, pp. 47–55.

Thibaudet, A.: *Conclusions sur Flaubert.* Nouvelle Revue française, 1st August 1934, pp. 263–8.

3. TRANSLATIONS

All Flaubert's main works and some of his lesser ones have been translated into English with varying success: *Bibliomanie* by T. W. Koch (1929); *Novembre* by F. Jellinek (1934); *Madame*

SELECT BIBLIOGRAPHY

Bovary by Eleanor Marx-Aveling (1886), H. Blanchamp (1905), J. L. May (1928), G. Hopkins (1948), Joan Charles (1949), and Allan Russell (1950); *Salammbô* by J. S. Chartres (1886), M. French Sheldon (1886), J. W. Matthews (1901), B. R. Redman (1928), and E. P. Mathers (1931); *L'Education sentimentale* by D. F. Hannigan (1898), D. K. Ranous (1923), and A. Goldsmith (1941); *La Tentation de saint Antoine* of 1856 by René Francis (1910); *La Tentation de saint Antoine* of 1874 by L. Hearn (1911); *Trois Contes* by A. McDowall (1923) and Mervyn Saville (1950); *Saint Julien l'Hospitalier* by M. D. Honey (1925); *Bouvard et Pécuchet* by D. F. Hannigan (1896) and T. W. Earp and G. W. Stonier (1936). The George Sand-Gustave Flaubert letters have been translated by Aimée L. McKenzie (1922) and a selection from the correspondence by J. M. Cohen (1949). Other letters and travel-notes are translated by F. Steegmuller in *Flaubert and Madame Bovary* (1939).

Index

INDEX

INDEX

INDEX

INDEX

INDEX

flaubert

a

biography

by

philip spencer

Flaubert's childhood in the bleak
Hotel-Dieu of Rouen; his friendship
with the unhappy Le Poittevin; his
love for Elisa Schlésinger and her own
strange history; his illness and its effects; his tumultuous liaison with
Louise Colet; his journey to the Levant
with the scintillating but perfidious Du
Camp; the writing of *Madame Bovary*
and his subsequent prosecution; his
friendships with George Sand, Louis
Bouilhet and Turgeniev, and his affectionate encouragement of Maupassant,
are all brilliantly described in this
biography.

This is the skeleton of events in which
we see Flaubert grappling with his
nervous malady, toying with unrealizable desires, struggling to master his
art, and finally emerging as almost the
symbolic figure of the modern novelist.
Philip Spencer introduces the general
reader to Flaubert and his writing and
at the same time supplies the needs of
the specialist in French literature; he
has made full use of recently discovered new material.